Gretna FC
Living the Dream

Gretna FC
Living the Dream

A Season with Football's Most
Remarkable Club

Andrew Ross

BLACK & WHITE PUBLISHING

First published 2007
by Black & White Publishing Ltd
99 Giles Street, Edinburgh EH6 6BZ

1 3 5 7 9 10 8 6 4 2   07 08 09 10 11

ISBN 13: 978 1 84502 155 9
ISBN 10: 1 84502 155 X

Typeset by Greengate Publishing Services, Tonbridge, Kent
Printed and bound by MPG Books Ltd

Acknowledgements

I would like to thank Brooks Mileson, Ron MacGregor, Graeme Muir, Rowan Alexander, Davie Irons, Craig Mileson, Jon Tait, Keith Melvin, Derek Collins, all the staff and players at Gretna FC, First ScotRail, Jack Gass, Michael Blanco, Douglas McDonald, Russell Dalton, Stuart Ross and all at Black & White Publishing.

For Lauren

Contents

Forewords

by Brooks Mileson

What a way to end a season! James Grady had always promised me that he would be the one whose goal would win us the Scottish First Division Championship but I didn't, for one minute, believe that this would happen in the dying minutes of the last game of the season. If I had known how nerve-racking this encounter would be, I would probably have heeded my doctor's advice and stayed away from this one.

My ambition, since I became involved with Gretna, has always been to gain promotion to the SPL. I thought we would get there some day but never did I think we would get there by winning three promotions, three championships, on the trot. Doing so is an incredible testament to the dedication and talent of the players, coaching staff and all connected with the club.

The 2006/07 First Division campaign proved to be an incredibly difficult one with many ups and downs along the way. Fortunately, they are all captured in Andrew Ross's excellent book. Reading the chapter on the season finale at Ross County, brought back all the emotions that I felt that day – from when my heart was in my mouth to the feeling of pure elation.

Those at the club and on the terraces will never forget what was achieved that day but Andrew's book guarantees that those historic achievements will be recorded for Gretna fans and football fans in general to enjoy for years to come.

by Davie Irons

When Andrew Ross asked me to write a few words about
our 2006/07 Scottish First Division campaign, my immediate
reaction was to ask how anyone could sum up the season just
gone. It was one full of highs, lows, frustration, elation, drama
and eventually sheer euphoria. That just about describes what
everyone connected to Gretna, from players to fans, went
through on the way to winning promotion to the SPL.

For those of you who watched from the terraces, Ross's
excellent diary of the season will serve as a reminder of the
most incredible season in the club's history. If you're new to
the Gretna story, Ross's account will allow you to experience
the ups and downs of an amazing season when the small club
from Dumfries and Galloway made it a record three successive
league promotions in a row – something which may never be
achieved again.

It was a truly memorable season, which saw the team involved in European football. There were thrilling local derbies
and many a hard-fought league game and it culminated in an
amazing title race that virtually went to the last kick of the
season. As Ross discovered throughout the season, we don't
do anything in half measures at Gretna.

I hope you enjoy his frank and honest account of a turbulent
yet exciting season.

I can't finish without thanking the magnificent group of
players, the loyal and dedicated staff and fans and, last but
not least, Brooks Mileson for supporting the team throughout
and for making 2006/07 a season to remember.

Prologue

I'm not sure where it all started. Yes, as a sports reporter, Gretna Football Club's meteoric rise up the echelons of Scottish football had caught my eye but that wasn't it. Maybe it all started one sunny May afternoon during a visit to my parents in the Highlands. I switched on the television anticipating a feisty FA Cup Final encounter between Liverpool and West Ham only to see a completely different spectacle – the Scottish Cup Final. Hearts versus who?

Gretna won the admiration of a lot of neutrals that day, not least myself. No Second Division outfit had ever reached the final in the modern era before and to take the game to penalties – fantastic. To go on to play in the UEFA Cup that same summer was a fairy tale and all this from a club from a village of only 2,700 inhabitants. It beggars belief. I registered it all but not for one minute did I think I'd end up following the club as it closed in on its greatest achievement of all.

To be honest, the real moment I decided that I *had* to write a book about Gretna was that unforgettable day in August 2006 when MSP Tommy Sheridan walked out of Edinburgh's High Court having won his case for defamation against the *News of the World*. Sheridan stopped in front of the throng of international press, composed himself and spoke:

> Gretna have made it into Europe for the first time in their lives but what we have done in the last five weeks is the equivalent of Gretna taking on Real Madrid in the Bernabeu and beating them on penalties.

In the weeks after Sheridan's famous speech, I thought about Gretna a lot. I began scouring fan sites and publishers' websites but couldn't find any evidence of a book being done about the record-breaking club. It didn't make sense. To me, it was one of the greatest sporting stories of our time. But it was more than that now. Gretna had crossed over from the football world. Sheridan's speech made me realise they were now firmly rooted in the public psyche. My mind was made up.

Indeed it was the very next day that Gretna's season commenced and I started following the 'Black and Whites' from afar. They started well. In fact they started very well – a 6–0 defeat of Hamilton Academicals put them top of the First Division on goal difference. They'd lose their next three matches, including a historic UEFA Cup tie against Northern Ireland's Derry City. But it didn't matter – I was hooked. From that day forward, Gretna's was the first result I looked for in the Sunday papers.

One thing I noticed was that Gretna's results were never dull. It played havoc with my plans to get a publishing deal. I'd send off a proposal to a publisher and then cross my fingers that Gretna would keep winning while the proposal was being considered. As one publisher mulled over the idea, Gretna got beaten 6–0 by Hibernian in the CIS Cup. 'Thanks but no thanks,' came the reply on Monday morning.

Resolutely I contacted another publisher later that week. 'I'll have a look at it,' they said. Gretna beat Partick Thistle 6–0 in the league the following Saturday. The call came on Tuesday. 'You might be on to something here. Leave it with me.'

The following Saturday Gretna got beaten 2–0 at home by lowly Airdrie. Monday morning my phone rang. 'I think it's too much of a risk,' said the fickle publisher. 'Feel free to come back to me if they win the league.'

It went on like this for weeks, during which time Gretna's league position fluctuated. With each game, I felt like I was running out of time but they were always in or around the top half of the table so I never gave up hope. The loss to Airdrie was followed by a 3–3 draw away to fellow promotion hopefuls St Johnstone in early October 2006. Another 3–3 draw came the following week against Clyde and Gretna rounded off the month with a 3–1 win against Hamilton. Things were looking up for the First Division new boys from the tiny Borders village.

During this time, one particular publisher had my proposal sitting on his desk all along and was watching Gretna's results as keenly as I was. He didn't seem to be as put off by Gretna's unpredictability, which I liked – the way I saw it, it was a great story whether they got promoted to the SPL or not. Winning wouldn't hurt the prospects of a book – indeed, it would make sure it brought the Gretna story to a wider audience. As I was expecting to hear from him any day, I crossed my fingers that November would see a continuation of the club's good form – I was living in London at the time and I was desperate to get up to Scotland to follow the team first-hand.

Football being football, it started badly. Dundee beat Gretna 3–1 on 4 November 2006. Things improved the following week when they hammered local rivals Queen of the South 5–0 at home. Gretna's unpredictable form continued the following weekend, however, when they got beaten 2–1 away to fellow promotion chasers Livingston. It was frustrating and, all the while, I never heard a word from the publisher. With the season nearly a third of the way through, I knew that Gretna's game at home to Partick Thistle on 25 November was key. Nay, it was make or break. With both teams tied on twenty-seven points at the top of the table, anyone winning the match would go three points clear.

I was on edge the day of the game and wished I could be transported all the way from my North London flat to Raydale Park. It was strange because, although I hadn't *physically* started following the club, I had in another way. I was already emotionally involved in the club's fortunes. I also knew that, if I didn't hear from a publisher soon, the window of opportunity for doing the book would have passed – forever. I was desperate for Gretna to get back to winning ways.

That Saturday I followed the game closely on Ceefax and cheered every time each of the four goals Gretna scored went in. My girlfriend Lauren thought I'd lost the plot. It was a good win. A significant three points – Gretna were top of the table. In truth, I'd almost given up hope of ever hearing from a publisher by then. I was sitting in a pub with Lauren, bemoaning the fact. 'I can't believe no one wants to commission this book. I guess publishing just doesn't work like that,' I said. 'These life-changing telephone calls out of the blue just don't happen.'

Just then my mobile rang. We both looked at it for a moment, vibrating on the table, before I answered. It was an Edinburgh number. 'This is Campbell Brown from Black & White Publishing.' Gulp! 'Sorry to call so late in the day. I just wanted to say we've read over your proposal and we'd really like you to do the Gretna book with us . . . Hello . . . are you there?'

I was but I was speechless. Within a week, I'd left my job and moved back to my native Scotland for the first time in a decade. I didn't need my arm twisted as, in truth, I'd been pining to do just that for years. Come Saturday, I was on the terraces at Raydale Park for the first time. It happened that quickly. With fifteen out of thirty-six games gone, I had no time to waste. An unforgettable six-month journey had begun . . .

1

'You're Nothing but an English Pub Team'

30 August 2006

Before a publisher finally took the plunge, I'd done endless research about the feasibility of doing a book on the team from the tiny Borders village. I got a measure of what I'd be up against when I called Gretna's press officer Jon Tait for the first time. I was seated at my desk in my flat with the sounds of the city blowing in through the open window. At that precise moment, London and Gretna's remote Raydale Park seemed poles apart. I wondered why I was even considering upping sticks and moving back to Scotland to do a book on a team that had been playing English non-league football just five years earlier. The barman in my local, a Clyde fan, had already pointed out that the favourite chant for visiting teams to Raydale Park was:

English pub team!
You're nothing but an English pub team.

I had everything here I could ask for – a great job, a great girlfriend (with a pair of Arsenal season tickets), a great circle of friends and a great flat. But Gretna was a *great* story and no one seemed to be telling it. It was that rare thing in sport – an incredible, untold tale. They are like hen's teeth and, once I had hatched the idea to do the book, there was no talking me out of it. I wanted a ringside seat as the plucky Borderers set about rewriting the history books forever.

I phoned Tait to see how much assistance the club could be if I followed Gretna's quest for promotion to the Scottish Premier League (SPL). If they achieved the feat, it would make it an unprecedented three promotions in a row. I got a bad feeling from the start. It wasn't that Tait was being obstructive, he just wasn't committing himself to anything.

'Can I get access to the manager?' I asked.

'You'll just have to come up and see what happens,' replied Tait.

'And what about the owner, Brooks Mileson? I know he's been ill but surely you could get me some time with him?'

Again Tait filled me with trepidation about the task ahead by laughing off my requests for access to the eccentric club owner. With no access to Mileson, there would be little point in doing a book. I knew ME (myalgic encephalomyelitis or chronic fatigue syndrome) sufferer Mileson had recently undergone an operation to stem serious internal bleeding. I also knew that he'd recover as he had done from two previous heart attacks. This, after all, is the man who broke his back at the age of eleven, losing a kidney in the process, and was told he'd never walk again. Far from it – Mileson bounced back to become a national cross-country champion and a four-minute miler. He later made his fortune from insurance. Mileson's story is every bit as fascinating as Gretna's.

From the way the conversation was going, I was getting an inkling that Tait didn't want me to come to the club at all. Having written a book on another football club (Wigan Athletic), I knew this was not an uncommon reaction. It's a slow process and you have to take the softly-softly approach but Tait was giving me no cause for optimism whatsoever. It was a major problem because I wanted to go to a publisher with a complete package in place. As it stood, I'd have to lie about having been granted the elusive 'access all areas' that I really wanted and cross my fingers.

With no publishing deal anyway, my plan was only really half-baked. I had an idea that, if I could swing a deal, I might live in Edinburgh for the remainder of the season. Gretna was also an option, I suppose, if I wanted to go down the full *Shining*-style immersion route. I asked Tait what he thought about the idea.

Tait laughed uncontrollably.

'Sorry?'

'You don't want to live in Gretna, man,' said Tait in his thick Geordie brogue. 'There's nothing here apart from the football club!'

'Don't you live there?'

'Not bloody likely. I live doon in Carlisle,' he said.

I started to get a sense of what I was letting myself in for. Tait hadn't just made me feel uneasy about the project – he'd made me feel like an outsider. Something I'd soon learn about the Gretna press man would explain his vagueness and initial reluctance to help me out. Either way, I sensed there were going to be some testing times ahead.

28–9 November 2006

Having practically boarded the next train to Edinburgh (with Lauren in tow) after taking the call from the publisher, the next two days are packed with flat viewings, missed appointments and disappointments. We establish two things by the end of the first day of viewings. Namely that, while I am a property snob – wood-effect laminate flooring and faceless Ikea furniture are anathema to me – Lauren is a location snob. This means that either one of us is going to be disappointed (I somehow doubt it will be Lauren) or we'll find a nice flat in a great area and live happily ever after.

After increasing our rental budget by 30 per cent, day two of the flat-hunt proves more fruitful. We find a garden flat

(I'm happy) in the Stockbridge part of the city (Lauren's ideal location). Amusingly, our landlord's name is Johnnie Walker. It's almost too good to be true.

2 December 2006
Gretna FC v St Johnstone
Raydale Park, Gretna

A fitting first game as I follow Gretna FC on their unlikely quest for promotion to the SPL. Pre-season league favourites St Johnstone, lying fourth in the First Division with twenty-four points, make the long journey south to face Gretna, table-toppers with thirty points. It's a veritable championship six-pointer.

With the Black and Whites just hitting top spot in the league, it seems like the perfect starting point for this fly-on-the-wall account of the club's promotion push. That and the fact that I have only just signed the book deal. Come to think of it, I've yet to actually receive a signed copy of the contract so *please* don't let me down today, Gretna – not before my publisher has inked the agreement. Anything less than a win today and the project might be over before it has even begun. No pressure then.

Wearing five layers, looking like the Michelin Man and feeling like eight years in London has turned a tough – well, let's say moderately rugged – Highlander into the quintessential southern softie, I set off. I've got ninety miles to cover, mostly by way of a two-and-a-half-hour train journey from Glasgow (where I stayed with a friend last night) to Gretna Green, at a snail's pace. I've never been to Gretna or Raydale Park before and really have no idea what to expect. The train is ominously empty, especially of football fans, and there's not a black-and-white Gretna scarf or blue-and-white Saints scarf in sight. It makes me wonder if I'm even on the right train. I ask a woman (travelling with a child pumped up on a diet of Irn-Bru and

4

crisps at 10 a. m.) and she assures me I am. Nursing a fairly savage hangover, it's all I can do not to throttle the young kid who keeps me awake for the duration of the journey. Note to self: no more big nights out before matches.

Two hours of screaming, biting, chewing, jumping and shouting later – the E-number-filled child, not me – during which time the kid's poor mother lies slumped over the table, defeated, only occasionally rising to feed her child more junk food, and we're in Gretna Green. *Welcome to Scotland – the future's bright, the future's (Irn-Bru) orange*, I think as I step off the train, alone, on to the deserted platform.

There is no station to speak of. As the train pulls away, I survey the scene. A deserted platform, no longer than three train lengths. A graffitied shelter. On one side an expanse of green fields and a small conurbation of houses – Gretna Green. On the other side the busy M74 and a small village beyond – Gretna. I've rarely seen such an uninspiring stop on the national rail network.

There's a certain dislocation that can only be achieved by stepping off a warm, busy train on to a deserted platform and watching that train – your security blanket, if you will – pootle off into the distance. At this exact moment, as the wind stiffens, cutting me to the bone, I'd give anything to be back on the train – screaming kids and all. Come back – all is forgiven! And save some of that Iru-Bru for me.

I shouldn't complain. This is what I wanted. I didn't want to travel here by car. I didn't want to plan my journey to the nth degree or read anything about Gretna or the football club before I experienced it for myself. I didn't want to bring a friend along or my girlfriend . . . OK, honestly, she's at the Arsenal v Tottenham London derby as we speak so couldn't come and hold my hand even if I'd wanted her to . . . which I did.

I realise that I don't even know where the stadium is. It's 2 p. m. and there's not a football fan in sight. Then I notice a man walking a dog. He disappears into the tunnel beneath the platform that leads to a barren field and the village in the distance. I instinctively follow. After ten minutes, I enter Gretna for the first time. Still there's not a soul in sight, but rounding a corner, I see what I'm looking for – football fans, twenty of them, dressed from head to toe in the blue and white of St Johnstone, some eyeing me threateningly for signs of my allegiance. I decide to merge with the 'crowd' and follow. After five minutes, the throng enters a pub – nice work.

I drag myself out of the warm pub, however. It's half an hour to kick-off and I haven't even found the stadium. I'd happily while away the time over a quick hair of the dog but I've arranged to make myself known to Gretna's press man before the match. I don't think we've got off on the best footing on the telephone so I'm determined not to miss him today.

It only takes five minutes to find Raydale Park and catch my first glimpse of the Borders club's fans – the Black and White Army – swarming towards the stadium like ants. I get that buzz of anticipation you can only get from visiting a football stadium for the first time. I'm excited but it also feels like my first day at school. I know that I need to make a good first impression to have any chance whatsoever of getting the access that my publisher demands. I've been down this road before and know the entire project rests on whether people at the club like and trust you. There's no predicting the response I'll receive. For some reason, Gretna being a smaller club makes me less confident of a warm reception.

It is with trepidation that I enter the stadium. I have no further instructions from Tait other than to 'come and find me and say hello'. I'm desperate to see the pitch and the players warming up, though, so I bypass the chaotic collection of Portakabins that house the club's off-pitch operations. Through one steamed-up window I see a photographer in North Face all-in-one winter wear, looking like an overgrown infant in a Babygro. That must be the press office. It can wait. I want to savour my first view of Gretna's field of dreams. Raydale Park

– an unassuming arena yet the scene of so many historic moments in the Scottish League. It wasn't always that way. Once English non-league football was played here.

I quickly realise that I'm nervous as hell and lost to boot. I follow the river of black and white through a narrow doorway in single file. This bottleneck is the main entrance to the ground! Apart from its atrocious layout – one that would make a health and safety officer wince – the first thing that strikes you about Raydale Park is its intimacy. As you enter at the left-hand corner, you're immediately confronted with the contractible players' tunnel that traverses the main thoroughfare.

Gretna's manager, Rowan Alexander, is standing at the end of the tunnel, a picture of concentration. The players are milling around too. Some are out on the pitch examining the playing surface. Others stand talking to fans, signing the odd autograph. It's unlike anything I've ever seen at a professional football club. No cordoned-off areas. No surly security guards barring your way. I get the feeling that I could walk up the tunnel, into the dressing room, pull on the Gretna number 9 shirt and no one would object. Well, no one but Gretna's star striker, Colin McMenamin.

Walking past the tunnel next to one of the corner flags, I soon come to the supporters' club bar and hospitality area – a modest building in keeping with the ramshackle nature of the ground. Inside, red-faced sponsors in ill-fitting suits are shoulder to shoulder drinking English bitter. The pitch is barely three yards to their left, separated only by a low wall and a narrow path that leads along the edge of the pitch to the main stand. It has to be seen to be believed.

This narrow corridor is as congested as the M8 at 6 p. m. on a Friday night. Everyone entering at the home turnstiles must tread the path along the touchline as far as the halfway line before the stand begins. I stop and ask a steward where the press box is. A Cumbrian accent replies that it's further up on the right. I walk along, keeping my eyes right, averted from Rocky the Raydale Rooster – Gretna's ebullient mascot who's dancing like a madman in the centre circle. Rocky Radio – Gretna's match-day radio station and an exclusive one at that with a mere 1,744 listeners today – provides the soundtrack of high-octane pop and rock.

It's not long before I've passed the tiny, decrepit main stand and the temporary stand that wouldn't look out of place at a school sports day. From the far corner of the ground, I look back up to where I've come from. Raydale Park is a sight to behold. To the right, running along behind the goal, is a new stand, split seventy–thirty between home and away fans. On the far touchline is a long, low-roofed terrace. 'Shed' might be a better description. The seven-foot-tall structure runs the length of the far touchline like an elongated bus shelter. The SPL may be beckoning for one of today's teams but we are a long way – a *very* long way – from the heady heights of Ibrox and Parkhead.

There's no stand or terracing at all behind the other goal. This has been demolished to make way for phase one of Gretna's new 6,000-capacity stadium – a requirement for entry into the SPL. Locals are up in arms about rumours of a possible delay to the plan that could see the club miss the March deadline for completion. The delay would mean that, if promoted, the club would be forced to seek a ground-share in order to gain entry to the hallowed SPL. When I eventually do meet Jon Tait, he will give me a titbit of gossip about a potential ground-share. None of the fans seem aware of it but spotting a Motherwell FC director in the stands during the game gets my own journalistic radar going.

I've been at the small ground for ten minutes and still haven't tracked down Tait. Taking a wrong turn back past the temporary stand, I find myself beneath the Meccano-like structure next to a line of portaloos. At the other end, a man in a club jacket furtively rolls a cigarette and lights it while simultaneously scoffing a meat pie. I walk over, surprising him. 'You don't know where I could find Jon Tait, do you?'

'What do you want to speak to him for? He's a fookin' wanker,' comes the reply.

'Oh, right.' I'm momentarily stunned.

'Nah, it's me, man. How's it gannin'?' says Tait, punching me in the arm.

I've been to lots of football grounds across the UK to report on matches and you're never sure what to expect from press officers. Some welcome you with open arms. Others see your presence as an inconvenience. Tait was a hard one to figure out. On the telephone, he'd been guarded – I'd later learn that this was because Tait was 30,000 words into his own tome on the club's history that he intended to self-publish. Once I met him face to face, however, I realised I'd misread him. Tait had an informal, laid-back, dare I say 'amateur' manner. It was a trait that ran through the club from top to bottom. Not in a bad way, I might add. I found the atmosphere quite charming.

Tait, a bricklayer-turned-journalist, proceeds to take me on a whistlestop tour of Raydale, introducing me to anyone of interest who happens to pass. We meet Craig – everyone dispenses with surnames at the club – a colleague of Tait who he leaves me with in the Portakabin-cum-press office while he disappears in search of another pie. Tait's colleague is rewatching Gretna's recent Scottish Cup Final appearance. Because of the informal manner of the introduction, I assume he is Tait's assistant but as we talk I become nigh-on positive that the young man sitting across from me drinking stewed tea and discussing the finer points of Newcastle nightlife is none other than Brooks Mileson's son and heir (to a reported £80-million fortune). I'm still not absolutely certain so I venture some ambiguous questioning.

'What's your day-to-day involvement here, then?' I ask.

'I do a bit of everything, mate. The old man wants me to take it all over one day.'

I knew it. 'Really? How is your dad? Is he coming to the game?'

'Aye. He's getting better. He'll be here but will head off straight after,' says Mileson Jnr.

'It would be really good to speak to him for my book when he's feeling up to it,' I say.

'No problem, mate. Just tell me when you want to do it and I'll sort it out with the old man.'

This was more than I could have hoped for from my first visit to the club. Having expected the wealthy Milesons to be aloof and hard to reach, I'd had sleepless nights about gaining access to them. But here I was helping the affable Mileson put together the journalists' correct result sweepstake. I pick 4–3. After monitoring Gretna's results for the first half of the season, I know that they are rarely involved in no-score draws but the real reason I am burdened with the prediction is that 1–0, 2–0 and every other feasible winning Gretna scoreline are already taken. I could plump for a 1–0 or 2–1 to today's visitors but, with Mileson standing over me, I know what needs to be done. Plumping for a Gretna win seems to appeal to Mileson, who smiles and nods in approval. It is a pound well spent.

Tait returns with white-haired club chairman Ron MacGregor. MacGregor is one of the few staff to have witnessed the Mileson revolution first-hand. As club chief executive Graeme Muir joins us for a chat, MacGregor excuses himself but not before inviting me back to see him next week.

Among other things, Muir is working on the redevelopment of the ground and ground-share plans for next season. I find him to be approachable and down to earth. Aside from Mileson Snr, I've now met every key member of the off-field management. It's a good day's work. The players and coaching staff will be a completely different kettle of fish. They are the centurions, the untouchables of club hierarchy at any level of the game. To get on first-name terms with the manager and his squad I'll have my work cut out. Still, there'd be over twenty games to attend before the end of the season and I'm optimistic.

'You're Nothing but an English Pub Team'

With kick-off nearing, Tait shows me to my seat in the windswept press box before disappearing to a far warmer-looking seat at the back of the stand. Tait tells me I'm seated next to two journalists from a German magazine who are over to write a feature on the upwardly mobile club. Except they aren't. The seats are empty now and would remain empty (yet reserved) at every game I'd go to that season. (Tait often asked me if they'd turned up yet. They never did.)

Far from being a heated, luxurious vantage point, the press box is just a section of sixteen seats positioned directly behind the away dugout. Sitting on the front row of the press box, I am virtually on the pitch. And with the only means of accessing the main stand passing right in front of me, I'm repeatedly required to stand up to let people past. Still, it affords me my first brief meeting with club owner Mileson.

As he passes, the ponytailed and bearded Mileson says hello and stretches out a frail-looking hand. For a moment, I think he knows who I am but then I notice he does this with everyone. He's the club's saviour and a man of the people and everyone wants to wish him well after his recent operation. Mileson is nowhere near as intimidating as I'd imagined. Indeed, he seems at least as down to earth if not more so than everyone else I've met at the club. Far from being suspicious at my presence, I've been made to feel at home at Gretna and as welcome as if I'd just dropped in on an old, much-loved friend. I admit that any attempts at journalistic impartiality start to crumble there and then.

Despite the strong wind, it is a clear, sunny day but one where the daylight is living on borrowed time. No sooner have the club's very own cheerleading troupe – the Annan Angels – finished their pre-match interpretation of the song '500 Miles' than the floodlights are illuminated and kick-off beckons.

This is my first proper look at the Gretna team. To a certain extent, my own fate will be intrinsically tied to this group of players for the next six months so I'm keen to see them in action. I already know of ex-Ross County defender Martin 'Canso' Canning (more on whom later) who joined Gretna in January 2006. I know of influential midfielder Steve 'Tosher' Tosh too. The former Aberdeen man is renowned for his goal-scoring ability – twenty-two goals in almost seventy games for the club confirms it.

I also know of Alan Main, Gretna's thirty-nine-year-old goal-keeper who spent time with Dundee United and St Johnstone earlier in his career. As a member of United's youth set-up, I'd once played snooker with Main though I doubt he'd remember it. Kenny 'The Good Doctor' Deuchar is the only other Gretna player that I know anything about. Deuchar, a doctor and accomplished striker, has become a crowd favourite since his transfer from East Fife in July 2004. He scored a staggering forty-one goals in the 2004/05 season as Gretna were promoted from the Third Division to the Second. He scored no fewer than six hat-tricks, equalling Jimmy Greaves' long-standing record in the process. With each hat-trick earning the player a week's use of Brooks Mileson's Aston Martin, the club owner barely got to use the car last season.

Deuchar isn't playing today, however. He isn't even on the bench. Having not started a match for a month, the Good Doctor – the nickname bestowed on him by Sky Sports' Jeff Stelling – has shocked the fans by submitting a transfer request. It is the topic on every fan's lips and the fact that Deuchar is profiled in *Anvil*, the official match-day programme only serves to fan the flames of speculation. Deuchar may be on his way out of the club but not before we learn that his favourite food is sticky toffee pudding and his favourite drink is Irn-Bru (what else?).

Gretna line-up today as follows:

*Alan Main, Derek Townsley, Danny Grainger, Steve Tosh,
Martin Canning, Chris Innes (c), Erik Paartalu, David
Nicholls, Colin McMenamin, David Graham, Gavin Skelton*

'You're Nothing but an English Pub Team'

Subs: Craig Barr, Matthew Berkeley, Greg Fleming (GK), James Grady, Jamie McQuilken

St Johnstone may be lying fourth in the table but no one is in any doubt that the former SPL team are favourites to win the First Division and the sole promotion spot to the top tier. It's on-form Gretna that start brightest, however, and their 4–4–2 formation quickly takes on a more attacking bent with Tosh and local boy Skelton on either side of midfield making repeated forays up the wing to support Gretna's young strike partnership of McMenamin and Graham. It's exciting stuff and the standard of football on display impresses me.

The crowd is unexpectedly vocal. I'm not sure why that surprises me but it does. Maybe I just don't associate the Borders with football. It's rugby territory in my mind but I find myself looking forward to spending my Saturdays for the foreseeable future in the company of the jocular Gretna fans. A turnout of 1,744 may be poor on the face of it but for a village of 2,705 people it is probably hard to beat on a per capita basis anywhere in the world.

It only takes ten minutes before a group of home fans start taunting Saints manager Owen Coyle. Among them is Rowan Alexander's partner, Clare, who is sitting behind me. The exchange ends with Coyle mouthing an X-rated response before turning to apologise a moment later. This is football at the sharp end, at the coalface, where fans' taunts can be heard by players and managers alike. The intimacy would be foreign to a player in a better league.

I spend the first twenty minutes, during which Gretna dominate, trying to familiarise myself with the home team. Derek 'Degsy' Townsley at right back looks every bit the journeyman pro, his greying hair belying a never-say-die, combative style of defending. His height makes him a target for attacking set pieces too. In the middle at the back, captain Chris Innes and Martin Canning look imperious in the air and

I doubt I'll see a better defensive partnership in the league all season. Aggressive, tall and agile, the two also cause a threat at set pieces. Young Danny Grainger at left back is not blessed with the height of his counterparts but is solid in the tackle and ventures up the left wing at every opportunity. With Alan Main between the posts it makes for an extremely solid defence and it's easy to see why the team have only leaked one goal in their last three matches.

In midfield thirty-three-year-old Tosh provides the flair on the right. A player who wears his heart on his sleeve, he's quick to challenge every decision by the referee and is involved in every good Gretna move. Davie Nicholls in the middle provides a bit more grey hair to temper the raw – and sometimes rash – enthusiasm of Tosh. More of a classic holding midfielder, he and young Australian Erik 'Skippy' Paartalu – who bears a passing resemblance to Steven Gerrard – repeatedly break up St Johnstone attacks before sending Tosh and pacy left-sided midfielder Gavin 'Gav' Skelton – twice voted Players' Player of the Year – on counter-attacks. Skelton is the club's longest-serving player and Gretna to the core.

Paartalu's presence is the only fathomable reason I can think of for there being an inflatable kangaroo being brandished by St Johnstone's noisiest pocket of fans on the terrace opposite. Someone sitting next to me suggests it's because Australia routed England in the latest Ashes Test and that some people view Gretna as an English team. Oh, how I've missed Scotland's particular brand of insularity and petty jingoism.

In Davie Graham and Colin McMenamin, manager Rowan Alexander has two in-form strikers. The industrious Graham, at twenty-one years of age, is full of running and, having recently made the number 10 shirt his own, has become a fans' favourite. Graham was voted man of the match in Gretna's 4–0 victory over Partick Thistle the week before, despite strike partner McMenamin having scored a hat-trick. The taller McMenamin is more of a classic centre forward and the former

14

Newcastle United youth flourishes from the opportunities that Graham's mazy runs create.

It's not long before Gretna's dominance starts to pay off. With only Saints' Trinidad and Tobago international, Jason Scotland, posing any threat to Gretna's defence, the team is able to keep the pressure on the Perth men. On twenty minutes that pressure pays off when Tosh intercepts a sloppy Steven Anderson pass across his own eighteen-yard box and rounds keeper Michael McGovern to give Gretna a deserved lead. The crowd erupts and it takes a moment or two to realise that I'm clapping. I receive some withering looks from my colleagues in the press box as a result. I feel sheepish for getting carried away but the atmosphere at Raydale Park is contagious.

The goal seems to wake up the lethargic visitors. I know it's a good two-and-half-hour drive from Perth but they have been dreadful in the opening spell and certainly don't have the look of title contenders. However, on thirty-five minutes the visitors actually have the ball in the net, only for it to be ruled offside. The scare elicits an immediate response from Gretna. On thirty-eight minutes a cross to the back post is fumbled by McGovern and headed back across goal, where Paartalu arrives to steer home Gretna's second. I'm up out of my seat again – this time with a little more reserve. (At the time I found it inexplicable why Rocky Radio played the jingle for Antipodean insurance company Sheila's Wheels after the goal. On reflection it's obvious. Needless to say the inflatable kangaroo went wild.)

The final seven minutes of the half seem to be spent waiting for replacement balls after the first, second, third and fourth are punted out of the park and over the low corrugated-iron roof of the away terrace and into the gardens of the houses which run adjacent to the ground. When half-time arrives I wait hopefully for Tait to fetch me and lead me to an unseen press lounge for a complimentary pie and Bovril. This is not

15

the SPL, however. Five minutes later, with the cold wind biting, I'm still waiting so, resignedly – yes, I know I sound like a spoiled child – I go and join the queue at the pie stand. As I near the front of the queue I see that there are four pies left and three people in front of me. When the first person in the queue buys two I know that's that. I deserve it, I suppose. I console myself with a hot dog with dubious meat content and a cup of thick Bovril. It's a good job. I don't think I would have survived the second half without it. Raydale Park's proximity to the Solway Firth and the unsheltered nature of the ground give it an arctic feel.

The second half is only minutes old when the crowd start chipping away at Coyle again. The Saints manager, at first annoyed by the intrusion, seems to warm to the crowd and enjoy the repartee. There's certainly nothing for him to enjoy on the pitch. With the temperature dropping to near freezing, Saints just don't seem up for it. Their indifference enables Gretna forward Davie Graham to run riot. The first twenty-five minutes of the second half is some of the scrappiest, most disjointed, mundane football I've seen anywhere, however. Only the introduction of James Grady for the injured McMenamin injects any sort of pace into the game. Still, with the form McMenamin is in – he's the league's top scorer on sixteen goals – Grady needs to make his mark.

Grady is instrumental on seventy minutes when he crosses to Tosh, who unleashes a rasping volley that whistles past the post. Saints do briefly offer some resistance but never really look like scoring. With hypothermia setting in, I lapse back into counting how many footballs have been kicked out of the ground. My records show that balls five, six and seven sail out of the ground into the inky darkness on seventy-five, eighty and eighty-three minutes. I'm starting to realise that six months of this could test my patience to the limit. (If I knew then how the season would unfold, and ultimately end, I'd curse myself for getting so maudlin so early.)

'You're Nothing but an English Pub Team'

There are few people in the stadium – players included – who are disappointed to hear the final whistle. The game wasn't a classic but it's three valuable points against one of the title contenders and the players celebrate as if they've won the league. In that moment I glimpse a togetherness in the squad that St Johnstone just didn't display today. As Gretna's very own anthem, 'Living the Dream', plays over the tannoy system I can't deny the veracity of it. If First Division football sees tiny Gretna already living their dream, it's hard to grasp what promotion to the SPL would mean.

In the press room after the match Rowan Alexander keeps the hacks waiting and when he arrives he's serious, deter-mined and businesslike. I've seen that look before in young managers like Paul Jewell at Wigan Athletic. I decide not to introduce myself just yet. Nobody else offers to so I assume that now is not the time to meet the mastermind behind Gretna's record-breaking success.

No one seems very at ease around Alexander though that's often the way football managers like it. I suppose it's part of their job description. My view of him changes slightly when I see him outside the ground, embracing Craig Mileson in a manly hug. You can tell how much it means to both men to have beaten one of the league's so-called 'big' clubs. The gesture also hints at the close-knit feel that runs through the club from top to bottom. Money or no money, this club has worked hard to climb up the Scottish leagues. It means everything to those involved to take another step closer to the SPL by opening up a five-point lead at the top of the table.

I leave Raydale Park happy and intrigued to learn more about the club. As I stroll alone through the darkness to the station I realise that not only do I need to go back to Gretna, I actually *want* to.

6 December 2006

That return to Raydale comes quicker than expected. I realise
I'll have to wait a very long time for Jon Tait to arrange anything for me so decide just to head down on the off chance.
Even if Mileson and Alexander are not around I know that
club chairman Ron MacGregor will be.

I'm not wrong. When I arrive, and Tait gets over the shock
of seeing me, he tells me that neither Mileson nor Alexander
are anywhere to be seen. MacGregor is in, however, and Tait
takes me to see the chairman. 'Make sure you've got plenty
of tape in your recorder!' he says as he leaves.

Like all of Raydale Park's off-field operations, the boardroom and MacGregor's office are housed in Portakabins. It
has the temporary look of an Antarctic research station and
is about as warm. I receive the warmest of welcomes from
MacGregor, however. I can see why the white-haired pen-
sioner and his wife Helen, the club secretary, are so popular
at the club.

Sitting down with MacGregor at his large, leather-bound
mahogany desk, surrounded by some vaguely maritime-
inspired decor, I feel like I'm aboard a tall ship rather than
inside a prefabricated Portakabin. I'm sure I almost detect a
gentle undulating motion but realise I actually *am* rocking
on the teak swivel armchair on the plush but lumpy carpet
salvaged from the office of one of Brooks Mileson's many
companies. I like the anachronisms. I like the mentality that
completely ignores the infrastructure and says, 'This is our
boardroom and this is all we've got so let's make the most of
it.' It sums up the can-do attitude of the club that has got it
where it is today.

MacGregor has been at the club since the English non-
league days and is the perfect person to tell me how the club
went from there to the cusp of the SPL in such a short space
of time. He provides me with the perfect potted history of

the club. I didn't expect him to do so without pausing for breath, however – Tait had been right about the tape.

'As the only Scottish team to play in England, the club has always held a lot of interest for football fans,' starts MacGregor with very little prompting – it's like listening to your favourite grandpa tell war stories. 'I first got involved fifteen years ago when the club was playing English non-league football. It was halfway through our penultimate season in England that Rowan Alexander joined the club. We'd harboured ambitions of getting into the Scottish League for a long time and had applications rejected in 1993 and 1999. The question of whether we could ever be self-financing always came up.

'When Airdrieonians folded in 2002 the league launched a contest to replace them so we put together a brochure and started canvassing all the league teams. Everyone thought Airdrie United would win the ballot because they were the natural successors to Airdrieonians but we won, much to the dismay of the other applicants. That was in late June and we had to have a team and have the club in order for the start of the season in August.

'There was a fearsome checklist. We had to remove the gravel from the terraces, level the pitch. It was endless and because the contractors knew we had a tight deadline we didn't exactly get the best deal for any of this work.

'We somehow made the deadline but due to all the outlay we started to toil as the season went on. The crowds were good. I remember our first fixture was against Greenock Morton and it was a 2,200 sell-out. Matt Henney scored for us in sixteen seconds. It was a dream start on the pitch – we'd finish the season fifth in the league – but off it we'd lost sponsorship now we were playing in Scotland. By the end of the season we had a hefty financial burden, and a local business who'd helped us with the government Skillseekers programme said they were going to pull out.'

With MacGregor lost in reverie, I let him continue uninterrupted and sip my tea dutifully.

'Brooks was known in the area for his interest in Carlisle,' he continues, 'but his offer to buy the club was refused. He first came to Gretna as a fan, paying his money like everyone else. One of our committee knew Brooks and asked him if he could sponsor the Skillseekers programme. He agreed and was happy just to pop along now and again to see how things were going. He didn't sweep into the boardroom or anything like that.

'In that second season in the Third Division we saw that we weren't making any headway with the finances whatsoever. Brooks agreed to give us a bit of advice. We did the best we could with the benefit of his nous but still made no progress so we asked him if he'd be willing to get more involved, take a seat on the committee. Brooks said, "If I'm to get involved you have to transform yourself from a committee-run organisation to a limited company. I will help you with that. I also do not want to control the club or be announced as the new owner."

'Of course we said, "Yes please!" No money changed hands but Brooks agreed to take on the financial commitments of the club. Getting the squad to go full-time was the first thing he did. At that time we only had one full-time member on the playing staff. That was Rowan. He'd joined as player, manager and groundsman after leaving Queen of the South under a bit of a cloud. He never complained. He rolled up his sleeves and did very well.

'When Brooks got involved he said to Rowan, "If you really like your groundsman work you can do that full-time but if you'd prefer to manage full-time the job is yours. I know which one I'd prefer." It took Rowan a microsecond to accept the manager's job. We moved towards being a full-time football club from there and gathered momentum. We finished third in the league that season and got our first promotion the next. The season after, we were promoted again and somehow reached the Scottish Cup Final. It's hard to take in even now but it happened that quickly . . .'

MacGregor pauses and I'm about to ask him a question when he continues. I keep the tape rolling.

'It was an emotional day at Hampden. It was a dream come true. We took four thousand fans. There's not even that many people in the village! It was a fantastic atmosphere . . .'

(In case you're wondering, this is where I did actually run out of tape. I could have happily listened to MacGregor all day, however.)

2

No Sleep till Airdrie

9 December 2006
Airdrie United v Gretna FC
Excelsior Stadium, Airdrie

Despite just moving into a new flat in Edinburgh I decide to break up the trip to Airdrie with an overnight stop in Glasgow at my mate Doug's. (Honestly? OK, the missus has gone back down south again, this time for a job interview, leaving me high and dry.)

Doug was the first of my friends to get married and now, sadly, he's the first to get divorced – I think he'll appreciate the company. Little do I know that Doug had also invited Russ – conversely the most recent of our friends to get wed. We're a pretty incorrigible trio but recent rumblings in the conjugal ether make me doubt that I'll escape the night without a crushing hangover.

I'm not wrong. After an early start, we're soon three sheets to the wind, back at Doug's fighting over what to play on the stereo. I take a photo of Doug and Russ wrestling drunkenly over control of the music with my mobile phone and send it to another friend. Half an hour later, and true to form, the pair are passed out on the sofa, beer cans in hand. I can't resist taking another photo and sending it too. I spend the next half-hour playing all the songs I want to play before passing out myself.

I wake with a hangover but it's a 3 p. m. kick-off and Airdrie is only a thirty-five-minute train ride away. It's a trip into the unknown. As with Gretna last week, I've never been to

23

Airdrie in my life. This project is going to be a real eye-opener in so many ways. It's an opportunity to reconnect with my homeland after nearly a decade away and to go to places I would never otherwise have reason to visit, or probably ever visit again.

I'm glad to be making the trip to Airdrie even on such an especially cold day as this. The Gretna press man Jon Tait told me that he never goes to away games and that the travelling support is usually extremely modest, often no more than a coachload. I'm pleased to be in the minority.

Being just a short hop from vibrant, regenerated Glasgow, I'm not sure what to expect of Airdrie. As the train passes through the city centre and then on to the delights of Easterhouse and Shettleston, I begin to get a feeling of foreboding. Again, I could have driven here, planned it all on Multimap or used sat nav but I didn't. I wanted the trip to be part of the experience. All I knew was that I was to alight at Drumgelloch – the end of the line – and that the stadium was a fifteen-minute walk away. I say I could have driven but what I really mean is I could have asked a friend to drive. I don't have a driving licence and until I do it will be First ScotRail's finest for me. So long as there are no buses involved, it suits me just fine.

The grim sight of endless housing estates and derelict buildings scrawled with sectarian slogans makes way for a narrow band of countryside after thirty minutes but it doesn't take long for the urban decay to return. Some of the stops on the line look genuinely nice, if a little run-down, but nothing could prepare me for Drumgelloch. Now I'm not sure how many people from the town will ever read this book but I'm just going to stick my neck out and say this anyway: I've never been to such an uninspiring place in all my life. This makes Gretna and its rows of well-kept council houses look like a setting from *Last of the Summer Wine*.

My plan is to follow the stream of supporters that I'd assumed would be on the train, from the station to the ground.

It's more reliable than any map or directions I know. The problem? There is not another soul on the train when we reach the end of the line. As I step off it and survey the endless – and I mean *absolutely endless* – lines of grey council houses, I get a sudden sinking feeling. I feel like an intrepid travel writer whose luck has finally run out.

The most striking thing is that there is not one single shop or pub in sight. I can, however, see a set of floodlights in the distance at what must be the Excelsior Stadium. In between is a sea of grey, decaying real estate. I suddenly don't blame the majority of the Gretna loyal for staying at home and going Christmas shopping.

After walking for ten minutes, I've still not seen a shop where I could ask for directions. In fact I've not seen a soul. I've been barked at by numerous pit bull terriers but not seen one person. The only sign of life is the occasional garish display of Christmas lights adorning the tired-looking houses. It's eerie and threatening – the most sinister sort of maze imaginable. Thank God I've got the floodlights and I'm using them as a ship caught in a storm uses a lighthouse. OK, I'm exaggerating – my hangover must be contributing to the paranoia.

After the grimness of Drumgelloch the grandly named Excelsior Stadium shines like a beacon. Most First Division teams would kill for a stadium like this. It's modern, comfortable and probably the right size should a club like this gain promotion to the SPL. It's ironic that one of the clubs best equipped for the SPL is worst placed to win it – Airdrie are rock bottom of the league. At the other end of the table Gretna are five points clear but as I pop into the press box to pick up a team sheet *Mail on Sunday* reporter Jon Coates reminds me not to take anything for granted. 'What makes the league so good this year is that all the teams are capable of beating each other,' he says.

I settle down for the first half next to Gretna's affable web editor, Keith Melvin, and two of Rowan Alexander's backroom staff. The duo are here to operate the ProZone software – a video analysis tool which produces extensive feedback on player and team performance. It's a surprise to see the system being used by a small club like Gretna but it's a statement of intent from the Black and Whites.

Aside from the derelict coal mine visible through one of the open corners of the ground, the Excelsior feels like a proper football stadium. Despite the crowd being reported as 1,169, it's hard to believe there are that many here. There are no more than fifty Gretna fans and only one of the four stands is open. After scrounging a press ticket I've been exiled to the stand opposite. It's got to be the coldest day of the year and with the press box open to the elements and no tea and certainly not a pie in sight, I decide there and then that I'll sit with the Gretna fans at future away fixtures.

The Gretna line-up is unchanged from last week:

Main, Townsley, Grainger, Tosh, Canning, Innes, Paartalu, Nicholls, McMenamin, Graham, Skelton

Subs: Berkeley, Fleming, Grady, Jenkins, McQuilken

On the back of the win over championship rivals St Johnstone it would seem that the journey north by the Gretna fans would be one worth making. Saying that, Airdrie also beat Saints three matches ago. Ominously, Airdrie beat Gretna at Raydale Park in late September too. It is one of the results that threw the form book out of the window for this division. Relegation candidates or not, Airdrie are not to be taken lightly.

The first twenty minutes of the match offer little to suggest that we're watching top versus bottom, the teams with the most goals scored (Gretna) and conceded (Airdrie). Without a shot on goal to cheer the fans, the biting cold suddenly becomes more evident and the prospect of the half-time whistle and a warm pie excites more than the prospect of a goal. Yet one comes. A quick look at the teams before the match shows that Gretna tower over their opposition. Set pieces from the visitors are always going to be a threat. And so it proves. A Danny Grainger corner is fumbled by the keeper – a reminder that it is pantomime season – and Derek Townsley has the easiest of tap-ins.

The feeling with Alexander's ProZone boys is that we can now expect a bucketload of goals. Yet Gretna somehow conspire to self-destruct. On twenty-seven minutes the usually reliable Alan Main fluffs a clearance directly into the path of Airdrie's Gary Twigg. With Twigg bearing down on the eighteen-yard box with an open goal at his mercy it is only a last-ditch tackle by Martin Canning that denies the Airdrie striker an easy tap-in. The rash tackle earns Canning a red card and it is some consolation for the Gretna support that the referee does not give a penalty too. Instead the official awards a free kick right on the edge of the box that is duly wasted.

With Gretna down to ten men I suddenly get a feeling of foreboding. It is not only promotion and Gretna's five-point lead at the top of the table at stake but the prospects for my book too. I can't decide which worries me more but before I know it I start to shout, 'Come on, Gretna!' My outburst draws some cursory glances from the impartial press box. Stuff them – 'Come on, Gretna!' I repeat.

With Steve Tosh reluctantly drafted back from midfield to right back and Townsley moved into the centre, Gretna still look good for their one-goal lead. The pressure from Airdrie begins to mount, however, and when a through ball from Twigg is latched on to by Graeme Holmes it takes a great point-blank save from Main to deny Airdrie an equaliser. It's not long before the home team are on the attack again and deservedly draw level on forty-two minutes when Stephen McDougall cuts in from the right and fires the ball low into the left-hand corner of the net.

As the half-time whistle sounds talk in the press box turns to whether Alexander will stick with two strikers or bring on a defender to shore things up. No one includes me in the conversation. Press boxes are places where you're not easily let into the inner circle. You've got to do your time before you're accepted by the lifers, the old-timers who haven't missed a game in twenty years, who know everyone at every ground and who seem able to conjure up cups of tea and pies out of thin air. It's from these old stagers that you usually hear the best gossip, and when I overhear some of the senior journalists talking in whispers about Gretna's owner my ears prick up. 'Brooks looked grey last week. He looked like an old man and was walking with a stick. It didn't look good to me at all,' says one reporter gravely. It's a sobering thought. Mileson is key to my book. He's the man who's made it all possible at Gretna and the thought of him shuffling off his mortal coil before I interview him terrifies me.

The ProZone boys are more concerned about the game. 'What do you reckon?' I say. 'I think Gretna can still nick it.'

'We'll do well to get a draw,' replies one of the boys, eyeing the statistics on his screen. He must know something I don't. Airdrie are still there for the taking. Alexander proves it, defiantly fielding an unchanged side for the second half. This is brave management but it worries me for one reason – in the first half Tosh was looking more and more frustrated at being pinned back in defence. He's a ticking time bomb as far as I can see.

Hats off to Alexander for sticking to his guns. It's a gamble but Gretna start the second half strongly and look the more likely to score. It's a disciplined display only blighted by an inevitable yellow card for Tosh. The booking seems to precipitate a collapse and Airdrie go straight for the jugular. On sixty-one minutes Twigg rises in front of a stationary Gretna defence to head home. Twigg scores a carbon copy of the goal ten minutes later to make it 3–1.

No Sleep till Airdrie

On seventy-five minutes Gretna briefly rally for a comeback after Townsley gets a second from a set piece: 3–2. As Gretna chase the game and tire, however, Twigg is granted acres of space and completes an impressive hat-trick. It's all I can do to stay till the final whistle and witness the sorry spectacle. My legs have seized up with cold, the ink in my pen has frozen and my fingers are so cold that I can't write anyway.

It's a toss-up whether the increasingly frustrated Tosh will make the final whistle or not. The looks he casts towards the bench throughout the second half suggest there'll be a few words said in the dressing room after the match. Who knows what is said in the aftermath but on Monday morning it is announced that Tosh is leaving the club by mutual agreement. It's a bolt out of the blue. Tosh has scored eight times this season, is arguably the club's most influential player and has eighteen months left on his contract. The newspapers speculate that it's the first of a series of cost-cutting exercises from owner Mileson and his recently hired, and instantly unpopular (with the fans), director of club development, Mick Wadsworth. When I later catch up with Tosh he says, 'The manager said he wanted to keep me but it was down to finances. I don't think I will be the last to go.'

I just don't buy it. Despite the miserable defeat to Airdrie allowing Partick to narrow the Black and Whites' lead at the top to two points, Gretna are on the cusp of the promised land. Why would they dispose of their star midfielder now? It was time to get to grips with what was really going on at the club. I owed it to the forty-nine crestfallen fans who'd witnessed the Excelsior debacle. Maybe it was the cold, maybe it was a dodgy pie, but I think I was starting to feel their pain and I didn't like it one little bit.

15 December 2006

I was on good terms with Jon Tait but he'd still shown no willingness to arrange meetings with Mileson or Alexander. I didn't want to push it so decided that I'd keep attending games and see where I went from there. In truth I was pretty preoccupied during the week by Gretna's next fixture: Ross County away. It was a match I'd been dreading and relishing in equal measure since I'd seen the fixture list. Gretna, the team I've hitched my wagon – nay, my literary career – to for the season, versus Ross County, my home team, the team that are in my blood, that my dad played for, that my two brothers played for, that my nephew recently represented at under-thirteen level. In fact I'm the only person in my family not to have donned the famous (locally) dark-blue strip.

I plan to attend the match with my parents, girlfriend and nephew Callum, who is a diehard County fan despite recently leaving the club's youth programme. The move was not of his volition. The powers that be in County's youth set-up found him to be extrovert and a constant mischief-maker. Huh? He's a goalkeeper, for goodness' sake, of course he's a bit off the wall!

The match will be the first true test of my loyalty to struggling Ross County following the incident and of my new-found affection for the other woman, my bit on the side that is Gretna FC. I've never felt so conflicted.

First we have to get up to the Highlands. Lauren offers to drive so we decide to hire a car. Not just any car but the mighty Kia Picanto 1.1L. It's the smallest car I've ever seen and it feels like it's made of cardboard. It's just over a three-hour drive to my parents' . . . in a proper car. God knows what it will be in this.

In the hire car office we're in a queue behind a sweet old woman who's picking up a car arranged by her insurance company. 'How long will you be needing the car for?' asks the young assistant.

'It depends how long it takes to get my car back,' says the lady.

'Did you have a wee scrape?'

'Yes. I rolled down a ravine on the roof,' she says quite matter-of-factly.

'And would you consider upgrading to the premium liability waiver insurance policy that we offer?' asks the hire car employee hopefully.

It takes an age for us to get our hands on our car. The guy serving us spends so long walking round the car checking for any bumps or scratches that I consider walking out and using a different firm. It's not me that's driving, though, so I bite my lip. Finally, we get the keys. We pull out of the forecourt slowly and as we do I spot a rather stylish chair that's been discarded in the street. Our flat is crying out for such a piece of furniture so we pull over. As we proceed to perform the *Krypton Factor*-like task of fitting the object into the back of the car, the man who assisted us begins to take an interest. He gets up from his desk and walks to the door. 'Everything OK?' he shouts.

Just as he does so, I force the chair through the small boot and hear the roof fabric tear. 'Yes, we're fine. We'll be on our way now.'

Within twenty minutes the Picanto is doing 81mph down the north end of the Forth Road Bridge, causing the needle on the speedo to shake like a divining rod. Everything is vibrating, actually. I think we might just have broken some sort of record for the Picanto. I doubt anyone else has ever been stupid enough to propel it to such velocity. Trying to maintain speed in the Picanto is an art form. You have to judge roundabouts perfectly so as to be able to slingshot out of them with the minimum loss of pace. Momentum is key. Stopping is not an option – you may never get this tin can moving again.

As it's the first time Lauren has driven the road, I advise on downhill stretches where we can pick up the pace and on uphill sections where we must prepare by hitting maximum speed at the base of the climb. Somehow by squeezing every last ounce of power out of the Malaysian motor we complete the journey in a little over three hours. And we've used only about three pounds' worth of petrol. The car seems to run on fresh air.

I'd called Ross County earlier in the day to arrange tickets for the game. As my dad is a former player, I can usually ring up and arrange the odd complimentary ticket. And so it proves. One of the directors, known as 'Sugar' Kennedy, will leave some tickets for us at reception. It didn't take much to sweeten him up.

16 December 2006
Ross County v Gretna FC
Victoria Park, Dingwall

Match day comes and I still can't decide whether to sit in the main stand where we've been allocated tickets or leap the security barrier and sit with the thirty or so Gretna fans in the away section. I'm impressed even that many are here. The supporters' bus had to leave Gretna at 7 a. m. to make it here in time for kick-off. This is their furthest away trip of the season – one they'll have to make again on the final day of the 2006/7 campaign. Already, with Gretna riding high and Ross County languishing near the foot of the table, that fixture is taking on an ominous look.

Gretna backroom staff and directors are thin on the ground today. The trip has been deemed inadvisable for a person in Brooks Mileson's medical condition but I spot omnipresent web editor Keith Melvin and the ProZone boys. While we take our seats my nephew pesters me to go to the 'Jail End' with him. For the uninitiated, the Jail End is where you stand if you're a County diehard. The shed-like stand is behind one of the goals and the atmosphere within is raucous. I make a deal – we'll sit in the main stand for the first half, after which I'll move to the Jail End with him and Lauren, who looks strangely enthused by the prospect. What have I done in my life to deserve her?

I'm in a quandary about what I want to happen today. County are just three points above the drop zone. Gretna, on the other hand, are top of the league, two points ahead of Partick and six ahead of St Johnstone. It's too close to call at the top and bottom but I know in my heart of hearts that County will survive the drop this season. I say that, but I know I'm just trying to justify rooting for Gretna, whose slender lead could do with bolstering. I've got to take County's ill-treatment of my nephew into account too. I consider the many pros and cons. The outcome? I reckon I'm the only person there praying for a draw.

The Gretna team has a familiar look about it, save for former Blackburn Rovers youngster Craig Barr coming in at right back, with Townsley moving to the centre to cover for the suspended Canning. Allan Jenkins comes in too, in place of Tosh in midfield. On the bench fellow veteran Jamie McQuilken has lost his place to the more youthful Ryan McGuffie while Brendan McGill is in for thirty-six-year-old James Grady. Can you see a pattern?

Here's the full line-up:

Main, Barr, Grainger, Jenkins, Townsley, Innes, Paartalu, Nicholls, McMenamin, Graham, Skelton

Subs: Berkeley, Birch, Fleming, McGill, McGuffie

Just before the match starts I corner Graeme Muir who, as usual, has his mobile phone fixed to his ear. No doubt he's arranging for the disposal of another ageing Gretna legend. Shockingly, it turns out that he is.

'I hear there's been a bit of turmoil at the club this week,' I say.

'Not really, Andrew,' says Muir.

I ask him if there's any truth in the Tosh story.

'He's been transfer-listed, simple as that,' says Muir. 'So have McQuilken and Grady. I don't like doing it but it had to be done.'

I can hardly believe what I'm hearing. Tosh, McQuilken and Grady, though ageing, are all SPL class. They're arguably the type of players that are required to fight it out of this tricky league where only the champions are promoted. I sense the hand of Mick Wadsworth, Bobby Robson's former number two at Newcastle. The director of club development is rumoured to be casting an eye over Gretna's squad of some thirty professionals and is known by some fans as the Grim Reaper, plus a number of less-flattering monikers.

'What's going on?' I ask. 'Is it cost cutting?'

'No. They're all the wrong side of thirty and their contracts were not going to be renewed. It's as simple as that,' says Muir with the icy calmness of a contract killer. He falls short of being sinister only because his expression is as serene and calming as ever.

When the match gets under way I have to admit that it is fairly forgettable. Gretna look out of sorts – and who wouldn't after a five-hour bus trip here on the back of last week's defeat. Much to my amazement, County take the game to the league leaders. They dominate possession but fail to create any meaningful chances. Still, it's encouraging stuff and contrasts with a pretty uninspiring display from the visitors. There's a lot of route-one football from both sides and I have to say I find myself questioning the wisdom of letting Tosh leave the club. He may be the wrong side of thirty but he still knows a few tricks with a football and keeps it on the deck where it should be.

Gretna are at sixes and sevens. Twice County players find themselves through on goal with just Main to beat. Martin Scott first fluffs his chance by curling the ball into the side netting. Next it is SPL-bound Don Cowie's turn but he just fails to latch on to the clever through ball from Stuart Anderson. County actually have the ball in the net in the half. An uncharacteristic fumble by Main in his six-yard box sees Sean Higgins steal the ball and square it to Michael Gardyne, who passes it into the empty goal. Unfathomably, the strike is disallowed and the scare seems to spark Gretna into life. Even an improved Gretna can't break the deadlock, however, and with the rain starting to fall heavily a dreary 0–0 seems like the most likely outcome.

At half-time we move to the Jail End. I briefly consider standing on the uncovered away terrace but my nephew reminds me that if I'm spotted there I'll never be able to set foot in the Jail End again. It's just not worth the sacrifice so the Jail End it is. I wonder where I'll watch from next time Gretna visit?

It's immediately livelier in the Jail End and a really pretty poor mystery meat pie gives us that energy boost required to keep up with the County faithful. Their song repertoire is pretty blue. This is the club that coined the chant 'If you cannae beat the County, beat your wife' after the goalkeeper from a visiting team was exposed as a wife beater.

County's local rivals are SPL outfit Inverness Caley Thistle, of 'SuperCaleygoballisticCelticareatrocious' fame. County fans hate Caley and their best song – possibly the best football song ever – is reserved for the team that play on the site of a former gypsy settlement. It goes, 'The wheels on your house go round and round, round and round . . .'

My favourite song of the day is one my nephew and his friends belt out at will:

I can't read and I can't write,
but that don't really matter.
Because I sup-port the Ross County,
and I can drive a tractor!

Superb.

Gretna FC – Living the Dream

I see lots of familiar faces in the Jail End. This is where I spent countless Saturdays as a youth as County climbed the lower leagues in a slightly more sedate fashion than Gretna. County seem to have hit a glass ceiling in the First Division, however. Hopefully Gretna can smash through it.

In the Jail End you are literally in the back of the net. I pray Alan Main, whom I've run into a few times at the club, won't recognise me in amongst the crowd who start singing 'You fat bastard' and the like when the teams reappear.

As the second half gets under way I bump into an old football friend. In fact we'd often visited Victoria Park together for games in the Under-18s Highland League. 'Why is it we never played for County, Kev?'

'We weren't good enough,' he says nonchalantly.

Gretna will only win promotion this season if they overcome teams, like County, that just won't lie down. The first twenty minutes of the second half is a war of attrition, both teams reverting to long-ball football. With ball at feet Gretna are one of the most watchable teams in the league, but with the midfield bypassed completely they struggle to take control of the match. But they persist and somehow on sixty-six minutes take the lead. The nature of the goal is unfortunate – the County left back gives the ball away cheaply on the edge of his box. This would be OK against many strikers in this league but the last person you want to offer up a chance to on a silver platter is top scorer Colin McMenamin. The Gretna striker coolly tucks the ball away.

I'm gutted. But I'm not. I know County won't bounce back from this. I have seriously mixed emotions. I don't feel like jumping around and celebrating – if I did I'd no doubt be on the wrong end of a beating – but I know how important it is for Gretna to pick up the three points. It's OK joining in the celebrations away at Airdrie or any of the other teams in the league because I have no emotional attachment to them; but this is Ross County – my team – and it still hurts to see

36

them concede a goal. My old mate Kev sees my inner turmoil and offers a few words of solace. 'Don't worry about it,' he whispers. 'At least a win for Gretna is a win for your book.'

He's right, of course, and with their noses in front Gretna don't look like they are going to lose. Indeed, it is a shock when in the dying minutes veteran County striker Derek Adams finds himself one-on-one with Main with a great chance to nick an equaliser. Adams wastes the chance but it should have been 1–1. It's not; Gretna have edged it. With other results going their way it's a good win – it stretches their lead at the top back to five points. It is a fact echoed by McMenamin, who I bump into after the match. 'To take three points up here is massive,' says the number 9. 'We keep reading that no one's been consistent in this league. But in our last seven games we've won six and beaten all the teams around us. I don't think we're getting the credit that's due.' It will be a familiar theme as the season wears on.

Rowan Alexander is equally happy and sums up the game perfectly: 'We came up here expecting a battle and we got one. It wasn't a pretty match. It was a roll-your-sleeves-up type of game. We knew it would be tough but we worked hard and earned a massive three points.'

There's no denying it's a good win but I can't hide my disappointment at County's loss. I imagine I feel like someone whose team has lost but who has backed their victors at the bookies before the match. It's a funny sort of silver lining.

We all squeeze into the Picanto after the match. 'The roof's ripped,' says Callum. Damn, I'd forgotten about that. (So were we charged for the damage? Let me offer you a tip: if you've defaced the interior of a hire car make sure that you return it five minutes before the rental office closes, preferably when it's dark and after you've removed the bulb from the interior light. Trust me, it's foolproof.)

23 December 2006
Gretna FC v Hamilton Academicals
Raydale Park, Gretna

This is the quintessential one that got away. Thanks to the arcane public transport system I have a decision to make. It's miss Christmas with my family or miss the match. Such are the transport connections from the Borders to Edinburgh and from the capital to the Highlands, there is no way I can take in the match and make it home for Christmas Eve. I'd really love to say that Gretna won over my family and that I spent Christmas alone as a result . . . but it did not. In all honesty this was one match that I was destined to miss. Being a rescheduled Boxing Day fixture, the fact that I even had the slightest chance of seeing it on 23 December was a miracle.

The fact doesn't stop me from feeling guilty all morning as I do some last-minute Christmas shopping . . . oh, all right, *all* my Christmas shopping. I know I've only been to three Gretna matches so far but I'm hooked. With three o'clock nearing, I call up a match reporter and ask for the starting line-ups. Gretna are largely unchanged from last week save for the return of Canning from suspension at the expense of Barr. The reporter says the crowd is poor, at 1,226. I'm not sure if that makes me feel better or worse about not being there.

This is a match that Gretna should win but if I've learnt anything from the past few weeks it's that the Borders team seem to struggle against the poorer teams and raise their game for the top-of-the-table clashes. With Hamilton lying fifth it's anyone's guess what will happen. With none of Gretna's title rivals in action today a win will put Gretna eight points clear at the top of the league.

Throughout the first and second half I badger the match reporter until he doesn't answer his phone any more. By the time my line of communication to Raydale is cut, Gretna have toiled and persisted and managed to eke out a 1–0 lead courtesy of a fifty-seventh-minute Colin McMenamin header. The game sounds missable but McMenamin's celebration does not. After hitting the back of the net for the eighteenth time this season, the league's top goalscorer hoists up his shorts to reveal his underwear. It's a fortnight later before I get chance to ask him what it was all about.

'It was a bit of fun aimed at Davie Graham because he wears a different pair of boxer shorts to training every day,' says McMenamin. 'The last pair were Spiderman efforts! Our physio had the last laugh that day by turning up in a red and black thong!'

A new pair of pants every day – whatever next? I continue to follow the game on Ceefax but, underwear aside, McMenamin's goal is the only thing that separates the teams on the day. It makes it seven wins from eight for Gretna. It's an achievement that sees Alexander and McMenamin win Manager and Player of the Month awards. More importantly the win gives the Black and Whites a comfortable eight-point cushion going into the Christmas period.

The next time I'm down at Raydale Park, I pick up the programme from the Hamilton game. Inside is an interview with Gretna's Australian midfielder, Erik Paartalu, accompanied by a photograph of the player wearing . . . a kangaroo suit. The mind boggles as to where they'd got hold of the outfit in the remote Borders village.

3

Wandering in a Gretna Wonderland

28 December 2006

Still in a hungover fug after the excesses of Christmas, I call the Queen of the South press office to grovel for a ticket for the 2 January match. The first person to answer the telephone at these clubs always seems to be the person you're looking for.

'Can I speak to the press officer?' I say.

'Speaking,' comes the reply.

'Actually, I think I need to speak to the commercial director' I say.

'Erm . . . that'll be me too.'

'Who would I speak to concerning the whereabouts of Osama Bin Laden, Lord Lucan, Shergar and the Holy Grail?' I enquire.

'You can speak to me about that too, sir.'

I introduce myself and say that I'm doing a book on Gretna. There's a lengthy silence before the response comes: 'You should wash your fucking mouth out. That's a swear word round here.'

He is serious. This is my first experience of the Gretna–Queens rivalry. I never expected it to be this fierce. I explain what I'm doing and try to make small talk to gloss over the awkward pause that followed his outburst.

'Should be a good match?'

'It will be for us when you're chased out of Palmerston leaving the three points behind,' says the Queens' employee sinisterly.

Later in the day I call Jon Tait to confirm I'll be down for the game against Dundee on Saturday ahead of the local derby. Tait answers the phone in fits of giggles. 'What's going on?' I ask.

Tait fills me in on what will be known as the Curious Case of the Gaffer and his Biscuits. Alexander is famous at the club for his penchant for the odd chocolate digestive. The problem: his players have a penchant for putting their fingers in the cookie jar. Relations between players and manager had deteriorated to such a level recently that the gaffer took to locking his office during training sessions. The plan worked until today, when Alexander returned to his office, unlocked the door and walked in to find a crumpled, empty biscuit wrapper and a desk covered in crumbs. With no sign of forced entry, the gaffer was bemused.

'So what happened?' I ask. Tait tells me that all will be revealed in Saturday's programme.

29 December 2006

Noon. Back in Edinburgh after a Highland Christmas. I'd sooner have stayed there and avoided the circus that Edinburgh will turn into in the next few days as millions descend for New Year. Needs must, however. Hogmanay is at the back of my mind. In the forefront, tomorrow's match with Dundee.

Having just heard from Lauren that she won't be taking her car back when she returns tonight, I realise that I've got to plan alternative means of transport to the game. The train it is then. No matter what people tell you about Scotland's extensive and punctual rail service, I can tell you that getting round the country in a timely manner by train is easier said than done. For example, I need to travel to Gretna Green tomorrow for the match at 3 p. m. Easily done, right? Wrong. Sure I can get from Edinburgh to Carlisle in just over an hour, and normally I'd be able to connect to the First ScotRail service on to Gretna Green. But this is *me* travelling. I need only book a flight and the skies darken in an apocalyptic manner. Here are some examples:

Caught in a hurricane and evacuated from Key West during spring break to Florida? Check.

Force-ten gale during summer ferry journey from Portsmouth to St Malo? Check.

Freakish May blizzards during a sunshine break to Barcelona, causing plane to land in Madrid? Check.

Flash floods, electrical storms and landslide near Perth during my train ride north for Christmas? Checkity, check, check, check . . .

It is because of my rotten travelling luck that I returned to Edinburgh from my parents' place near Inverness via Aberdeen. That's five and a half hours to travel 170 miles. I could have just about flown to New York in that time. OK, I admit it: I could have taken the bus replacement service on the direct route via Perth, but as a closet claustrophobic – God, even typing the word 'closet' almost induces a panic attack – and chronic travel sickness sufferer, buses are always the last resort.

Nothing strikes fear into my heart more than those three little words: 'I lov—' No – 'bus replacement service'. And that is exactly what it said when I consulted the train times from Carlisle to Gretna Green tomorrow. Now I know it's only a half-hour bus journey but I was only stuck in a tunnel on the London Underground for half that and in an elevator at a tube station for around the same time – see what I mean about me and travel? – and both were enough to bring on panic attacks. Good thing my current project will see me traverse the country (repeatedly) on public transport! Travel and me: it's just not meant to be.

Safe to say that it's probably no bad thing that my fledgling professional football career never survived beyond my eighteenth birthday. By then I'd been playing competitive football for ten years and had gone green and vomited on coaches in every corner of Scotland. From Aviemore to Elgin, Kyle of Lochalsh to Portree, I'd done it all. I'd been there, bought the T-shirt, vomited on the T-shirt, put on my spare T-shirt and vomited on that too. I'm surprised that my disgusted team-mates didn't nickname me 'Hugh'.

So, in true claustrophobic, borderline-obsessive-compulsive fashion, I spend the entire morning seeing if there is any way at all to reach Gretna without stepping on to a bus. Of course there isn't. I look at maps, local taxi services, consider cycling – everything, but to no avail. I bite the bullet and commit my-self to the bus replacement service, in both directions, no less.

I feel somewhat vindicated when a *Poirot* rerun playing in the background on the television sees the legendary Belgian detective utter the immortal phrase, 'Poirot does not travel by bus!' Solidarity, brother!

30 December 2006
Gretna FC v Dundee
Raydale Park, Gretna

Despite the prospect of a problematic journey I'm looking forward to getting back to Raydale Park. I board the packed 10.52 a. m. Carlisle service to find that the seat reservations I'd made have not been honoured. Without a seat, I consider dis-embarking and abandoning the whole enterprise. I've missed one game; what difference would another make?

I find a seat – just – and proceed to call Virgin's booking line to make a reservation for the return service much, much later today. It's not as easy a trip from Edinburgh to Gretna as I'd anticipated before renting a flat in the city. The multiple border crossings that are required have only added to the dislocating feeling of follow-ing a team that I didn't previously have any emotional ties to. Yet our fates are intertwined and I have butterflies in my stomach at the prospect of today's game. Maybe it's because I'm dreading the bus journey or maybe it's because something is happening between this club and me. I can't quite put my finger on it.

Needless to say Virgin has no record of my reservations for the return journey either and their agent recommends that as all northbound trains are fully booked for the next two days, I shouldn't even consider travelling. Oh. New Year in Carlisle train station it is, then. I'm sure it wouldn't be as bad as it sounds. As the train pulls in to Carlisle station, I still haven't decided whether I'm going to just turn back round and try and get on the first train back to Edinburgh or push on to Gretna. In that moment I empathise with fans who faithfully follow their teams all over the country every weekend. I'd been doing so for just under a month and was already realising that, without a car, you truly are at the mercy of the rail companies.

Alighting at Carlisle I have a decision to make and I have an hour before my connection to Gretna in which to make it. At least all the stress is taking my mind off having to take the bus. (I know, I know, it's pathetic, isn't it? But I am who I am and who I am is someone who was subjected to a three-hour round-trip bus journey to school every day for thirteen years. I'm the kid who was 'fortunate' enough to be in the school football, basketball, athletics and volleyball teams. I'm the one who spent every weekend in living memory between the ages of twelve and sixteen on winding, sickness-inducing roads going to ever more obscure destinations in search of ever more obscure sporting glories.)

In the blink of an eye, as the coach looms into view I realise it is coaches and not common-or-garden buses that I despise. It's those elevated seats with not quite enough leg room that force you to rub shoulders with the person sitting beside you; those tinted windows; that inexplicably blacked-out rear window; those ashtrays that are still full of ash despite smoking long having been banned; and that vague whiff of vomit, urine and alcohol wafting down the coach from the coffin-like toilet cubicle (if you're lucky enough to have one) that is regurgitated through the air conditioning system, that has turned me off the subspecies that is the 'luxury coach'. Seeing the coach fill up and knowing there's a local bus service to Gretna that I can catch instead, I give it a body swerve. A stopping service may take twice as long but at least it stops every two minutes, giving me the chance to leap off if I start to feel queasy.

Enough of that. Rant over.

I'm on the bus and as it motors the eight miles to Gretna – don't say a word, a phobia is a phobia – I try to take my mind off the fact that I'm on a bus for the first time in ten years. Overcoming phobias or passing milestones like this doesn't give me the euphoric feeling that I thought it would. I just feel pathetic at having gone out of my way to avoid buses in the past. Still unsure whether I'll be able to get back to Edinburgh after the match, or even back on this bus, I feel like I am truly going into the unknown.

You know it's funny: I moan and gripe about travelling around the country following Gretna – it always seems to be a case of *Planes, Trains and Automobiles* (and Buses), and it's always so damn cold. But once I get within sight of Raydale Park and hear the crowd and the crackly announcements from Rocky Radio over the tannoy system, all is forgotten. The excitement of going to watch live, professional football replaces it. It makes it all worthwhile. In this moment, when I can hear the fans sing to keep themselves warm and can practically taste my half-time pie I could forgive anything of the transport companies of the world that make my life such a misery. I really could. This is what Saturdays are all about.

I arrive early at Raydale Park in the hope that I'll be able to speak to some of the people behind the scenes who make this ambitious football club tick. Even though the crowd is small again today at 1,541, there's a buzz around the ground. And it's not just emanating from the fans. Everyone associated with the club seems to have grasped that they are living through special times. Having been promoted twice in the last two seasons and sitting eight points clear at the top of the table, there are great expectations. The prize of SPL football is so great as to be blinding.

It's sunny in Gretna as kick-off nears. It's deceiving. It's often sunny here but rarely warm. The sky soon starts to cloud over, however. The pitch has definitely seen better days after forty-eight hours of persistent rain. I pass the time by thumbing through the match programme. On page 46 I find an account of the 'biscuit' incident outlined by Tait. The article is accompanied by a photo of Tom Cruise in *Mission Impossible* get-up, suspended from the ceiling of a bank vault. Instead of Cruise's head, striker James Grady's has been superimposed. In his hands, instead of some hi-tech equipment, is a packet of McVitie's chocolate digestives. Grady et al., it seems, had climbed on the roof of Alexander's Portakabin-cum-office, removed the roof and lowered someone down to snatch the biscuits. Who says footballers are just big kids with too much time on their hands?

Before the match Steve Tosh, Gretna's mercurial midfielder who is to be controversially moved on in the January transfer window, is rewarded with a Rolex for services to the club by chairman Ron MacGregor. MacGregor cuts a Mr Burns-from-*The Simpsons*-type figure yet he's friendly and not in the least bit scary. After a hurried presentation he makes himself scarce, leaving Tosh standing alone, looking bemused. He eyes the pitch hungrily, studies the Rolex for a moment then shakes his head dejectedly. You can tell this isn't easy for him and he'd rather be in the dressing room getting stripped in preparation for what he does best.

Tosh's demeanour says it all. This was not his decision. He loves the club and is a firm fans' favourite and the announcement of his departure was as much of a shock to him as it was to the fans. Everyone is looking for answers about Tosh's departure and that of fellow seasoned professional Jamie

McQuilken. Having declared he intends to stay and fight for his place, James Grady's future is less clear. It's rumoured that he made a secret pact with Brooks Mileson that he'll score the goal that clinches promotion to the SPL in exchange for an extra year on his contract.

With time to kill before kick-off I slip into the press office. I'm not surprised to find Craig Mileson there, puffing away on a cigarette. Like father, like son. Despite being heir to a multi-million-pound fortune, the former BBC Young Magician of the Year seems at home swapping match-day banter with Tait, Keith Melvin and the group of photographers who clog up the place with their paraphernalia. They are a jocular bunch. While I'm in there someone knocks on the door and hands a ball back that disappeared over the stadium wall two weeks ago. That's the type of place Gretna is.

Mileson Jnr seems to prefer his role as operations manager of the club to his previous job working in insurance. Who wouldn't? Today he's watching Gretna's historic Scottish Cup Final appearance for the umpteenth time. The match has reached penalties. I stand over him and say, 'The result won't change no matter how many times you watch it!'

Mileson flashes a boyish grin. He always seems happy to see me though I'm never entirely sure if he grasps what I'm doing here. 'How's your dad?' I ask.

'He's good, thanks. We're expecting him down just before kick-off,' says Mileson.

'Did you tell him about the book?'

'Yeah, I told him there might be a book in the pipeline.'

In the pipeline! I've got to submit the first few chapters in a matter of weeks. 'Do you think you could introduce us today?'

'I won't have time today, mate, sorry. Why don't you just go up and see him in the stand?' he says.

'OK. But how will I find him?'

'He's the one with the camera crew following him around,' says Mileson wryly.

Wandering in a Gretna Wonderland

Truth be told, I've been hanging around the club for weeks in the hope that I might bump into Mileson Snr. I'd seen neither hide nor hair of him, however, and no one was making any effort to introduce us. I'd later learn that Mileson's illness, the seriousness of which was played down by the club, was the main reason his son was shielding him from me. I'd also been going about meeting him in completely the wrong way. I knew that Mileson was supposed to be a man of the people but I didn't realise it stretched to slumming it with the fans in the stand. Mind you, you slum it wherever you go at Raydale Park!

Coming out of the press office and through the warren of corridors I immediately filter into the thoroughfare that leads to the stand. Up ahead I see a microphone boom winding its way through the crowd to a ripple of applause. I follow the microphone through the crowd, like a lion stalking a baby giraffe in long grass, as Mileson makes his way to his seat at the back of the Corries Stand. I follow as close as I can without arousing suspicion and take a seat a few rows away from Gretna's enigmatic owner.

As the match kicks off the stand is full. I pick up snippets of conversation from people sitting around me such as: 'Did you make it last week? No? Me neither – it was just too cold.'

And: 'I think Bill went to watch Carlisle today instead.'

It's not what you'd expect to hear in the home end of a football ground. Although there is a hard core of support here (and as the game goes on it becomes evident who those fans are because the temporary structure feels like it will collapse under the constant stamping), it strikes me that for all the promotion buzz surrounding the club its supporters can be laissez-faire at times. You'd never hear a Celtic fan say, 'We're away today – let's go to Rangers instead.' It just doesn't happen. I know, I know, this sounds hypocritical coming from me but there you go.

I'm suddenly aware that with a ground-share with Motherwell being mooted should Gretna be promoted, the loyalty of the club's fans will be put to the sternest of tests. A 152-mile round trip for a home game will test the resolve of even the most loyal members of the Black and White Army. But that's talk for another day. Today's visitors, Dundee, bullied Gretna off the park last time they visited and ended the match 4–0 winners. No one has done a job on the league-toppers this season like Alex Rae's combative team. Still, the table doesn't lie and Gretna should win today.

It strikes me as the game gets under way that the secret to Gretna's success is the rod of steel that they have through the centre of the park. From Alan Main – probably the best keeper in the league – to the central-defensive pillars of Canning and Innes, to the veteran Nicholls in midfield complemented by the sheer physical presence of the six-foot-four Paartalu alongside, it's a daunting prospect for the opposition.

Gretna's line-up today numbers:

Main, Townsley, Grainger, Jenkins, Canning, Innes, Paartalu, Nicholls, McMenamin, Graham, Skelton

Subs: Barr, Berkeley, Fleming, McGill, McGuffie

In the first half it is only the excellent, if at times eccentric, goalkeeping of Dundee's French stopper, Ludovic Roy, that keeps the tie scoreless. Early on Roy drops a couple of easy crosses and parries a weak shot to the waiting Colin McMenamin, who is only denied by a brave recovery save by the Frenchman. On seventeen minutes Roy makes amends again when he turns a powerful Davie Graham shot around the post. It is instinctive stuff. When Roy has time to think is when the trouble starts.

Throughout the first half I keep half an eye on Mileson, who is sitting with Mick Wadsworth. Despite his recent health scare Mileson puffs away on an endless chain of cigarettes – the ban on smoking in public places is blurred here at Mileson's own club, situated just a few hundred yards from the border.

Mileson's pen name of 'Puff Daddy', under which he writes a column on smoking for the *Sun* newspaper, is well earned.

It's great to see a club owner in with the fans. Mileson seems happy to eschew the directors' box in favour of the cheap seats. He exchanges comments and criticism with supporters during the first half and seems as ardent as any other fan there. I guess that is what makes him so popular here.

The startling thing about the Corries Stand is its proximity to the goal. It's a mere two metres from the goal line, meaning the goalkeeper is well within earshot. After a few more shaky clearances the home fans sense the fragility of the Dundee keeper. Every goal kick is greeted by a drum roll and the cry of 'Ohhhhhhhh, you French bastard!' The crowd truly go to work on him and any other Dundee player that comes within earshot.

When a Dundee player appears to suffer a broken nose and is treated in front of the stand, someone shouts, 'At least it won't spoil your looks, you ugly brute!' It is one thing getting paid £90,000 a week to play in front of 70,000 prawn-sandwich-munching fans who sing songs about your wife's sexual proclivities, but quite a different prospect to spend forty-five minutes being subjected to some of the most hideous character assassination ever voiced. The goalkeepers who get involved with the crowd's banter are warmed to. The ones who ignore it are taunted even more. God knows what poor Roy has done to deserve the sheer vitriol being dished out today.

On twenty minutes Derek Townsley almost breaks the deadlock with a headed effort from an Allan Jenkins corner. Dundee, who until this stage have been spectators, soon have their first cast-iron chance. A counter-attack sees Gretna stretched at the back and they are lucky that Jay Shields' through ball finds Derek Lyle alone but in an offside position.

The chance sparks Dundee into life and they take control of the game as half-time nears. Twice they almost take the lead through Brian Deasley and a venomous twenty-five-yard free kick from Paul Dixon. The half ends goalless, however. I expect to see Mileson make a sharp exit to Raydale's modest hospitality suite to warm up but he does not. He stays put while those around him drift off, discussing the first half with a fan seated in the row in front of him. This is as good a chance as any to meet him.

I sidle up to the club owner and hover a metre away while he chats to a fan. The conversation pauses; I see my opportunity. 'Brooks, hello. I wonder if I could introduce myself. My name's Andrew Ross. I'm doing a book about Gretna's promotion push.'

Having only seen Mileson in the flesh once before, it strikes me that he looks at least ten years younger now than he had two weeks earlier. Then, quite frankly, he looked at death's door. In any case he looks older than his fifty-nine years.

Confirming what I'd suspected, Mileson knows nothing of my book. He listens intently as I explain a bit about it. Having turned down some twenty-plus offers to do his autobiography, he knows a thing or two about the publishing game. I sense that he's weighing me up as we speak, figuring out if my intentions are good. To my relief, he doesn't seem perturbed at having me hanging around his club for the rest of the season. Indeed, he invites me to come down and spend some time with him when he's back to full health. It's a huge weight off my mind.

When the second half kicks off it is indistinguishable from the first, apart from the directions the teams are facing. It's gritty, scrappy, nip-and-tuck stuff, with nothing between the teams. There are no real chances until the sixty-fifth minute when Gretna confirm they are one of the league's most dangerous teams from set pieces. A Jenkins corner is headed away but only as far as Paartalu, whose looping header is goalbound before Chris Innes makes sure of it on the line: 1–0. It is the hundredth goal in matches involving Gretna this season.

The goal doesn't really elicit the fightback that might be expected of an Alex Rae team. The game continues to be a physical affair, however. With ten minutes to go the combative

Wandering in a Gretna Wonderland

Davie Nicholls sustains an injury that will keep him sidelined for weeks. Late on Dundee player-manager Rae almost salvages a point for his team. Showing a glimpse of his top-flight pedigree, Rae goes on a mazy solo run and skips over three challenges before finding himself five yards out with just Main to beat. A player of Rae's quality should score but Martin Canning seems to come from nowhere to block Rae's shot and secure another valuable win.

The victory gives Gretna a massive eleven-point lead at the top of the table after title rivals Partick and St Johnstone see their head-to-head clash postponed. If things get tight as the end of season nears, the Christmas period, where others faltered, may yet prove to be the making of Gretna. Goalscorer Chris Innes, for one, is astounded that the Black and Whites have opened up such a lead, saying of the eleven-point margin, 'If you were to tell me that at the start of the season, I probably wouldn't have believed you. St Johnstone and Partick will still mount a fair challenge but as long as we keep winning that's the main thing.'

It's been a good day. I get on the bus back to Carlisle without a second thought. The win has put a spring in my step and a double-digit lead in the league at the halfway point of the season is a dream come true for the club and its fans. I'm cautious about Gretna's promotion credentials, however. The chasing pack of SPL old boys St Johnstone and Partick Thistle have games in hand and in the January transfer window they will no doubt strengthen their squads with experienced professionals who've been over the ground before. Whether Gretna do the same remains to be seen. It could prove decisive come season end.

That thought and the sight that greets me as the Edinburgh-bound train pulls into Carlisle brings me back down to earth with a bang. The carriages are packed like cattle trucks and I feel the possibility of a night in the waiting room looming large. I fight my way on to where my reserved seat should be and, miracle of miracles, there, bathed in the halo-like light from the reading lamp, like a vision, is My Seat. Maybe things are going to work out after all.

2 January 2007
Queen of the South v Gretna FC
Palmerston, Dumfries

It's 2007. Will this be the year that Gretna achieve what many said could never be done? Is it just possible that with a convincing lead at the top of the table and confidence at an all-time high that the promised land, that Shangri-La known as the SPL, is within their grasp? What better test of character for the club than a New Year clash with local rivals Queen of the South?

It's my first South of Scotland derby and as I set off for Carlisle on the first leg of my journey I'm still slightly hungover from a raucous Hogmanay. Most of my fellow passengers lie slumped over tables before we've even pulled out of Waverley. Typically, and because the train company again failed to honour my reservations, the only seat I can find is on a table with a mother and two young children. The kids play nicely and look well behaved. Perfect. It's 10 a. m. and I settle into my seat for a little snooze. I'm woken ten minutes later, however, to hear the mother tell her son, 'If you don't eat all your Mars bar you're not getting any crisps and Irn-Bru.'

Uh-oh. I get the feeling that this little kid is an incendiary device waiting to be triggered so I slip back into a deep slumber as quickly as I can. I am awoken ten minutes later by the child repeatedly banging his Matchbox car on the table. I give him a look that says, 'I really don't need this today, shut up!' But there's nothing there. The lights are on but there's nobody home. The kid is caught in the midst of some euphoric sugar rush and can barely even focus. His mother gives him a crayon to do some colouring-in and calm him down but he proceeds to scribble erratically across the paint-by-numbers picture, oblivious to the stark black outlines on the page. He's oblivious to everything. The mother tries to pacify him occasionally by threatening to put him off the train by himself at the next stop. She's a nasty piece of work. Part of me thinks that would be the best thing that could ever happen to the boy.

At the next stop it's me who gets off, alone, to find that my connecting service to Dumfries, home of Queen of the South, has been cancelled. There's not even a bus replacement service. The next train gets into Dumfries at 2.57 p. m., leaving me exactly three minutes to find my way to Palmerston Park. Not for the first time I consider giving up and going straight home.

In contrast to Scotland, 2 January is not a public holiday over the border. Carlisle is buzzing. In Edinburgh there was still very much a feeling of the morning after the night before the night before. Dumfries will be the same. It is one thing getting there just before kick-off, but the possibility of the return train being cancelled doesn't even bear thinking about – so I don't and board the train.

I wouldn't miss this much-anticipated derby match for love nor money. It's a sell-out and expectation has been building in Gretna all week. There's been a war of words in the local press, especially because Gretna players Tosh and McQuilken are mooted to be joining Queens in the January transfer window. Tensions in the two towns have been running high.

It's my first ever visit to Dumfries and I'm not sure what to expect when I arrive. I'm convinced that I'll be able to get a taxi outside the station but that's because I've already forgotten that I'm travelling back into Scotland, where it's still a public holiday. Unsurprisingly the station car park is deserted when I arrive. Worse still, there's not a signpost for the stadium in sight or anyone to ask for that matter. I feel like I've stepped into the Twilight Zone. I have two directions to choose from so I start to jog off in one of them. In five minutes I'm in Dumfries town centre and see a taxi. I flag it down.

'Palmerston, please,' I say.

'No, you're not going there,' comes the reply from the cross-eyed driver. I almost expect to hear some banjo music, *Deliverance*-style.

'Sorry?' I say, feeling for the door handle. 'Has the stadium moved or something?'

'No, the booking says Annan Road, 3 p. m.'

I realise that I've stolen someone's taxi. 'Sorry. Can you tell me where the stadium is?'

The Neanderthal taxi driver points and grunts. I think I've found the missing link.

I finally take my seat at the tired-looking Palmerston Park at 3.10 p. m. Fortunately there is no score, not on the pitch anyway. As I arrived at the stadium the police were escorting a Queens fan out of the ground. He looked drunk and confused and blood was pouring from a head wound. It didn't look like he'd suffered the gash in a fall.

As I take my seat in Palmerston's museum-piece wooden main stand I realise that I'm seated with the home fans. Still, it's a great seat, high above the halfway line and with a view beyond the far stand to the green pastures of Dumfries and Galloway. Half of the opposite stand has been allocated to Gretna fans and there must be upwards of 800 of them. To the left is the home terrace, which is rowdy and vocal. The atmosphere is electric. It's the biggest and noisiest crowd I've seen in the First Division.

Though the pitch looks like a ploughed field both teams are apparently trying to play football. Gretna are unchanged from the Dundee game save for McGuffie deputising for the injured Nicholls.

The starting eleven comprise:

Main, Townsley, Innes, Canning, Grainger, McGuffie, Jenkins, Paartalu, Skelton, Graham, McMenamin

Despite the disparity in league position Queens dominate the early part of the ill-tempered match. Gretna are lucky not to go a goal down when rising star Willie Gibson's shot from twenty-five yards is tipped round the post by Main. Indeed, it takes until the twentieth minute for Gretna to piece together any sort of possession at all. The poor playing surface is not helping.

That perseverance pays off on twenty-five minutes when Davie Graham picks up the ball, drives past Jim Lauchlan and squares it to Colin McMenamin for the easiest of tap-ins at the back post. It is his nineteenth goal of the season. This goalscoring record has attracted the attention of a number of SPL and Football League clubs but my sources at the club tell me that the player, whose contract runs out at the end of the season, is set to repay the club's faith in him and ink an improved deal within days. I can't help thinking how great it would be to see the predatory McMenamin in the SPL, especially in the black and white of Gretna. It is the first club at which the young striker has really fulfilled his promise. After spells with Falkirk and Livingston, the twenty-five-year-old has been subject to three free transfers in his career. His blossoming into a prolific striker is one of many Gretna success stories overlooked by the media.

McMenamin celebrates like he's just scored the winner in the World Cup Final and does a lap of honour past the home fans with a hand cupped to his ear. He earns a yellow card for his trouble and a fistful of death threats but the Gretna fans lap it up. McMenamin is their talisman. Losing him to the SPL at this vital part of the season is unthinkable.

The three drummers in the Gretna stand strike up a beat and the fans break into song. I suddenly feel isolated in the home stand. I want to stand up and sing along but know I'd be signing my own death warrant if I do so. When the urge passes I ponder what I'm currently feeling. Yes, it's fantastic for my book, nay, essential, that Gretna have a great season but what I feel is something else. I desperately want to be amongst the Gretna fans. I feel a growing affinity with them.

As long as I can remember I've given friends a hard time for having more than one team. You know the type – 'Celtic are my Scottish team but Real Madrid are my Spanish team, etc., etc.' What utter bollocks. You only have one team and you are born to them as you are to your family. People who follow Chelsea now but have never been to West London in their lives are charlatans. It's just not right.

Suddenly I was at risk of becoming the biggest hypocrite of all. I had no emotional or geographical ties with Gretna yet here I was desperate to cheer them on. It felt like infidelity to suddenly have feelings for another team. What was happening to me? Was I weak, was it a midlife crisis, was the relationship I was in (with my beloved Ross County) failing or was I just suffering from a crush that would pass?

Whatever was happening, I was glued to the action at Palmerston. I was starting to learn more about the players, see what makes them tick, their strengths and weaknesses. Take centre half Chris Innes. My admiration for the captain was growing with every game. He is a true leader for Rowan Alexander's troops on the field. He's level-headed and talks to his teammates throughout the game, whether it be to offer a bit of advice, some encouragement or to lambast them for a mistake. The former Dundee United player, like McMenamin, deserves to return triumphantly to the SPL with Gretna.

As the half-time whistle nears the game begins to heat up. The home side force two good saves from Main but these are overshadowed by a series of rash challenges that go unpunished from the referee, who is having a terrible game. The remainder of the half is played out without incident to a backdrop of 'The referee's a wanker' from the home fans. When they cease the Gretna contingent applaud. For the first and only time this afternoon everyone is in accord.

At half-time I try and rendezvous with Jon Tait but the press man did not even receive a ticket from Gretna's local rivals. 'typical queens' replies Tait via text when I try to track him down. I decide to stretch my legs and maybe search out a half-time pie and disappear into the bowels of the stand. There I spot a sheepish-looking Steve Tosh. Not wanting to harass him, I hover with intent waiting for a good opportunity to introduce myself.

I realise that as I am loitering, waiting to meet him, Tosh in turn is loitering outside the Queens boardroom, waiting, I presume, to speak to the directors of both clubs about his mooted transfer. I bite the bullet and introduce myself. I explain I'm doing a book and Tosh seems interested, if a little on edge. 'What's going on, then? Are you going to Queens?' I ask.

'I don't know,' confides Tosh in a hushed voice, holding his palms up. 'I genuinely don't. I'm still training but just not getting picked. No one has really said anything to me. I'm desperate to be out there and play.'

It's the words that would drive any Gretna fan to distraction, knowing that Tosh, who has provided so many magical moments in the past, is sitting in the stands, itching to pull on the black and white jersey.

'So when are you going to know?' I ask.

'I don't know. I'm in limbo. It's a nightmare,' says Tosh.

The second half is barely two minutes old when Gavin Skelton chips home a second for Gretna from nine yards. Skelton is a firm fans' favourite and they go wild when he celebrates in front of them before running over to Rowan Alexander and assistant manager Davie Irons. Irons has been at the club almost as long as Alexander and shares his passion and drive. His celebration is zealous to say the least.

It's no more than eight minutes later when ex-postman 'Degsy' Townsley receives a delivery from Graham after a good run, shimmies past a defender and dispatches the ball under the advancing Colin Scott into the net. Degsy too is a club legend. It seems that Gretna have them in abundance from numbers 1 to 11 and on to the subs bench. I suppose when there have been so many highs in the past two and a half years there is going to be a fair share of heroes in the ranks.

Gretna's third goal prompts a chorus of 'Easy, easy, easy'. No disrespect to Queens but it really is easy for Gretna from here on in. At 3–0 the game is wrapped up and it's just a case of how many more Gretna are going to score before the final whistle. Some Queens fans feel a bit hard done by. I overhear one fan murmuring, 'It is easy when you've got Scotland's answer to Abramovich backing you.'

The Gretna fans are more vocal than they are at home. They're clearly taking great pleasure in routing their local rivals. At the risk of sounding like a glory hunter, I'd give anything to be over there with them, joining in with their rendition of 'Walking in a Gretna Wonderland'.

When the action on the pitch resumes some of the Queens players, sensing the match running away from them, get increasingly physical. Martin Canning is the first casualty. He suffers a head wound and is hauled off. It's an opportunity to see how quickly the Black and Whites reorganise. Almost instantly Jenkins slots into the right-back position with Townsley moving across to join Innes in the centre. It's seamless and works better than when they went down to ten men at Airdrie.

Rowan Alexander doesn't seem to like the treatment being handed out to his players one bit and his remonstrations with the fourth official attract the attention of the local constabulary. The police remain in the vicinity of the Gretna dugout for the rest of the match, during which vitriol and abuse rain down from all sides on the former Queens manager and Dumfries resident.

When Skelton drills home a fourth on eighty-seven minutes the home stands begin to empty. The man who has sat next to me groaning and booing the entire match says, 'I should have left earlier, truth be told.'

'What, like ninety minutes?' I reply, perhaps inadvisably. There's a brief pause while the fan tries to decide whether I'm a Gretna fan in disguise or an ironic Queens fan. He seems to settle on the latter and shrugs resignedly.

By the time the final whistle sounds the home stands are all but empty and only the 800 Gretna fans of the 3,714 in attendance remain. The players stay on the pitch after the match and go over to celebrate the victory with the fans. It's a wonderful moment. Alexander, who joins them, is clearly delighted with the result. Again in the congested Christmas fixture schedule his team have picked up three points. It's the sixth clean sheet for the team in seven matches. Alexander pays tribute to his defence when he speaks to the press afterwards. 'I thought Townsley, Canning and Innes were head and shoulders above everyone,' he says. 'It shows the resilience of our team at the moment.'

It's a mad dash from the ground to make the next train. Miss that and I'm in Dumfries for another two hours. I make the station in plenty of time but am stunned when I look at the departures board:

17.30 to Carlisle – cancelled
19.18 to Carlisle – cancelled

'What are you going to do?' I ask the unfortunate member of staff behind the perspex screen. 'You can't just abandon us here like this!'

The flustered rail worker gives me a withering look. She makes me realise my outburst would not be out of place in a 1970s disaster movie. She proceeds to try to find a sober taxi driver to ferry a small group of us to Carlisle. I pray that the driver I met earlier has clocked off for the night. The three guys waiting for the taxi with me could easily pass for celebrity lookalikes. I pass the next twenty minutes making small talk with Ricky Gervais, Bill Bailey and Billy Connolly, none of whom is very funny, before a taxi swerves round the corner erratically. On any other night I would run a mile but it's this or a night in the station so I jump in.

Gretna FC – Living the Dream

The driver definitely seems a little worse for wear as we negotiate the thirty-five miles of winding roads to Carlisle. I strike up a conversation with Connolly. It transpires he's on a quest to visit every football league ground. His anecdotes from the various grounds – best pies, cheapest tickets, most inaccessible stadium – erm . . . Gretna – pass the time. I fill the silences raving about Gretna while Ricky Gervais and Billy Connolly stay silent. Towards the end of the journey Gervais tells me he's a Queens fan and gives me a vicious look.

The rest of the journey is spent in silence as sleepy villages fly by. We make the train, just, and I find a carriage away from Gervais, who looks like he wants to punch me. It's been a hectic day. As I drift off into a slumber I replay the Gretna goals in my head and I hear 'Wandering in a Gretna Wonderland' being sung by 800 contented souls. Thoughts of Ross County, who have lost to St Johnstone and are hovering above the relegation zone, are banished from my mind. Gretna are eleven points clear at the top and all is well.

4

The Alexander Technique

6 January 2007
Clyde v Gretna FC: Scottish Cup third round
Broadwood Stadium, Croy

A break from the relentless quest for promotion today as Gretna travel to Clyde in the third round of the Cup. Gretna went all the way to the final in 2005/6, beating Clyde along the way. In last season's physical Cup encounter between the two sides Davie Graham had his leg broken, three players were red-carded and there was a post-match bust-up in the tunnel. It's made the fixture a bit of a grudge match. A recent league meeting between the two fanned the flames when Gretna's free-scoring Colin McMenamin netted a controversial injury-time winner after Clyde had put the ball out for one of their players to receive medical attention.

I'm looking forward to seeing if Gretna's Cup credentials are still intact or whether, like a cheap tea bag, they won't stay in the Cup for long. It's my first trip to Broadwood Stadium, which has been christened the Ice Station by visiting fans due to the biting winds that blow through the open end of the otherwise impressive ground. I dress accordingly and after boarding my delayed train from Waverley to Croy I synchronise my watch with the station clock.

The imposing Broadwood looks like a bit of a white elephant on its own in the North Lanarkshire countryside. It bears more than a passing resemblance to the Death Star from the *Star Wars* trilogy. Here's hoping that the force will be with Gretna today. Making the Scottish Cup Final last season as a Second Division club was the biggest upset in the history of the competition and the club are desperate to go one better. Due to their Cup pedigree the bookmakers have installed Gretna as sixth favourites ahead of no less than five SPL teams.

With his health improving – but still terrible by most people's standards – I know that Brooks Mileson is expected at today's match. Mileson is the man who intrigues me most at Gretna. The anywhere between £3 and £5 million (he never talks about exact figures) that he is rumoured to have put into the club seems purely philanthropic. Unlikely to ever make a penny from the club, it begs the question: why?

Mileson has been absented from any day-to-day involvement at the club for months following a burst bowel and bout of extensive internal bleeding. The man's medical records read like a script from *Holby City*. He told me at last week's game that he would be back any day soon and to pop in and see him, yet no one at the club keeps a diary or seems able to pin him down. Undeterred, I've decided that away games are my best hope of spending time with the club owner and when he's far more relaxed to boot.

When I arrive at the stadium I head straight to the press box to see Keith Melvin. He always has the inside track on team changes and any club gossip. I also need to ask him whether Mileson has made it to the game and where, in the stand opposite, he's seated. Melvin calls a friend in the away stand and asks them to have a scan of the crowd to see if Mileson is there. They can't see him but I decide to go over anyway.

Leaving the warmth of the press box to embrace the worst the Ice Station can throw at me, I pass the CCTV operator's office. The door is open. I have an idea. I watch the camera operators through the half-open door for a minute while my plan forms. As I'm about to retreat, dismissing my notion as crazy, one of them turns round and asks if he can help.

'Erm, maybe,' I say. While I explain what I want I swear the officers are in two minds as to whether to comply or arrest me on the spot. Mercifully they agree and soon their cameras are scanning the away stand. Mileson would stand out in any crowd. Six foot tall, bearded and with a mane of black-grey hair, he cuts a striking figure. His fondness for knee-length leather coats means he will never blend into the background. With Big Brother's help, it doesn't take long to locate him among the 300 travelling supporters. It crosses my mind that, as Mileson is an 'ill man', it would be terrible folly if anything were to happen to him today with me sitting alongside. When I walk round the pitch to meet the club owner it feels like a thousand eyeballs are burning into the back of my head. Maybe it's the raucous Clyde fans but I get the distinct impression that the CCTV cameras follow me for the rest of the afternoon.

Mileson seems surprised to see me and invites me to sit with him. I can't help noticing that his trousers are covered in animal hair and assorted feed stains. With a reported menagerie of animals at his Cumbrian estate perhaps it's not a surprise. It's little snippets of rumour, mixed with local myth, that make me want to get to know the man better. He has a reputation for never turning a sick or injured animal away from his sanctuary, whether it be hedgehog, llama or tortoise. I wonder if this benevolent characteristic is what attracted him to Gretna. This, after all, is the man who is said to have donated money to well over a hundred league and non-league clubs in Scotland and England with an emphasis on fan participation in the boardroom.

It's a hard game to call today but with Rowan Alexander's men looking for a seventh clean sheet in eight games it's going to take something special to beat them. Then again, with a physical Clyde side expected to take the field, the loss of Nicholls and McGuffie to injury in midfield might tip the balance in Clyde's favour. A midfield of Skelton, Jenkins,

Paartalu and McGill looks a bit lightweight and inexperienced on paper.

The full Gretna line-up is:

Main, Townsley, Grainger, Jenkins, Canning, Innes, Paartalu, McGill, McMenamin, Graham, Skelton

Subs: Barr, Berkeley, Bingham, Birch, Fleming

Throughout the first half Mileson and I chat. It's typical football talk: 'How did the ref miss that!' 'He should have buried that chance!' That type of thing. From his easy-going demeanour you would have no inkling that Mileson is one of Britain's captains of industry.

I resist probing him too much during the game. He's just a fan watching his team on a Saturday afternoon. I join in the singing and stamping with the Gretna support alongside Mileson. I think he approves. When I stand up and have a go at Gretna captain Chris Innes, shouting, 'Come on, *Colin*, you can do better than that!' I cringe and hope that it has gone unnoticed. It is by Brooks but not by a young Gretna fan sitting nearby who gives me evils for the rest of the half.

The Gretna support are in fine voice this afternoon. Numerous choruses of 'Skippy' are given a run-out in homage to Erik Paartalu who is starting to put himself about in midfield in response to the physical way that Clyde have started the game. I also hear Gretna's techno-like chant: 'Black and White Army. Woo! Woo!' for the first time. Mileson comments on how noisy the fans are and how lively they were at Palmerston the week before. 'I wish we could be like that every game,' he bemoans. He's got a point. Raydale Park can be eerily silent at times.

The game is tense and scrappy and after McMenamin cracks a shot off the bar before scooping the rebound over from twelve yards early on, there are no real chances to speak of until some twenty-five minutes later, when Clyde's Gary Arbuckle fires in an angled shot which is parried by Alan Main.

The Alexander Technique

The tension is driving Mileson to distraction. 'I hope they let me out for a fag at half-time,' the hundred-a-day man says in a strained north-east accent. 'My nerves can't take much more of this.'

It is by no means a feast of football and for much of the first half my gaze wanders to the man stood behind a fence at the open end of the ground. He watches the game intently, occasionally turning to take a frisbee from his dog's mouth and launch it 200 metres across the field beyond. Animal lover Mileson smiles when he sees me observing the spectacle.

Just before half-time Gretna finally break the deadlock. Davie Graham capitalises on a defensive blunder on the edge of the box and drills home from fifteen yards. The strike hasn't come a minute too soon. Rowan Alexander took the player aside in training recently and told him he's got to weigh in with more goals. Nearby, Graham's father has his own reasons for celebrating – namely a substantial bet on his son being the first scorer.

At half-time I duck down inside the stadium in search of a pie. Like a good restaurant and its house wine, a football club can be judged on its meat pie alone. I hear some Gretna fans bemoaning the fact that they're £1.70 each. It doesn't deter me. I plump for what turns out to be a rather excellent steak and gravy pie at £1.90. Coming back up the stairwell I see Mileson pleading with a steward to let him out for a cigarette.

As I tuck into my pie the unctuous puff pastry flakes off and blows in the wind. I feel a little guilty. This is a genuine culinary treat. Pies at football grounds shouldn't be this good and their very existence lends weight to the argument that the game is being taken over by the middle classes. Not that I am myself, of course. We're working class and proud of it, as my mum likes to remind me between glugs of New World Cabernet Sauvignon.

When Mileson returns we have a good chat about Clyde's ground. 'It's a council stadium, you know,' he enthuses. I get the impression that he'd love to be able to count on such backing from local government in Gretna. We also talk about potential signings in the transfer window and Mileson rules out following the lead of some of their title rivals who are stocking up on experienced pros. It's a proven method of getting out of this tight league.

Mileson says the club will be investing in youth and reveals that Steven Hogg, a twenty-year-old six-foot-three left-sided midfielder who came through the Manchester United youth system, will be the club's first signing. 'Mick Wadsworth rates the teen highly,' he says, showing the faith he has in the Gretna fans' new hate figure.

I like Mileson's frankness. I've noticed he's like this with everyone when it comes to footballing matters, which is why I'm amazed none of the fans who're outraged by the imminent departures of Tosh et al. have bothered to ask the man who is bankrolling the whole operation why they're going. If, like me, they did, Mileson would be more than happy to explain that with the maximum twenty-two over-21s allowed in his squad (as per SFL rules) it is time to stop being a retirement fund for the ageing, expensive pros the club has collected on its climb through the leagues and bring in new players who are capable of making the step up to the SPL.

The teams come out unchanged after half-time. Before kick-off Mileson asks me to come and meet him during the week.

'Are you sure you'll be there?' I say, having been let down before.

'Yeah, I should be. Just check with Craig,' he says, smiling.

'Great. I'll come down midweek and pop my head around your door,' I say, somewhat doubtful that the meeting will ever occur.

'I don't have a door!' Mileson says. 'I don't even have a desk. I sit wherever I can.'

Early in the second half Danny Grainger charges upfield and unleashes a left-foot thunderbolt from thirty yards that the Clyde keeper somehow manages to push around the post. On sixty-nine minutes Gretna go one better when Graham's penetrating run and clever cut back leaves Erik Paartalu free to slot the ball home from sixteen yards. Less than ten minutes later and McMenamin atones for his earlier miss, steering a Skelton deflection into the net for a third. Almost immediately the Clyde stand empties, to a chorus of 'Cheerio, cheerio, cheerio!'

I part with a jubilant Mileson on the final whistle and head round the pitch to speak to some of the players. As I pass a steward I'd spoken to earlier she says, 'What are you going to write? That Clyde were shite?'

It had crossed my mind but that would ill-advised. I know Gretna will be back here in the league soon enough, needing three points to take the club one step nearer to promotion. Unlike today, Clyde will be no pushovers.

Predictably, in the tunnel the press pack are talking up Gretna's chances of a repeat Cup Final appearance. It's early days for that type of talk and you can see a few raised eyebrows among the players. I corner Davie Graham before I leave and he tells me in no uncertain terms where the club's priorities lie. 'Another Cup Final? Who knows?' says Graham. 'But the league is our bread and butter and getting promoted to the SPL is our main focus.'

10 January 2007

I'm due to go down to Raydale today but a strain of respiratory flu keeps me bed-bound. Having recently nursed Lauren through the same lurgy, and ribbed her for being a pathetic patient, I brace myself for the storm.

If I'd known now that Brooks Mileson would prove so hard to pin down in the coming weeks I would have dragged myself out of my sickbed to make our meeting today. However, I am very wary of infecting the club owner or the playing staff for that matter. Gretna's next opponents, Partick Thistle, have already postponed one match and lost another one due to an outbreak of flu at the club.

Over the next couple of days I console myself with buckets of chicken soup and copious amounts of daytime television – opium for the housewives and homeworkers. The flu will clear up soon enough but an addiction to Channel 4's *Deal or No Deal* is something that will stay with me for months. Will we ever be set free from the clutches of Noel Edmonds?

13 January 2007
Partick Thistle v Gretna FC
Firhill Stadium, Glasgow

I wake to the sound of gales and torrential rain and my first instinct is to check if today's match is cancelled. It's not, though three other games in the division are. My heart sinks a little. Having just kicked the flu that has brought the country to its knees I can think of nothing worse than sitting in the wind and rain for two hours. The two matches to be given the go-ahead are Gretna's at third-placed Partick and second-placed St Johnstone at Livingston. Gretna are fourteen points clear of Thistle, and eleven clear of St Johnstone. It makes today's matches must-win affairs for all concerned.

It's Saturday, it's Scotland, it's public transport and it's me travelling. It can only mean one thing – complications. I've dragged Lauren along to today's game and, as we arrive at Haymarket for the 11.49 a. m. First ScotRail service to Glasgow, we find that the train is cancelled due to flooding on the route. Typical! When the line reopens an hour later all subsequent trains are packed and we're lucky to get on.

The plan is to arrive in Glasgow early, have a look around the city centre – I know this will involve shopping but that's the deal I've struck – before heading to Firhill Stadium. The weather puts paid to any serious shopping and I escape with two brief visits to similar-looking upmarket shoe shops with similar-looking staff and stock before we call it a day.

'Firhill for thrills,' I tell Lauren in the taxi. 'It never fails to deliver.' She looks out of the window at the driving rain falling on a Maryhill crime scene and raises an eyebrow. (Yes, *that* Maryhill of *Taggart* fame.) Lauren asks what's happened. 'There's been a MUURDUUR!' I say. She eyes me with a look of genuine confusion.

Inside the ground the away fans are bearing the full brunt of the weather. There can be no more than fifty bedraggled-looking Gretna fans in attendance. As kick-off nears a few more trickle in, having been stuck in traffic. Lauren comments that it's a shame they'll miss the start of the match. 'No matter,' I say. 'Gretna never start quickly.'

Gretna's starting line-up is unchanged from Broadwood save for Ryan McGuffie replacing McGill in midfield.

It comprises:

Main, Townsley, Grainger, Jenkins, Canning, Innes, Paartalu, McGuffie, McMenamin, Graham, Skelton

Subs: Barr, Berkeley, Bingham, Fleming, McGill

Just moments before kick-off I see Mileson trudge in with a friend. Despite the torrential rain both are eating from soggy-looking fish-and-chip wrappers. The pair have arrived just in the nick of time. First Erik Paartalu continues his rich vein of scoring since signing a permanent contract when he slots home from just outside the box on twenty seconds. From the restart, Allan Jenkins nicks possession from Thistle and feeds the ball to Colin McMenamin, who exchanges a clever one-two with Gavin Skelton before bending the ball around helpless Thistle keeper Jonathan Tuffey to make it 1–0.

No one inside the ground can believe their eyes. It's certainly the most bizarre start to a match I've ever seen. Gretna have scored twice before eight of the home side have even touched the ball. It's a sucker punch and having conceded ten goals in the previous two meetings between the clubs the Partick support have every reason for suspecting they are about to be on the receiving end of another drubbing. 'You were right,' says Lauren ironically. 'They don't start quickly!'

Fortunately for Thistle, the onslaught never materialises. Alexander's men seem as shocked as the home side to have scored two goals with such ease and the worsening weather makes it near impossible for either team to play any football. Undeterred by the boos ringing out around the stadium, Thistle inevitably pull one back on twelve minutes when Derek Young volleys Simon Donnelly's flicked-on free kick past an outstretched Alan Main. It's a lifeline for the home side and shuts up the boo boys in an instant. It seems to rock Gretna slightly, being the first goal they've conceded in five games. But the defence soon settles. Derek Townsley's excellent performance is particularly poignant as I was told by a source before the game that he will be the next ageing star to be shown the exit at Raydale Park. I can tell by Degsy's body language that he's yet to be told.

It's a real shame. The thirty-five-year-old fullback has been Mr Consistent this season, works as hard as anyone and has weighed in with a handful of crucial goals. His exit is a continuing statement of intent by Alexander, Wadsworth and the powers that be that they are committed to preparing for the SPL sooner rather than later. It's a brave step and one I hope does not hamper the club's quest for promotion. What was it Alan Hansen said? 'You don't win anything with kids.' (Then again, look how accurate *that* turned out to be.)

As conditions deteriorate at Firhill it's commendable that the two teams are able to produce any sort of spectacle at all. It's freezing cold and the biting wind causes Lauren to ask if we can swap seats so I can be her windbreak. Nearby I can see the Partick directors shuffling in their seats, looking forward no doubt to a half-time pie and warming glass of red. It's one of the rare days when I envy football's 'haves'. There is some inkling that someone up there is most definitely not part of the prawn-sandwich brigade, however, when the roof above the directors box springs a leak and a veritable Niagara of water gushes in, soaking the club's dignitaries. A ripple of laughter spreads around the ground but stops as everyone looks up to their own section of roof to see if it is holding up.

I bump into Brooks Mileson at half-time. Typically, he's looking for somewhere to escape for a cigarette. I ask him if he enjoyed his fish and chips and he tells me that the meal is an integral part of his match-day ritual – Mileson's photo next to his column in the Gretna programme has him tucking into a big portion of the national dish. 'The quality of those fish and chips can affect the result,' says Mileson, jokingly. Of the Clyde victory last week he says: 'Good fish and chips mean a good performance. The omen worked with a great second half.'

'What about today then?' I ask.

'We had to take them into the ground – a first for us,' he says. 'Wasn't sure if this was a bad omen or not. After two goals in seventy-one seconds we thought we'd be setting a new trend in our eating habits but the rest of the game has put paid to that!'

It's a toss-up if the teams will even turn out for the second half. There's lying water on the pitch and the rain is showing no sign of letting up. Partick, who played with the wind at their backs in the first half, must have some sort of pull with the gods because as the second half commences the wind changes direction, prompting Lauren to ask to change seats again. I comply reluctantly.

Thistle's Mark Roberts takes advantage of the gusting wind straight away and within two minutes of the restart has netted a superb goal from twenty-five yards that sails over Alan Main's head into the top corner. It silences the Gretna support and prompts the noisy Thistle support to break into a chorus of 'Scottish by a molehill, you're only Scottish by a molehill . . .'

The equaliser sparks the game briefly back to life. Thistle almost snatch a third through Allan Russell but for a spectacular block from Main. From there the game descends into something resembling *Bambi on Ice*. Players slide in recklessly for tackles, seeing Partick pick up three bookings in as many minutes while the ball gets endlessly caught up in puddles to comic effect. The game hits a nadir when Townsley's thirty-yard shot swerves away from goal, caught by the wind, and ends up on the opposite side of the park some twenty yards behind the player. It's a forgettable final act in a Gretna jersey.

When McGuffie fires over from eight yards with the open goal at his mercy you sense that it's destined for a draw. The final whistle comes as a relief to the 2,678 supporters who have braved the elements elsewhere. Livi's victory over St Johnstone gives Gretna fans more reason to celebrate than today's draw. It extends Gretna's lead at the top of the table to twelve points. When the result comes through I hear one of the country's top sports writers in the press box behind me say, 'That's the league over then.'

Outside the dressing room after the match Partick's scorer, Mark Roberts, confides to the huddled hacks, 'They can only throw it [the title] away now.'

Goalscorer Erik Paartalu, who looks harrowed by his first proper taste of the Scottish winter, says, 'We play the other teams in the top four this month and if we can take points off all of them we'll be in a very strong position.'

He makes it sound easy. It will be far from it. Each of Gretna's promotion rivals know that they must halt the Borderers' march to the title now or risk seeing the Black and Whites disappear over the horizon into the SPL.

20 January 2007
Gretna FC v Livingston
Raydale Park, Gretna

It's sunny but cold as I board the 12.52 p. m. train to Carlisle. Surprisingly, it's on time, there are no scheduled engineering works or known acts of God in our path and there's not a child with E-number-induced attention deficit disorder in sight. It's a relief as I am nursing a mild hangover in the wake of Lauren's sudden departure to Australia for a month. Having settled into Edinburgh life in recent weeks, the news that she's to train as a surf instructor on the other side of the world came as a bombshell. But with the first instalment of this book due in mid February, it may prove to be a godsend. It just doesn't feel like it after my first night home alone in front of *Celebrity Big Brother* and *CSI* repeats. One beer soon turned into six, leaving me with one of those hangovers that lingers all day and, no matter what you do, will not recede.

As the train travels south, the carriage remains blissfully silent. The sunshine continues to hold until the train slows as it passes Carstairs State Hospital, home to Scotland's most dangerous criminals. I always get a sense of foreboding here, wondering if a group of bloodthirsty escapees are about to mount an ambush. One day it will happen, mark my words. We pass the grim-looking detention facility unscathed but as we do so the sunshine starts to fade. I've noticed that it does this a lot round these parts.

As the sky darkens my sense of foreboding stiffens. I hope it's not a sign of some sort of sea change in Gretna's fortunes. After last week's draw at Partick, I've begun to question Gretna's promotion credentials for the first time. Today's visit of fourth-placed Livingston will be as good a test as any of Gretna's mettle. Having parachuted into the league from the SPL at the end of last season, Livi were touted as one of the favourites for promotion yet started the season poorly. Fifteen

75

points separate Gretna and Livi but after two wins on the bounce against Hamilton and St Johnstone, Livi are back in the hunt.

After seamlessly making the connection to Gretna Green (sharing the carriage with a youth travelling with a motorbike), I get soaked in the rain as I walk to the stadium. My mood is worsened still by the loss of a glove – essential survival kit for the Scottish football fan. This is nothing short of a tragedy on a day like today. If you're climbing Everest and you lose a glove you can kiss goodbye to your hand; you just have to choose which one. Walking into the biting wind blowing off the Solway Firth, that doesn't seem so far-fetched.

Despite the inclement conditions there's a buzz around Raydale Park. The stadium seems to be the only source of excitement in the sleepy village. Even on match days I rarely see a soul until I'm within earshot of the ground. Today is no different and such is the noise coming from inside I wonder whether I've missed kick-off. Fortunately, I haven't. It's 2.45 p.m. I bump into Brooks Mileson at the turnstiles. Mileson has just arrived in his black four-by-four. It's the first time in months that he has travelled to a match alone and I take it as a sign that his health is returning. True to form, he is attired in a knee-length jacket, today's variation being a brown sheepskin number, and, again, I can't help but notice that his trousers are covered in animal hair. We exchange pleasantries and Mileson asks me to join him up in the Corries Stand for a chat at half-time.

As I walk along the front row of the stand I see my usual seat, uncovered and already wet, waiting for me. Next to it are two seats reserved for the German reporters. Yet again they're conspicuously empty. I wonder whether somewhere in Dumfries and Galloway there's a pair of confused German journalists wondering how the hell to get to Gretna. If they're relying on public transport to get around they could be anywhere.

The Alexander Technique

Call me soft but I just cannot face sitting in the wet today. The loss of the glove has pushed me over the edge. My salvation comes in the form of Keith Melvin. Seeing me dithering near my seat the Gretna web editor waves me up to the shelter of the stand and a seat beside him. I sit between Melvin and match reporter Jonathan Coates. Coates eyes my hands – one gloved, one at the mercy of the elements – and raises an eyebrow. 'It's not a Michael Jackson thing,' I say.

The wind is blowing so hard that I wonder whether the temporary-looking structure that passes for the stand roof will last out the match. Indeed, as the teams take the field the wind is blowing so hard that some of the more lightweight members of the squad such as Davie Graham and Brendan McGill can barely stand upright.

Gretna's team is:

Main, Townsley, Grainger, Jenkins, Canning, Innes, Paartalu, McGill, McMenamin, Graham, Skelton

Subs: Baldacchino, Barr, Bingham, Fleming, McGuffie

It's clear that the swirling wind is going to play a massive part in today's game. Kick-off is even delayed while the fourth official removes a number of woolly hats and caps that have been blown clear off people's heads on to the pitch. No sooner is the wayward headgear collected than Gretna's resident clown, face-painter and balloon-animal-maker, Daffy-Dyl, watches in horror as the giraffe/snake/whatever it's supposed to be she's just made is caught by the wind and flies out of her hand, straight into the face of a Livingston player before travelling the length of the pitch in the blink of an eye and bursting unceremoniously under the foot of a steward.

Far from dampening the atmosphere, the wind encourages a Blitz spirit amongst the boisterous crowd. I've rarely seen Raydale Park so lively, despite the meagre 1,310-strong crowd. Livi have taken three buses from Central Scotland but are making noise enough for double that number. The home fans, too, are in high spirits. I sense that they're starting to believe that a fairy-tale third straight promotion is becoming a real possibility. News that top scorer Colin McMenamin has finally inked a deal to keep him at the club until June 2009 is also cause for celebration. Sources at the club tell me McMenamin cites his belief that Gretna are SPL-bound as the key reason for him sticking around.

The first ten minutes of the match are dominated by the wind, more so even than last week's debacle at Firhill. Gretna are playing into the wind and Alan Main can barely clear the halfway line with his goal kicks. One flies high into the air before spinning back and landing in his hands on the penalty spot. I'm sure it's an infringement worthy of a free kick.

The wind is so strong that it takes Gretna five minutes to even get into the Livi half. It looks ominous, especially as Livi have started brightly. Gretna dig deep, however, and in only their second foray into the opposition half Erik Paartalu performs one of his signature corner-like throw-ins. The ball sails into the Livi box like an Exocet missile, is flicked on by Allan Jenkins and slotted home from four yards by Martin Canning. It's a scrappy goal and one scored totally against the run of play. It's exactly the type of goal that can win a team promotion.

Livi bounce back almost straight away and Stephen Craig's close-range header hits the crossbar for what is the first of an agonising hat-trick of shots off the woodwork for the striker. The slack Gretna defending prompts an elderly fan in the row in front to mumble, 'Come on, Gretna, wakey, wakey!' At least that's what I think he says. For the entire match the man shouts incomprehensibly. I realise that I've heard him before at both home and away games but only from a distance. He's a bit of an in-joke at the club. I've even seen the odd player chuckle at his indecipherable shouts.

On the forty-minute mark Livi's defence is as toothless as the mumbling fan when an innocuous in-swinging free kick from the left takes the subtlest deflection off captain Chris Innes's head and sails into the net past the poorly positioned keeper. Gretna are 2–0 up against the run of play. If they can maintain this form they'll be crowned league champions within weeks.

At half-time the ground staff work overtime to repair the sodden pitch. Just before the break I saw a Livi player replace a divot in the manner of a considerate golfer. Off the pitch, too, running repairs are made to the stand. For the whole of the first half I lived in fear of the corrugated iron above my head ripping free in the wind and decapitating me. The stand seems to be made entirely of corrugated iron and scaffolding poles held together with duct tape. It's like grown-up Meccano. Melvin sees me eyeing the stand and rolls his eyes. 'Just don't ask to see the health and safety certificate,' he says.

It's so windy at half-time that Gretna FC's resident cheer-leading troupe have to make an eleventh-hour decision to abandon the pompoms. I swear that if they throw one of their number in the air they would fly straight out of the ground and over the border to England. The other half-time entertainment consists of the 50–50 draw familiar to so many small clubs. The £65 top prize highlights the problems the club are going to face if they do make the step up to the top division. An attendance of 1,310 for a home game just isn't economically viable in the long term, nor is only 10 per cent of that number participating in the 50–50 draw.

I go up and see club owner Mileson in his favourite seat in the back row of the Corries Stand. When I reach him, he is holding court with a couple of fans. He then turns to speak to a ten-year-old girl. I overhear the end of the conversation. 'They're a bit like camels only smaller,' enthuses Mileson, 'and I feed them on carrots.'

Mileson is alluding to the llamas in his animal sanctuary at his nearby hundred-acre estate. Searching later on the internet for 'Brooks Mileson + llama', I bring up a website called Celebrity Death List. The macabre site contains a list of the thirty celebrities most likely to die this year. Mileson and the Dalai Llama (*sic*) both feature highly on the list . . .

But the man in front of me looks far from death's door. Mileson said a few years back: 'I'm very passionate about the things that I do. I've got one kidney that operates at fifty per cent, I've got ME, so the whole buzz of the way that I am and the way that I operate helps me,' and he's living proof. Mileson has even had major bowel surgery since that proclamation but is bouncing back from illness. And Gretna's very own Dr Doolittle wants to talk football. 'We'll win this one,' he whispers conspiratorially. 'If Livi couldn't score with the wind they won't score against it!'

I don't know why I expect Mileson to be more impartial. Yet I find it refreshing that he is as blindly enthusiastic and biased as the next Gretna fan. It's infectious and it's part of what makes him the enigma that he is with the Raydale Park faithful. As the teams take the pitch for the second half he asks if I fancy coming down during the week to spend a day with him at the club. Having missed all our previously arranged meetings I jump at the chance. 'See you on Thursday then,' he says, tailing off as I head back down the steps. He adds, 'I should be around then . . .' I turn back but Mileson is already engrossed in the game. Thursday it is then. I'll be there, but will he?

Just four minutes into the second half Livi's Craig rounds Main but, with the open goal at his mercy, he inexplicably hits the post from just three yards. No one can believe it, least of all Craig. It's the miss of the season. Midway through a forgettable second half Livi get the goal they deserve when Scott Mitchell curls the ball into the top corner from twenty yards. On seventy-two minutes they come close again but man-of-the-match candidate Canning is on hand to deflect a goal-bound shot wide. He does that a lot.

It is to be Livi's last real chance of any substance. Three minutes later McMenamin shows why he is the hottest property in the division when he heads in McGill's clever cross. The 3–1 scoreline already flatters Gretna but soon after McMenamin makes it four after he chases a through ball and bravely knocks it past the advancing Livi keeper to take his tally for the season in all competitions to twenty-three.

As the match restarts my eye is drawn to Rowan Alexander, who usually leaves the touchline remonstrations to assistant manager Davie Irons. He is desperately trying to attract McMenamin's attention. When the striker looks over, his manager makes a clenched-fist gesture that the player returns. I'd love to ask Alexander about the exchange but thus far I have not been privy to such insights. Ever since I've started following Gretna, Alexander has been the only key figure at the club who has not acknowledged my presence. I understand it, I truly do. That's the gaffer's job: to be the disciplinarian, to be aloof and hard to reach, to appear to have no time for the press and to be feared by everyone at the club.

I think that rings true for Jon Tait. The press officer has ignored my requests for time with Alexander. Like many people at the club, he seems on edge around him. How bad can he be? By hook or by crook I need to get some time alone with the gaffer. Like Mileson, Alexander's input is vital for the book – a contractual obligation, even – and I haven't uttered a word to him in two months of following the club.

The match finishes 4–1. It's a good win for Gretna and a travesty for Livi. It's only when I squeeze into the press office after the match that I realise how many reporters are at the game. At last the press seem to be taking Gretna's push for promotion seriously. While we wait for the Gretna manager to arrive the members of the fourth estate confer about any ambiguous moments from the match (as long as everyone agrees on everything no one gets in trouble with their editor for getting something wrong). The group also decide which player interviews will go in the Sundays and which the Monday papers (this means no one gets an exclusive but also that no one gets in trouble with their editor for missing out).

It's a cacophony of noise. 'Was it a Paartalu cross or throw-in for the first goal?' someone says.

'Are we agreed that the second was Innes's or did Skelton's free kick go straight in?' says someone else. It doesn't matter what really happened. As long as the match reporters agree.

'Shut that fucking door! It's freezing,' says one of the photographers.

Everyone takes a pause from writing up their match reports before another snapper points at the screen of his laptop and says, 'Could this pass for McMenamin celebrating his goal? I missed it completely!'

Alexander's arrival is greeted with an awkward silence. He seems surprised to see so many faces – there are usually no more than five reporters here. 'Must have been a big game,' he jokes as fifteen Dictaphones are activated simultaneously. It's the most relaxed I've seen him with the press. Perhaps he too is starting to feel that promotion for the small club is not as outlandish a prospect as it might once have been.

It is the question on everyone's lips but Alexander is typically moot on the topic: 'We'll never allow the "P" word to be used until it's mathematically certain. The league is not over.'

Alexander's sound bites sound rehearsed. It is this detachment that makes me doubt I'll have any luck breaking through that tough exterior. To him I'm just another hack. As he prepares to leave I try to make eye contact but his head is down and he's making for the door. He pauses there to chat to Colin McMenamin, who's here for his post-match interview.

'Will you shut that fucking door?' shouts the photographer again without looking up from his laptop. Everyone falls silent. Alexander shoots a withering look at the photographer, who gulps, wishing the ground would swallow him up. As the photographer looks away Alexander's features soften. Encouraged, I follow him out into the cold. There a flustered radio reporter has cornered him but can't get his DAT machine to power up. Alexander says, 'Can't you run it off the mains? We do have electricity down here, you know!'

Seeing the radio reporter completely flummoxed I offer him my Dictaphone, happy to help a fellow 'professional'. He accepts and as the reporter looks over his list of questions I look at Alexander and raise my eyebrows. He smiles and we proceed to make small talk. I think I've caught him on a good day, having just seen off another promotion rival. I tell Alexander about the book. He seems to warm to me when he learns I'm not just another reporter. I ask him if he could spare a bit of his time to talk properly.

'Sure, no problem,' he says to my surprise. 'I'm here on Tuesdays and Thursdays. Just come and knock on my door if you're down.'

When Alexander finishes his radio interview he shouts over: 'See you next week then?'

'Aye,' I say, feeling a dozen sets of intrigued, jealous eyes boring into the back of my head through the press office door.

Having missed my train and with time to kill until the next, I wander away and find myself out on the pitch. It is floodlit and eerily quiet. On this pitch are heroes made. The silence is broken as Rocky Radio crackles into life. The club anthem 'Living the Dream' blasts out to the empty stadium. When you're down to ten men and getting beaten 4–2 away at Airdrie nothing could be further from the truth. But today, having won a match they could have lost (to maintain a twelve-point league lead), having extended an unbeaten home run to seven games, and with only next week's opposition St Johnstone seemingly between Gretna and the promised land, its hard to deny that they are doing just that. Witnessing the quest at such close quarters makes me feel like I am too.

5

Purgatory at Perth

25 January 2007

It's an exciting day today, not only because it's Burns Night
– one of my favourite nights on the social calendar – but
because I'm due in Gretna for my first proper meetings with
Brooks Mileson and Rowan Alexander. I'm scheduled to meet
Mileson at 2 p. m. and Alexander straight after. It's the type
of access than money can't buy. The only problem? As I write
this I'm stuck on a train to Carlisle and have been for thirty
minutes. If we're held here any longer while overhead lines
are repaired I'll miss my connection to Gretna and my meeting with the club's two most important figures. It's agonising
but after a further ten minutes the train finally starts to move.

I'm given a warm welcome at the club by Melvin and Craig
Mileson. I learn that Jon Tait has left the club, and Melvin is
to take on his responsibilities. It's a shame for the amiable
Geordie but it's a relief in some ways because I could never
tell whether Tait was a help or an hindrance to me.

Melvin and Mileson are instantly more enthusiastic and
at ease with having me around. I have a lot of time for both.
Today they seem occupied with thinking of things they can
post on the web forum of local rivals Queen of the South to
wind up their fans. I get the impression that it's an ongoing
battle, the pair of them popping their heads above the parapet
occasionally to fire off a pot shot.

When Mileson's mobile rings I know immediately that it's
his father. He's been held up somewhere and won't be able to

make it in today. 'Don't worry,' says Mileson. 'The gaffer has said he'll spend an hour with you.'

Right on cue Alexander arrives. It's only our second meeting and, as I don't want to appear pushy, my Dictaphone and notepad remain in my pocket. Alexander seems extremely relaxed though his presence seems to put Melvin and Mileson on edge. To start the ball rolling I mention how hard it's been to engage him in conversation on match days.

'Never expect anything out of me on match days,' he says. 'I become a different person to what I am through the week. The players are the same. We're totally focused and, with the press, concentrated on saying the right thing.'

Alexander takes a seat beside me and asks me a few questions about the book and what I hope to achieve. I tell him I don't expect the world from him straight away and that most of all I want to win his trust. 'Nothing we say will go outside these four walls until the book is published,' I say. 'I just want to get to the bottom of how the club works, what makes it tick. I'm not looking for any scoops, to dig any dirt. I just want to tell the story of the season, to capture the feel-good factor at the club.'

'You're the first, then,' says Alexander wryly.

'How's that?'

'The difference between you and the press is that they want to see us fail. Everyone wants to see us fall flat on our faces,' he says with a hint of bitterness in his voice. I listen intently. Warnings I'd been given from some of the match reporters about Alexander's growing paranoia ring in my ears.

'Some do,' I say. 'But you've had good press and after the success you've had surely it sells more papers if you falter?'

'But why is our success not a good enough story?' says Alexander. 'Ever since we've started to be successful people have been trying to discredit us. We've had people looking at how we run the club and whether we're breaking any rules but no one's found anything. We're squeaky clean. We're the cleanest club in the league. What we've achieved here has been done though honest hard graft.

'I've been here six years last November. I'm the longest-serving manager in Scottish football. Everything we're doing here is based on continuity but no one wants to know. No one wants to know about how we got this club into the Scottish League from non-league with no money. How we worked to turn it into a full-time club on a shoestring. No one asks about how we finished fifth and third in the Third Division before Brooks came along. And no one is interested in how we've spent his money, how we're always looking at new training methods, the work we're doing with the community and our academy, and how we're trying to build for long-term success here and not taking any short cuts . . .'

Alexander elaborates for a further five minutes. It sounds like he's getting five years of irritation off his chest in one fell swoop. Melvin and Mileson have obviously never seen the manager speak so frankly. They're engrossed.

Alexander is clearly a man with a lot to say but with no outlet to express himself. While he's talking freely I want to keep him here. After seeing the manager talk down any mention of promotion at the last four press conferences I've attended, I want to ask him what he really thinks. Again Alexander elaborates at length.

'The SPL is where we want to be. We're an ambitious club and that's the target. I cannot believe the lack of ambition of some of the clubs in this league. I know some are limited by finance but you should always strive to be better than you are. Take a look at the players other clubs are signing. We're the only club that are not looking for a quick fix. Other teams are signing older players with SPL experience who are coming to the end of their careers. We're doing the opposite.

'I don't think anyone has given us credit for the transition we've undertaken in the last few months. We're moving some very good older players out of the club and investing in youth.

Players who we think can make the step up to the SPL and that will be fit enough to cut it in the top division. If we win promotion we'll bring in more in the summer but I want to get some of the younger players bedded in now.

'We've got a combination of young players who're hungry to play in the top flight and a handful of experienced players who've played in the top flight before and are desperate to get back. It makes us a very determined team and means that every player is desperate to keep their place because if they don't perform we've got another fifteen players with the same hunger and ambition who'll step in . . .'

Suddenly I feel like I am in the inner sanctum, that I'm privy to things my colleagues in the press will never hear. It's a privileged position. As Alexander's words dry up the meeting reaches its natural conclusion. I think he's even surprised himself with the ground we've covered. I can't resist asking him just one more question before he leaves, however. I want to know why his celebration for Colin McMenamin's goal against Livingston was so public and deliberate. At 3–1 the goal surely had no significance?

'I was like that because that is exactly how I was as a player – aggressive and brave. That's how I like my players to be,' says Alexander.

It's clear that he is having great success inventing a team in his own image. Our time is up. 'What about St Johnstone on Saturday?' I say as a parting shot.

'It's a big match and the mind games between the clubs have been going on all week,' he says. 'We know all our doubters will be there waiting for us to fail and we know Saints will come straight at us from the start because it's probably their last chance to catch us. But we'll use that to our advantage as the game opens up.'

After Alexander leaves Melvin and Mileson nod simultaneously. It's gone well, they say. I prepare to leave and as I do

Purgatory at Perth

Mileson says, 'How would you fancy writing a column in the programme for the next home game?'

'I'd love to,' I say. After two months traipsing round Scotland, watching this club from the terraces, I finally feel like I've been accepted – no mean feat at a professional football club. It rounds off a near perfect day.

I say near because my journey home proves to be even more eventful than the one here. First I narrowly miss the Carlisle train. I consult the timetable and go for a wander to kill time before the next one. When I return, not only does the service not arrive, after calling the train company to complain I find that it doesn't exist. To make matters worse a poster in the unmanned station announces that there'll be a bus replacement service between Carlisle and Gretna for the Black and Whites' next two home games.

With another forty minutes until the next train and the temperature plunging below zero I take another walk. When I get stranded in Gretna (as I'm prone to doing) I feel like the village doesn't want to let me leave. It seems to have an overpowering pull on me. Sometimes I feel like Bill Murray in *Groundhog Day*. Every face in the village looks familiar because I've seen them at Raydale Park. Maybe it's more *Truman Show* than *Groundhog Day*. In the latter, the same thing happens every day. I'll soon learn that nothing could be further from the truth at Gretna Football Club.

I finally make it back to Carlisle around seven o'clock. With plans to attend a Burns supper back in the capital in tatters, I do what any red-blooded Scot would do on such an auspicious night. I make for the nearest chip shop and demand a haggis supper. I board the last train to Edinburgh sated and content. Euphoric, even, from the overdose of saturated fat.

26 January 2007

I'm sitting here contemplating tomorrow's showdown between Gretna and St Johnstone when the doorbell rings. It's
a surveyor here to value the flat. It's news to me and sends
me scrambling for my tenancy agreement. The surveyor provides a nice diversion from my faltering attempts to work this
morning, however.

'What's it you do, then?' he asks, peering over his half-moon
spectacles.

'Erm, I'm a writer, I suppose,' I say. 'I'm doing a book on
Gretna.'

'Ah, Miles Brookson. They'll be screwed when he stops
putting money in.'

I'm on the defensive immediately. I have it on good author-
ity that Mileson is in it for the long haul. A trust to look after
the club in years to come is also planned. I know from conversations with Craig Mileson that what hurts his father most
is the assumption that Gretna is a plaything that he'll tire of.
Far from it: Mileson has worked tirelessly to build a club that
could one day stand on its own two feet. A club at the centre
of the community linking it with any number of worthwhile
causes. As assistant manager Davie Irons says, 'Scottish football needs guys like Brooks. If they are going to scare people
like him away from Scottish football, close the door now.'

27 January 2007
St Johnstone v Gretna FC
McDiarmid Park, Perth

My excitement has been building all week for today's game
and I'm up early to set off for Perth for today's first-versus-
second clash. My train leaves and arrives on time, which must
be a first for this season, and my carriage is only half full until

a group of teenagers get on. The group look like they've got about twenty ASBOs between them. Like Scottish infants, Irn-Bru and junk food are their mid-morning snacks of choice, the only difference being that their Bru is laced with vodka. The group are pale, skinny and wear the preferred ned uniform – Burberry cap, Stone Island jacket, Matinique jeans and Lacoste trainers. As the vodka flows, noise levels increase and soon the whole carriage is bouncing to some ear-splitting happy hardcore tunes. It's two parts annoying, one part fascinating, and seven parts terrifying to see the face of Scotland's future.

Nothing can dampen my excitement for today's game, however. There have been lengthy previews in the newspapers all week and a fair degree of mind games emanating from St Johnstone's McDiarmid Park HQ. The biggest rumour, aimed at unsettling Gretna, is that former Saints keeper Alan Main is on his way back to Perth at the end of the season. That, along with disparaging comments from the Saints chairman in the weekend papers about Brooks Mileson, add more than a little spice to the occasion.

Not that it needs any. It's make or break for the home side's promotion hopes today. A loss will leave the Saints fifteen points adrift with just a dozen games left to play. A win for Saints, who also have a game in hand, will cut Gretna's lead to nine. When I arrive at the stadium I meet Keith Melvin. 'Did you hear about Degsy?' he whispers.

'Is he off too?' I say, rather too quickly.

'Yeah. How did you know?'

I just tap my nose and stay silent.

Truthfully, I'm surprised at Townsley's departure but admit that he could never cut it in the SPL. I cautiously applaud Alexander, and – dare I say it – Wadsworth, for being brave enough to overhaul the squad before promotion has been secured. It's a high-risk strategy, however. They're gambling with people's hopes and dreams and if they fail to reach the SPL fingers will surely be pointed.

The pre-match mind games continue at McDiarmid Park, right down to choice of music. 'Money, Money, Money' is played at full volume over the tannoy as Davie Irons puts the team through their paces on the pitch. Then 'Money' by Pink Floyd in a crass attempt to unsettle the visitors. Maybe it's working. Watching the pre-match warm-up, I can't help but notice that the Gretna squad aren't as relaxed as usual. Maybe increasing talk of their being 'Champions-elect' is getting to them. The press hammered home the notion in the morning's papers and have decreed that if Gretna win here, the title is theirs. With eleven games and thirty-three points up for grabs, I'd say it's premature.

I pick out a new face in the Gretna squad as they run past. I consult the team sheet and see 'A Trialist' is number 16. When Mileson arrives and takes his seat beside me I ask him who the mystery player is. He scowls. 'How should I know? I only own the fucking club!'

Mileson is not in good tune today. He's on his mobile straight away and Mick Wadsworth appears in the stands moments later, adding fuel to the rumours that he's having an increasing influence on first-team affairs. The pair wander away and start a heated-looking conversation. I'm watching the two men out of the corner of my eye, trying not to get busted when I'm interrupted by a voice from a few seats along: 'He's not a happy man.'

The speaker introduces himself as Jack Gass, a crony of Mileson's who travels to every match with him. Gass is an unlikely foil for multimillionaire Mileson. He looks like he's been plucked out of the nearest bar, one that he's propped up for the last twenty years, or from a farmer's field. He's ruddy-faced, good-natured and Gretna through and through. If you cut him he'd bleed black and white. He's been watching the club in its various incarnations since 1945.

'Sorry?' I say.

'Brooks isn't happy today.'

'Really? Why not?'

'That's all I can say,' says Gass mischievously.

'Can't you even give me a hint?' I ask, realising I've found an ally in the amiable Gass.

'Let's just say that the team was picked first thing this morning and it didn't look anything like the one that's going to take the field in ten minutes.'

'I see. So what happened? I thought Alexander was his own man. I thought Brooks stays out of first-team affairs.'

'You'll have to ask him. I can't say. I've said too much already,' says Gass.

'OK.' I change the subject. 'Did you get your fish and chips today?'

'Aye, it was good,' he says. 'The guy who owned the chippie was from Brooks's neck of the woods and gave us double fish!'

Just then Mileson returns with a face like thunder. He turns towards Gass and whispers. From the tone of his voice I can tell he's getting a few things off his chest. When Gass goes off to get a coffee the pair of us sit in silence. It's an awkward moment. 'Brooks, listen,' I say, 'if you'd rather I go and sit somewhere else today it's not a problem. I don't want to spoil your day and have you watch what you're saying.'

Mileson considers what I've said for a moment before replying. 'No, don't be bloody silly. You're fine where you are.'

'OK, only if you're sure,' I say, breathing a sigh of relief. We lapse into silence again before I pluck up the courage to ask about the trialist.

'Did you find out who the mystery number 16 is then?'

'Aye,' says Mileson, rolling his eyes.

'I'm surprised there'd be a trialist you didn't know anything about. Don't you get involved with transfers and signing players?'

'I don't at all!' says Mileson. 'I only get involved once the manager has identified a player he likes.'

I leave it at that. I've already pushed it and Mileson is clearly preoccupied with whatever has gone on that morning. I'll ask him about the incident again weeks later but he still won't be drawn on it. One can only speculate about what was said between the club owner and his manager. Whatever it was, it's my belief that from this moment forward the relationship between Alexander and Mileson never seems the same again.

All the unrest seems like a terrible omen for the game. I think it's got to the players because they look shocked and nervous. The tension between Wadsworth, Mileson and Alexander (who's pacing around like a cat on a hot tin roof on the touchline, occasionally glancing up into the stands) is palpable. It's worlds away from the usual camaraderie that the club and its staff enjoy and it's a massive subplot that will not help the players as they attempt to put the title beyond St Johnstone's reach. In contrast the Saints squad look relaxed but focused on the task at hand. With a squad including seasoned professionals such as Derek McInnes, Kevin James and Martin Hardie, they'll be no walkover for Gretna.

The changes in Gretna's starting line-up make me nervous. Nineteen-year-old Craig Barr, who hasn't started a game since October, is in for Degsy at right back while David Bingham, who hasn't started for a year due to an energy-sapping virus, is in for the injured Skelton in midfield. I wonder whether the highly regarded but rarely played Bingham was the subject of all the pre-match unrest.

The full line-up is:

*Main, Barr, Grainger, Jenkins, Canning, Innes, Paartalu,
McGill, McMenamin, Graham, Bingham*

Subs: Baldacchino, Fleming, McGuffie, Nicholls, Trialist

The match starts slowly and, contrary to expectations, Saints look as cagey as the visitors. It's scrappy and the only early chance is a McMenamin volley on ten minutes from a Paartalu throw. As the game settles down Saints take control. Gretna just don't look at the races and Mileson seems more interested in the latest scores streaming across the scoreboard than in the game involving his club – the club he's rumoured to have spent some £5 million on. Something or someone has rattled his cage, that's for sure.

On fifteen minutes the inevitable happens – Saints score through a Kevin James volley from twelve yards that leaves Main rooted to the spot. The 3,000-strong home support go wild and sing, 'He's coming home, he's coming home, he's coming, Main is coming home . . .' It seems to unsettle the normally unflappable Gretna stopper and his reaction is to wave to the Saints fans. It infuriates the Black and White army, who swiftly turn on their keeper.

A few fundamental errors as the first half progresses seems to unsettle the defence even more. It looks nothing like its usual solid self. At times Danny Grainger even covers the right back position for an overstretched Craig Barr. I ask Mileson, who seems detached and strangely unmoved by the scoreline, if he thinks the team are missing Townsley.

'I've got a lot of time for Degsy,' he says. 'He was at my house on Thursday. He was getting too old though.'

Just then Townsley's replacement, Barr, loses the ball high upfield but sprints back to tackle deep in his own half. 'Degsy would never have got back for that,' says Mileson as if to prove his point. Then again, Degsy might also not have lost the ball in that position.

It's all Saints as the half wears on. It's painful to watch. Gretna's midfield has gone missing and I don't think it will be found again this season. Even the usually impenetrable wall formed by Canning and Innes at the back looks shakier than an Elvis Presley convention. Repeatedly the pair go for the same ball while Main provides no instruction whatsoever. The apple cart is well and truly upset. It's expected that Gretna's form will slip at some stage but this sudden volte-face is staggering.

A pattern develops. Saints go on the attack. Gretna pick up the ball then punt it long up field. Six-foot-seven centre back Kevin James beats either Graham or McMenamin to the ball and Saints start another attack. It continues ad infinitum. High points for Saints are a stunning Jason Scotland shot from twenty yards that cannons off the post and a thirty-yard pile-driver from Willie McLaren that Main flaps at.

Gretna's best effort of the half is a Grainger free kick which flies just inches wide of Kevin Cuthbert's post. It's the nearest the Saints keeper has come to having to make a save in the half and the interval can't come soon enough. Going in at 1–0 down would be considered an achievement on the face of things but even that looks unlikely when Canning, in a display of uncharacteristic slackness, attempts to head a high ball back to Main only to deflect it into the path of the advancing Peter Macdonald. The chance is squandered but it rounds off the worst half of football I've ever seen Gretna play.

At half-time I leave Mileson and Gass griping about the performance. On the way back to my seat I see the familiar sight of Mileson trying to sweet-talk a steward into letting him out of the ground briefly for a much-needed cigarette. When he returns I try and lighten the mood by telling him about the pre-match music. 'I've heard it all before,' says Mileson with a sigh.

I'm keen to see what Rowan Alexander is going to do at half-time to change his team's fortunes. The midfield has been atrocious in the first half and I wouldn't be surprised to see either McGuffie or Nicholls make an appearance at the expense of either McGill or Bingham. Barr too is having a poor time of it at right back and is second to everything.

Gretna remain unchanged after the turnaround, however. The only discernible tactical change sees Graham pulled out wide on to the right. It's a smart move and encourages Gretna not to pump high balls up the middle. The Gretna midfield starts the second half in the same fashion it ended the first – they've gone

AWOL. I'm surprised Alexander hasn't made a change there but I'm prepared to give him the benefit of the doubt.

Unsurprisingly it's Saints that start the second half stronger. Jason Scotland is having one of his better games and he has two clear goalscoring chances in as many minutes. Gretna are actually unlucky not to be on level terms on sixty-four minutes when McMenamin has a powerful shot saved by the Saints keeper.

With Saints in the driving seat I ask Gass what he would do if he were manager. The question is designed to draw Mileson into conversation. Obvious, I know, but with Mileson out of sorts I'm treading carefully. 'We need to make a change in midfield,' says Gass. I nod in agreement.

Right on cue Mileson adds, 'The midfield has been like this from the very first minute and he [Alexander] hasn't made a change! It's been non-existent!'

It's strange to hear such stinging criticism from the mouth of the club owner. I get the feeling there'll be an interesting conversation between manager and club owner at some stage in the not-too-distant future. Oh, to be a fly on the wall then.

On sixty-seven minutes Alexander makes what the hundred travelling Gretna fans all seem to think is a long overdue change. McGill makes way for winger Ryan Baldacchino. 'Baldi' is held in high regard by the Gretna faithful and from the brief glimpses I've had of the pacy ex-Bolton winger I can see why. He has an immediate impact and makes a series of dangerous runs up the right wing. When fit he's an automatic starter in this team.

The look on Mileson's face seems to imply that he thinks the introduction of Baldi is too little, too late. On seventy minutes when A Trialist (ex-Airdrie left winger Xavier Barrau) comes on, Mileson shakes his head and tuts audibly. It seems like a desperate move and there are groans from certain sections of the Gretna support. The introduction of Baldi and Barrau for Gretna and Filipe Morais for St Johnstone injects some much-needed pace into the match. Despite the poor spectacle, the home fans have been singing their hearts out, creating a decent atmosphere. There are just not enough Gretna fans to form any sort of response.

Mileson's mood really hasn't lightened since his arrival. His ambivalence is getting to me because I'm desperate for Gretna to nick an equaliser no matter how undeserved. In quiet points of the game I've been going over in my mind whether I really want them to or not.

On the one hand, if they score then promotion seems all but in the bag, which will no doubt be a great boon to the prospects for this book – this may seem mercenary but I've already seen the postponement of publication of a previous book because of Wigan Athletic's faltering form.

A loss, however, has all sorts of connotations. It could be the start of a large-scale meltdown at the club as they throw away a twelve-point lead and promotion to the SPL altogether. Alternatively, it could mean that the title race will be blown wide open and make for a more exciting book. All sorts of thoughts are washing around my head. I've got mixed feelings but my overriding emotion is fear. I want more than anything for Gretna to win the league and I'm not sure I have the stomach for a fight to the last day of the season. If this keeps up, I might not have a choice.

As these thoughts fill my head A Trialist picks up the ball on the halfway line and heads for goal. In truth he's looked decent since coming on. He is thirty-five yards out when I'm dragged back to the present from my pondering. Now twenty-five yards out, with the defence backing off, he takes one look up before firing an unstoppable drive into the top-right corner of the net. Delirium ensues. The Gretna bench celebrate so wildly that a fracas with their Saints counterparts kicks off. I'm caught up in the celebration too. I'm up out of my seat, cheering wildly. The only person who isn't celebrating is Mileson. He's stony-faced. You couldn't make it up. A team that has been second best all day, that is playing worse than it has all season, and that has been unsettled by goings-on behind the scenes, has equalised through a player who has seen just fourteen minutes of action for the club. A player who, just one hour earlier, was unknown to the man who pays his wages.

The Saints supporters can't believe what they're seeing. They're seething at the injustice of it all. The bench are seething over Gretna's overzealous celebrations too. They've got a point. You would have thought Gretna had won the league, not equalised. Then again, at 1–1 they virtually have.

All credit to Saints. They regroup and win a corner within a minute of the restart. 'I daren't look,' says Mileson as the ball swings across. His feeling of foreboding is justified. Gretna fail to deal with the high ball and it falls to Saints midfielder Martin Hardie who hammers the ball home from ten yards. The Saints fans go wild and the goal sparks mad celebrations on the Saints bench. There's no love lost between the clubs but this time the local constabulary get involved after Davie Irons ends up on his backside on the touchline. It rounds off a bizarre day that has been out of character in every way. It is a day that has produced more questions than answers about Gretna's promotion push. More than that there's evidence of unrest at the club as it enters the most crucial stage of the season. I only pray that it's not the start of a meltdown because the next three months will be the most important in the club's history.

Yet as they enter the final straight the squad look devoid of spirit, when it's usually such a defining feature of how they play. The manager has, for the first time in many fans' eyes, run out of ideas. And the club owner, too, seems to me to be bemused and discontented with his manager. I wonder if, from nowhere, the club is suddenly teetering on the edge of crisis or if it is just a blip in an otherwise unerring ascent to the SPL? Only time will tell. The loss cuts Gretna's lead at the top to nine points with twelve to play. Saints have one game in hand and with the sides set to meet again at Raydale Park anything could happen.

Outside the ground I make my way through the Gretna fans. Their faces are painted with expressions of anguish and worry. I feel their pain. My motivations may be complicated but I want this team to do well. I really do. Further up the road I see another man who so desperately wants this club to taste success. It's Mileson. As I pass, he's puffing away frantically on a cigarette, mobile phone pressed against his ear. The expression on his face says it all. He's livid. I'd kill to know who is at the other end of the phone. With Alexander absent from the post-match press conference at that very moment, I can only guess.

31 January 2007

The last day of January and the day the transfer window slams shut until the summer. With stage one of the squad overhaul completed, following the departures of Townsley, Tosh and McQuilken, I'm expecting to see a few new faces at Raydale Park to replace them. However, with only Steven Hogg having signed on the dotted line so far it's looking like the revolution is getting off to a slow start.

I arrive at Raydale Park just after lunch and head straight for Rowan Alexander's Portakabin-cum-office. When Raydale Park is one day razed to the ground and rebuilt the one thing the construction company will not have to bring with them is Portakabins for on-site offices.

No one at Gretna seems to grumble about the state of their off-pitch facilities, however. That's what I like about the club. Everyone there is a pragmatist. They know what they have and, though their facilities may be amateur standard, they go about their business with increasingly dedicated professionalism. That's because everyone here knows that promotion will change everything. That means a new stadium where they'll all sit in ergonomic office chairs in centrally air-conditioned offices. The redevelopment may be controversial but it is the only way forward for the club if they are to grow. It's a shame. I like Raydale Park and its shambolic feel. It's been a privilege to see the club in its current state because it won't be long before all this is but a memory.

The humble surroundings at Raydale work twofold. They keep everyone's feet on the ground and also ensure that there are no big egos or unnecessary pretentiousness. Saying that, there is a hierarchy at the club and Alexander's Portakabin seems that little bit grander than the rest. From the brass nameplate on the door to the teak, leather-bound desk and antique furniture, it puts the press office to shame. Alexander's office is even replete with an ancient-looking Subbuteo table where the cerebral manager no doubt works out set plays and tactics.

I'm intrigued as to why Alexander has asked me down to meet him today. I assumed he'd be flying around the country looking for some last-minute deadline-day deals but when I enter his office he is sitting at his desk tapping away on his laptop. He doesn't seem to be in the best of moods. I'm not sure how to start so I make small talk. Before I can stop myself I've blurted out, 'No luck on Saturday.'

Alexander stops what he's doing and looks up. He's as surprised at what I've said as I am and though he's got a slight grin – or is that a grimace – on his face it's ever so slightly menacing. He says nothing but keeps staring at me, almost daring me to continue. I don't know what to say but I sense it's going to be hard work today. Alexander reverts his stare to the screen. I've clearly got the gaffer on a bad day. He looks stressed and preoccupied.

I rack my brains thinking of something to say, something to engage the manager. I haven't prepared any questions because the whole point of these discussions is that they are to be informal, relaxed (ahem!) and, hopefully, productive. By the time my brain engages I hear myself say, 'Maybe it will be the kick up the arse they need?'

Alexander looks up from his computer again, stony-faced. I think he's going to ask me to leave but his expression softens. 'Yeah,' he says.

I ramble on to fill the silence: 'A few of the fans said to me that they thought the team looked nervous and out of sorts during the pre-match warm-up at St Johnstone.'

'Who was that?' demands Alexander.

'Jack. Jack Gass,' I say, without thinking.

Alexander scoffs dismissively and goes back to tapping his keyboard. It's like getting blood from a stone. I up the ante. With no specific facts I'm just fishing for information. Alexander doesn't know what I've been told and what I haven't. 'Brooks didn't,' I stutter. 'I mean, I heard there were a few late changes on Saturday. Was that due to injuries or something else?'

Alexander glares at me. The expression on his face is unforgettable. I may be wrong but I get the feeling he's weighing up whether or not to throw me out of his office. Whatever – if anything – went on before kick-off on Saturday is going to remain a secret. Alexander averts his icy stare. Silence.

'I noticed Skelton was dropped. Was that injury? And Bingham started his first game for a long time . . .' I'm rambling.

Alexander stops what he's doing and speaks: 'Gav [Skelton] was the only one that was out.'

A little too quickly I reply, 'And there was Degsy too.'

Alexander dries up again. I ramble on, somehow working the conversation to whether Mileson – who's again cancelled our meeting today due to continued ill health – ever gets involved in football affairs. Alexander gives me daggers again. I've got to ask, though. What's the point in playing safe? Football is a fickle game and you never know when your last conversation with a player or manager will be before they to refuse to see you or are moved on.

'Brooks doesn't get involved in the football side of things at all,' says Alexander. 'The only time he does is if I go to him or if there's a player I'd like to look at. Then he'll get involved in negotiations. Brooks has got enough on his plate with the off-field development of the club but he mentors, he guides, he advises, and that's part of the good relationship we've got.'

At last he shuts the screen on his laptop. I tell him I sat with Mileson at McDiarmid Park and that he seemed mightily unhappy about Barrau's inclusion in the squad.

'That was a last-minute opportunity which arose. It's not something that's happened before,' he says.

Or again, I think. Alexander goes silent so I change tack and ask about the league run-in.

'The intention is to stay at the top. We've got to make sure that there's the belief here that we're stronger than the teams beneath us. The pressure is on St Johnstone. They've got to win all their games to have any chance of catching us,' he says.

With Alexander warming I ask about the team's capitulation in Perth. 'Do you think Degsy's departure and the other changes unsettled the team's rhythm?'

'Maybe. But that's just an excuse. You've got to adapt to the personnel you have available,' he explains.

I ask him if he's sat down and analysed why the game was lost.

'Why do *you* think we lost?' He throws the question back at me, catching me off guard. I'm speechless. I consider myself up there with the best of the armchair pundits but it's a luxury of my job to ask questions that I don't necessarily know the answer to. It makes no difference to Alexander, who stares at me, waiting for me to answer.

'I think it's the first game I've seen where you've played badly . . .' I venture before he interrupts.

'It's the manner in which we lost the goals that's important. How did you see the goals?' he says. I get the feeling he wants to test my football credentials. I know if I fail this will be the last of our private conversations. Here's a full transcript of my response with no editing whatsoever:

103

'Well . . . the first goal was the James one, wasn't it? That was the one that was deflected . . . I mean I thought . . . um . . . I felt . . . um . . . it was a corner, wasn't it? It was flicked on. No, it was a throw-in . . . no, it was a free kick. McInnes free kick, no?'

'It was a free kick from the centre line,' says Alexander. 'McInnes didn't take it. Somebody else took it. Hardie flicked it on from deep in the box and James got off his marker.'

'Who was his marker?' I ask.

'Exactly,' says Alexander. 'All the players have their responsibilities from set plays. They all know the individuals they've got to pick up. They're given those individuals for a reason and if they are not picked up things happen. We lost the goals because certain players didn't do their jobs. In response to all those punters and media' – Alexander catches my eye deliberately when he says this – 'it doesn't matter how badly we played. It's the manner in which we lost those goals that I look at as a manager. That's why I'm in this job.'

'I noticed that you pulled Davie Graham wide in the second half,' I say.

'That's because we weren't feeding our strikers. If you have two small strikers playing against centre backs that are six foot seven and six foot one, how would you feed them?'

'To feet,' I venture.

'Correct,' says Alexander.

'But why weren't you giving it to them on the deck?'

'Correct,' repeats Alexander.

I rephrase it: 'Why weren't you putting ball into feet?'

'Correct,' says Alexander again. 'You're asking me the right question. I asked the players that question at half-time because they knew the game plan.'

'So why wasn't it working?'

'You tell me!' exclaims Alexander, banging the desk.

I shrug.

'It comes down to mentality,' he says, opening a folder to reveal typed reports on each of the St Johnstone team. 'I give each of our players dossiers of their opponents. It tells them what they're like, how they'll react in certain situations and what their strengths and weaknesses are. It's up to the players if they want to read them or throw them in the bin. We've also got ProZone, which analyses individual players so there's no hiding place. If we concede a goal and it's something we've highlighted before the game then we've got a big problem.'

'It's frustrating,' I say.

'It's not frustrating – it's annoying. It's annoying because the players that we've got here, with the experience that they've got, with the places they've played, they should know better.' Alexander pauses for a moment contemplatively. 'Maybe that's why these players are here.'

The statement hangs in the air like a helium-filled balloon. I keep my mouth shut and wait for him to elaborate. I think I've opened up an unholy can of worms. I don't have long to wait. Alexander is in free flow and goes on to make a chilling prediction: 'If they are still making the same mistakes with us that they were making before they came here then we've got a big problem. We are not going to go too far. It's as simple as that.'

'So why was it against Saints that the majority of your players didn't do their job?'

'My opinion is that Saints wanted it more than our players. It was a game that was waiting to happen. There's possibly no better time for it to happen. The response that will happen will be tremendous. That's what I expect. Look at Chelsea. Not one player there goes out and doesn't do the job they've been given to do. It should be the same here every match,' says Alexander, now ranting wildly.

'So there's no truth in talk of a crisis at Raydale Park?'

'No, certainly not.'

'But you still didn't fancy facing the press after the Saints match?'

He smiles. I think if I'd asked this twenty minutes ago he definitely would have flung me out of his office. 'It wasn't that I was angry. I just wanted to take some time because after the match is not always the best time to speak to the press. Emotions could be high, you could be saying things that are misleading, disrespectful or derogatory that future opposition might use to motivate themselves against you. You could blame individuals for losing and that again will come back and bite you.'

'So you bit your tongue then?'

'Yeah.'

I ask Alexander what he thinks about some of the press saying the wheels are coming off Gretna's bid for promotion.

'The press always pick up on insignificant things,' replies Alexander. 'But that makes us stronger here. It makes us believe that what we're doing is right. I think we're victims of our own success. But it will only continue if we make it into the SPL after such a short time. We don't mind, though. We're still living the dream.'

And with that our time is up. It's been a strange encounter, and what would prevail in the subsequent weeks would shed dramatic new light on Alexander's behaviour. Gretna's quest for promotion may or may not come off the rails but if it does I'm in no doubt that the downfall will be traced back to the defeat at McDiarmid Park and the mysterious goings-on behind the scenes.

6

Twelve Hard Games to Go – Twelve Cup Finals

2 February 2007

Anticipation is growing for tomorrow's game. Forth 1 DJ Grant Stott (brother of TV presenter John Leslie) has been speaking about the match on his morning show. After being humiliated 6–0 in their last meeting I'm as intrigued as he is to see how Alexander's men will fare against the SPL team.

3 February 2007
Hibernian v Gretna FC: Scottish Cup fourth round
Easter Road, Leith, Edinburgh

Walking down Easter Road you are under no illusions that this is Hibee heartland. It's a sea of green and white and I'm within sight of the stadium before I see a Gretna fan. It's Rowan Alexander's partner, Clare, and some friends enjoying some fish and chips from one of Leith's finest. I give them a wave. I think Brooks has started a trend.

For those of you never to have had the pleasure of visiting Easter Road, I can highly recommend it. The view of the Firth of Forth from the vertiginous main stand is worth the trip alone. Not that you'll ever see it if you're an away fan because the main stand is reserved for home fans, guests, press and nondescripts like myself. If the away stand hadn't been sold out I'd have been in there.

I spot Keith Melvin as soon as I arrive. He fills me in on the team news. Ryan McGuffie is back in for Brendan McGill and David Bingham has not even made the bench. More surprising is the inclusion of young winger Matthew Berkeley. Berkeley has shown glimpses of what he's capable of from the bench this season and Melvin reckons he's earned his start after a recent fitness test showed him to be the fastest thing on two legs at the club. Only James Grady could come close – a fact, combined with a determination to stay and fight for his place, that Melvin claims has seen the veteran striker saved from the Raydale Park cull.

Looking at the team sheet I almost miss the fact that Alan Main's name is absent. His selection has been automatic this season and, because he's only missed three of thirty-two games, I take it for granted he'll be between the posts.

'What happened to Main?' I ask Melvin.

'Dunno,' he replies. 'Maybe he's been dropped for waving to the Saints fans too much.'

Melvin's evasiveness demands that I investigate further: 'Is he injured?'

'All I'll say is that he's got his feet up at home in Perth,' says Melvin.

'So he *is* injured, then?'

'Let's put it this way,' he says in hushed tones, 'I saw the gaffer yesterday afternoon and he said the only injury worry was Baldacchino. But I'd seen Brooks earlier in the day and he'd said that Main was ill and would miss today's game.'

As Melvin falls silent we're joined by a BBC reporter who says, 'I think it's a shame Main won't be there to see the SPL with Gretna.'

Melvin shoots me a sideways look. Neither of us respond. He emails me first thing on Monday morning to 'confirm' that Main was off training all week with a 'virus'. It smacks of a cover-up. When I later probe Alexander he says, 'We monitored Alan's situation closely during the week and he wasn't getting better quick enough.'

Again, it smells fishy and does nothing to scotch rumours that Main has played his last game for the club. The most persistent rumour is that he has signed a pre-contract to join Gretna's promotion rivals, St Johnstone. It makes me uneasy. This is the last thing the team needs. Main is the foundation upon which Gretna's solid rear guard has been built. Twenty-year-old reserve keeper Greg Fleming is an able deputy but just doesn't seem like the finished article yet.

I wander off to find my seat and realise I'm sitting near TV pundit Archie Macpherson.

'Are you here for the television today?' I ask as I pass.

'No, I'm just here to watch. It looked like the most interesting tie of the day,' says Macpherson.

'What do you think about today's visitors then?' I'm eager to hear a professional opinion.

'It won't be another six–nil like in the CIS Cup earlier in the season, that's for sure,' he says. 'Gretna have improved a lot since then. I think they've got a chance.'

By the time I take my seat the match has started. I'm soon joined by another latecomer. He taps the shoulder of someone sitting in the row in front as he takes his seat. When he turns round I see it's *Scotsport* presenter and panto stalwart Grant Stott. The man seated next to me is John Leslie. (Sadly, there's no sign of Abby Titmuss.)

I text a friend who keeps up with celebrity gossip to say that I'm sitting between Macpherson and Leslie.

He replies:

I wouldn't want to be the meat in that sandwich.

It has me in stitches of laughter.

Gretna line up as follows:

Fleming, Barr, Grainger, Jenkins, Canning, Innes, Paartalu, McGuffie, McMenamin, Graham, Berkeley
Subs: Grady, Mathieson, Nicholls, O'Neil, Skelton

It's the youngest team Gretna have fielded in a long time with an average age in the low twenties.

From the very first minute Gretna are clearly up for this match. Hibs struggle to get to grips with the First Division leaders in the opening minutes. Indeed, on three minutes Allan Jenkins picks up the ball thirty yards out and unleashes a shot that whistles just wide. It fires the Gretna support – numbering some 300 or more – into life. They spontaneously break into a chorus of 'Gretna! Gretna!' I'm surprised by the sheer volume. Why can't they be like this every week? It would silence some of their critics.

Gretna control the play for the first twenty-five minutes and by ninety the stats men have Gretna being just edged by Hibs with 52 per cent of possession. It's an encouraging sign. Gretna are responding to last week's capitulation in Perth just the way Alexander wanted.

Though Gretna dominate the first third of the match, when midfielder Scott Brown is on the ball it's hard to take your eyes off him. Brown seems to cover every inch of the pitch. All credit to Jenkins and Paartalu, however: their efforts make sure that Brown's influence on the early part of the match is kept in check. But the best chances still fall to Gretna. First Colin McMenamin latches on to a sloppy back pass but fires straight at the keeper, before Craig Barr's rasping thirty-five-yard effort has McNeill in the Hibs goal scrambling to make a low save. The young Barr looks more assured today and seems to be finally settling into the right-back berth.

The Gretna faithful are loving it and break into Scotland's only techno chant – 'Black and White Army, woo-woo!' This is a glimpse of how it could be in the SPL. While the away fans are allowing themselves to dream a little, Hibs ominously get into their stride. The lofty Rob Jones is the danger man for Hibs at set pieces and, mindful of Alexander's detailed dossiers, I notice that Canning has the task of marking him. And it's Jones who finds the back of the net on twenty-seven minutes with a back-post header from a sublime Brown cross. It's a dagger to the heart for Gretna fans and is only made worse by John Leslie's smug response to the goal. He scoffs. Yes, scoffs, for at least two minutes after the goal. It does not endear me to the TV presenter.

It's all Hibs from here on in. The introduction of Abdessalam 'Benji' Benjelloun after the break is the last thing Alexander's side need. Not only is the Moroccan a top-scoring clincher in Scrabble, he is also a bit handy with a football. He ties the Gretna defence in knots on a couple of occasions. The second half is only eight minutes old when Benji makes a mazy run into the box, appears to be felled, gets up, is felled again, gets up again, before somehow managing to fire off a shot which hits the post, rebounds straight back out and hits Fleming's shin before flying into the net. Cue more scoffing from Leslie. (It really is quite annoying.) Yes, it was the most outrageous own goal we'll ever see but this is SPL Hibs versus First Division Gretna. There's no need to be smug. To be fair, Leslie is very pleasant when we start chatting. 'I've got two–one on my coupon,' he says, adding, 'I like a bit of danger.'

'It's early days yet,' I say. I'm confident that Gretna have got a goal in them. Leslie is taking more of an interest in Gretna now his coupon depends on them. It doesn't stop him leaping out of his seat moments later when Benji curls in a fine shot to make it 3–0. 'It's party time,' says Leslie as Easter Road erupts.

'There goes your coupon,' I say.

'Yep, but I've also got a side bet for 3–0,' says Leslie, winking.

'Gretna will score. I promise,' I say. It's the least they deserve for their gutsy performance.

As the game wears on Gretna, though outscored, are certainly not being outclassed. They're unlucky to be three goals down. When Gretna win a free kick twenty-five yards out to the right of the goal I sense it is Danny Grainger territory. He could open a tin of peas with his left peg.

'Your bet's up here,' I tell Leslie. 'Watch the top right-hand corner.'

'No way,' he says defiantly, 'the left corner maybe.'

Grainger's shot shaves the bar above the right-hand top corner. Leslie exhales. 'I thought you liked danger?' I say.

'How come you're supporting Gretna?' he asks.

'It's a long story,' I say.

We banter back and forth about Gretna's title bid. 'What about Saints?' says Leslie. 'I think they'll give you a run for your money.'

We're interrupted when Gretna's Berkeley pops up at the back post and drills home a low strike to get on the scoresheet. Leslie crumples up his second betting slip of the day. I take great pleasure in goading the former *This Morning* presenter: 'Now you're going to tell me you have a bet on three–three.'

Leslie rolls his eyes. Two minutes later substitute James Grady finds himself clean through on goal but somehow manages to slide his shot past the keeper and the post with his first touch of the game. Somewhat stating the obvious, Grady says after the game, 'If that had gone in it could have changed the result.'

The game ends 3–1. 'Good luck with your book . . . and your team,' says Leslie as the other results ring out over the tannoy. St Johnstone are through to the last eight. With the league the absolute priority for Gretna their loss might be a blessing in disguise. At least the manner of the loss is some consolation to Rowan Alexander.

'I was very proud of the boys,' says Alexander. 'I thought they did fantastically well, especially in the first half. They've changed to a system which they haven't been used to, going to a four–three–three, and to produce what we did in the first half was very encouraging.'

Ever the analyst, Alexander will know a lot more about his team than he did at 3 p. m. More significantly he will be beginning to get an inkling as to whether the overhauling of his squad is going to plan. What he tells me after the match implies he's satisfied. 'They showed today they can compete against an SPL outfit,' he says. 'Although we haven't beaten a top-flight team yet, the signs are that it won't be far away.'

7 February 2007

It's the second of my weekly meetings with Alexander today. My last visit was terrifying and I'm not sure if I'm ready for another grilling from the Gretna gaffer. I spoke to my father – who enjoyed a successful professional football career – about what happened last time. He said, 'Maybe he just wanted to hear someone else's opinion from outside the club. Or maybe he's under a bit of pressure?'

I find the latter far more likely. I don't know of a manager who'll engage a journalist in a meaningful discussion about his team's failings. Even if I believe I'm in possession of one of the world's great footballing brains, I'm not so deluded to think that Alexander wants to pick it.

Just before I leave home I get a call from Craig Mileson. I am being summoned. Brooks Mileson is at the club and can see me any time before 2 p. m. I move double quick and get to Gretna for 1 p. m. 'The gaffer said you can go straight in,' says Mileson Jnr.

I look at him quizzically. 'And your dad?'

'He's not here.'

'But I thought you said—'

Mileson Jnr cuts in, 'Take the hint, man!'

'Seriously?'

'I'm only joking. My dad's still not a hundred per cent. He had to leave. When he's better you can have as much time with him as you want.'

I make straight for Alexander's office. I knock on the door and am summoned in. There's a white board on the meeting table in front of me. 'I hope that's not for me, is it?'

'Nah,' says Alexander, not seeing the joke. 'Take a seat.'

As is his custom he is tapping away at his laptop, going over the ProZone breakdown from the Hibs game. I tell him I'm surprised the club uses the expensive system and that he's probably the envy of other First Division clubs.

'We're not the only club to have funding available,' says Alexander defensively. 'It's what you do with the resources you have that's important.'

I ask him if he ever learns anything from ProZone that hadn't caught his eye during a match.

'Certainly,' he says. 'I'll ask a player on a Monday how he thought he did in the game. They'll usually say, "I thought I did well. I thought my passing was good . . ." Then I'll say, "OK, Let's have a look." His passing rate might be 50 per cent so we'll break it down further and see what areas his passing was unsuccessful and how we can improve on that. We'll work that into an individual player's training programme and that of the team.'

'But surely there's a temptation to overanalyse? How do you know where to stop?' I ask.

'You're right. There are numerous other programs you can add. It's endless. You become engrossed in it.'

Alexander's telephone rings and he answers it. My eyes wander around his desk. There's a *Simpsons* coffee mug with Homer, Marge et al. wearing Gretna kits. There's an unopened package from the *Sun* and there are a number of payslips scattered around the desk. I squint to see the names and amounts but daren't get caught doing it.

When Alexander finishes his call we talk about Saturday's defeat.

'The first half was decent,' he says. 'We had a lot of good chances that we should have converted. It's those things which determine whether you play at that level on a consistent basis or drop out of the league, so there was a lesson learnt. I thought that two of the goals were avoidable too.'

'What about Scott Brown's influence?' I ask.

'When you can sustain that level of work rate for ninety minutes it's something else. But that's what we want to aspire to. It was good to see that we were better equipped to cope with an SPL team like Hibs than we were in September.'

'Is that down to personnel?' I ask.

'Very much so,' replies Alexander. 'We've had a lot of younger players coming into the side as the season's gone on and I'm very contented with their progress because they're still inexperienced. If you'd seen the CIS Cup loss to Hibs you would have seen why we needed to make changes. It was glaring. We knew about it already but sometimes it's not easy to come to that point where you have to start telling players that where we're going is not for them. We had to make changes. That's where we are now and the signs are encouraging. I'd expect the experience at Easter Road to inspire the younger players to make sure that we are playing in the SPL next season.'

After facing SPL opposition I ask Alexander whether any frailties were exposed and whether he regrets not bringing more players in during the transfer window to bolster the bid for the SPL.

'Managers are never content with what they've got,' he says. 'They always want to do better and get better players in. We're no different here. Unfortunately . . .' he pauses, 'we decided we weren't in the position we have been in other leagues over the last couple of years. Then we've brought in older, experienced players to push us on from there. Now we're in the position where that's not good enough. Now it's crucial to bring in the right sort of people. Players that can give us a lift and take us right on through to where we're going [the SPL] and sustain us when we get there.'

Alexander has more to say. 'The problem we're facing is that we need the guarantee of SPL football to get the people we want to come to the club. There's others we could get but we don't want to go after the players who seem to go around the circuit offering a short-term fix.

'We're at a stage in our development where we can't just say, "We'll get him, we'll get him, etc." That doesn't do you any good anyway because you're just stacking them up. We've got to move players out before we move them in. It's a transitional period and that's the process we find ourselves in.'

I put it to Alexander that surely it's a gamble moving on consistent performers because you don't think they can cut it in the SPL. Surely promotion should be secured by any means, even if that is by playing ageing players who can't make the step up or by signing journeymen pros?

'I'm not going to criticise clubs like St Johnstone for who they're signing,' says Alexander. 'They're just doing what we did to get out of the Third and Second Divisions. They feel that bringing in experienced pros at this stage of the season will give them a lift. We've found that to be the case. But the proof of the pudding will come at the end of the season. Of course we'll kick ourselves if we don't go up knowing how far ahead of the rest we were. It would be incredibly disappointing if we find that we didn't have a squad that was good enough because we feel that this squad is certainly good enough to win this league.'

'So the current squad are all good enough for the SPL then?' I ask.

'I think we've got a squad here that we think should be more than good enough for *this* division. We sifted through a lot of players, some experienced pros who play the type of football we want to play. We haven't adapted our style to any individual. We've got players here who can contribute to good wing play, to high energy in the middle of the park and attack-minded football. This is all built on an experienced backbone.

'We've blasted through the leagues very efficiently and now we've got to push on again and concentrate on being more disciplined. It's a learning process for all our players and whereas before we've blooded younger players at an easier level, now, while we're in transition, they are getting thrown in at the deep end.'

The club's lack of activity in the transfer market is something that has surprised both fans and Gretna's promotion rivals. It's a bodacious policy but the press will continue to ignore it, instead focusing on the club's faltering league form.

The press have also been concentrating on the rumours that Alan Main is finished at the club after signing a contract with Gretna's promotion rivals St Johnstone. While Alexander is talking I slip in a quick question about the veteran keeper.

'Will Alan Main be with you in the SPL though?' I ask nonchalantly.

Alexander doesn't answer. I try another tack: 'Is he available for Saturday's visit to Airdrie?'

'We're not sure yet. He's had a virus that's flattened him.'

'So he's not moving to Saints then?' I ask.

'That's a rumour that's going to run until the end of the season when Alan's contract runs out. He's a Gretna player until the summer as far as I'm concerned.'

I fish for more information but Alexander remains tight-lipped. I pull out the fixture list and ask Alexander about the league run-in that will see Gretna face Airdrie (h), Ross County (h), Clyde (a), Queen of the South (h), Dundee (a), Livingston (a), Airdrie (a), Partick (h), St Johnstone (h), Hamilton (a), Clyde (h) and Ross County (a).

'They're twelve hard games. Twelve cup finals,' says Alexander. 'Twelve games we've got to try and win. We won't rely on other results going our way.'

'Surely there'll come a time when you start planning for the SPL?' I ask.

'No,' he says definitively.

'Not even a little?'

'Not at all,' he says. 'I'm only looking as far as the next game. We can't afford to get sidetracked. Our job is winning the next game. Airdrie have caused us problems in the past and they are fighting for survival so they are going to be dangerous. We need to make sure that we're mentally prepared because there's always a chance that complacency can creep in.'

On the train back to Edinburgh I ponder what Alexander said. With just twelve games to go every game is a must-win for Gretna. In a league of ten teams where three or four are candidates for relegation and anywhere between two and five can still win the league there will be no dead rubbers in the run-in. Every point will be a prisoner. Gretna may have a nine-point cushion at the top but they know they if they stumble St Johnstone will be there to pick up the pieces.

10 February 2007
Gretna FC v Airdrie United
Raydale Park, Gretna

Reports of the demise of the public transport system in the south of Scotland have proved premature. Instead of the promised engineering works no such obstacles materialise. By the end of the day I'll be stranded in Glasgow but that is just a minor detail – I've won this round of Ross v the Public Transport System.

Whether Gretna will win today against second bottom Airdrie is another matter. It's a big game but the stadium is eerily quiet when I arrive. There's not a single fan in the ground and Rocky Radio is conspicuously mute. I head for the press office but find my way blocked by a policeman. Inside, reserve team coach Andy Smith is being interviewed by the police. Smith's car broke down on the way to the game, causing him to abandon it on the hard shoulder of the motorway. The outcome? Three points on his licence and a £60 fine. As the police move out Craig Mileson and Smith look thoroughly displeased. A photographer enters and says, 'I'm sure I've seen one of those bastards at a Queen of the South game.'

It's distinctly gloomy in the press office and freezing to boot. 'Power cut,' says Mileson, pre-empting my question. 'Everything's off: the showers, the flood lights, tannoy system . . . We're trying to fix it but looks like the match will be postponed.'

Great. I've only travelled three hours to get here. I go for a wander. The stadium is completely empty with only thirty minutes till kick-off. I head to the al fresco men's toilet and I find the taps frozen and icicles hanging from the urinal. At the gates people are starting to congregate, wondering if the game is on or not. The Airdrie team coach arrives and you can see a few players shudder with cold as they make their way to the dressing room. That's before they're stripped. It might not even come to that.

I head back round to the press office which is acting as the nerve centre for the struggle to reinstate power. I see club chairman Ron MacGregor outside. 'I think you need to put a few fifty pences in the meter,' I tell him. He smiles wryly. I get the impression that he's seen it all before. This is new Gretna, though, and with the SPL spotlight on the club, how they handle situations like this is key. It would be catastrophic to cancel the match at 2.30 p. m.

Later in the season, when the days are longer, it might not be a problem but it's overcast and cloudy today and the floodlights will be required from the start. There's a lot of twiddling of thumbs while the ground staff run around like headless chickens. There's a back-up generator at the stadium but that has packed up too. Craig Mileson starts chain-smoking nervously.

I notice the match-day programme sitting on a desk and remember that my first column is in today. I've got a full page to myself and there's a picture of me at the top that has been crudely cropped so that I have narrow, squared-off shoulders. I realise that with the game looking like it's going to be called off at any minute the programme may never see the light of day. It may lie undiscovered for years before being unearthed in twenty years' time when I've just won the Pulitzer Prize for fiction . . . I'm awoken from my daydream by the sound of faint cheering. Gretna's electricity provider has guaranteed that the power will be back on if the kick-off can be delayed until 3.15 p. m. Game on. Let's shift a few of those programmes.

The column is a landmark for me. Three months ago I arrived at this club as a stranger with little knowledge of the team or the people that run the club. Now I was writing a hard-hitting editorial in defence of it. I was prompted to do so by a deliberately outrageous article in the *Daily Record* by radio presenter and Saints fan Stuart Cosgrove. I've included some excerpts from both below:

CASH FOR TITLES A POLICY THAT IS HARMING GAME
Stuart Cosgrove, *Daily Record*, 1 February 2007

Gretna are 'a good story'. But why has the media failed in its other duty – to report the deep feelings of resentment that Gretna's rise through the divisions has provoked, especially among lower league fans . . . the consequence of his [Mileson's] big-spending is it unintentionally harms the dreams of others. That is why it is unfair and that is where the Gretna project is fatally flawed . . .

Despite the attention heaped on them, Gretna's story is only romantic if you are emotionally retarded and we should stop confusing money with virtue . . . Their progress says more about the corrosive power of money than it does about small-town success . . .

FIRST IMPRESSIONS
Andrew Ross

At McDiarmid Park two weeks ago the pre-match announcer played 'Money, Money, Money' by Abba. It was as unsubtle as it was inappropriate. If the Perth club had looked at its own and other First Division clubs' activity in the transfer window they would have seen that they could have been accused of hypocrisy. While most clubs in the top half of the table courted expensive journeymen pros who could guarantee them a short-term boost in the promotion hunt, it was refreshing to see Gretna doing things differently.

Gretna's policy is brave, honest, a gamble even, but it epitomises what this club is all about. It is also at odds with the view that the club is cruising to the title on a wave of cash and quick-fix transfers. They're not. For that Gretna should be applauded.

120

Kick-off is nowhere near and I'm already stressing about missing my train at the end of the game. It leaves just after 5 p. m. I kill some time by going in search of a pie. 'Are they hot?' I ask.

'Yep,' says the vendor.

A minute later I'm spitting out a mouthful of cold, congealed grey meat.

It's absolutely freezing so I head back to the press office. There I find three photographers discussing the rumour that Kate Moss and Pete Doherty are going to marry in Gretna Green the following week. I ask Mileson what he's been up to.

'I went to the theatre last night,' he says, taking me by surprise.

'Really?' I splutter.

'Yeah, I went to see *The Woman in Black*. It's my favourite play. Have you seen it?'

'No, I don't think so.' I don't know why I'm surprised by his love of theatre. Maybe it's just that I've never, ever heard it discussed at a football club before. Cars? Yes. Glamour models? Yes. Nothing is quite what it seems at this club.

I take my seat at 3.20 p. m. As I've come to grips with the club and the players, I've looked forward to every match that little bit more. I've been waking up with mild butterflies in my stomach each Saturday, anticipating Gretna taking the next giant leap towards the SPL. The major team news is that Alan Main is back in goal while the talismanic Gav Skelton is back in place of Matthew Berkeley and the experienced Davie Nicholls is in for inconsistent Ryan McGuffie.

The full line-up is:

Main, Barr, Grainger, Nicholls, Canning, Innes, Paartalu, Jenkins, McMenamin, Graham, Skelton
Subs: Bingham, Fleming, Grady, McGuffie, O'Neil

As the match kicks off and the wind bites I think about a conversation I recently had with a friend who was surprised I'd been taking in so many games. When I described a typical home match he interrupted, saying, 'So you're taking a six-hour round trip to stand in a shed in sub-zero temperatures for ninety minutes watching twenty-two men chase a ball around a field?'

In Gretna's defence I have to say they're always good for a goal. But that's irrelevant, really. I've been bitten by the bug and relish my Saturdays. If my book deal was pulled tomorrow, would I still be here next Saturday? You bet. This has ceased to be a job. It's more than that.

Both teams start brightly and it is Airdrie who have the best chance of the opening ten minutes when a shot is deflected over by Martin Canning. Melvin, sitting next to me, says that Canning has earned the dressing-room nickname 'The Fridge' for his cool performances and being calm under pressure. Canning puts in a display worthy of the man of the match award. He'll never get it, though. Whichever boozed-up sponsor picks it will inevitably opt for Davie Graham. The boy has won so much champagne this season that he must have bubbly for breakfast.

The game is twenty minutes old before Gretna have an effort on goal. Airdrie's Paul Lovering's slack pass-back falls to Colin McMenamin, who shoots straight at the keeper. He does that far too often. The chance seems to give Gretna great encouragement and in the face of some poor refereeing they take control of the game. I count four free kicks in the space of three minutes that referee David Somers whistles for and I swear that not one was an infringement. Melvin, who records statistics for the club website, says that after twenty-five minutes Gretna have already got double the number of fouls against than they usually register in an entire match. Despite this the Diamonds' fans sing, 'You're nothing but a homer,' to the ref. Gretna fans retort, 'Don't we fucking know it!'

It's good fun but Somers is spoiling the game. I don't want to buy into the conspiracy theories that abound about the refereeing bias against Gretna but in three months of following them I've never seen them awarded a penalty. Curiously, it is at home that I think they are victim to some of the worst decisions. Today is no different and with each free kick against their team either Alexander or Irons strikes the roof of the perspex dugout in disgust.

Gretna stick resolutely to the task in hand, however, and on twenty-six minutes Davie Nicholls' shot from distance from a clever Allan Jenkins cut-back brings out a good save from Stephen Robertson. Gavin Skelton is having an inspired game. The next best player on the pitch is Skelton's opposite number, Steven McDougall. He remains Airdrie's principal threat for the full ninety minutes.

On forty-two minutes Erik Paartalu draws another excellent save from Robertson. You get the feeling it is going to be one of those days. At half-time I pop up to the Corries Stand to have a chat with Brooks Mileson. He's not looking in the best of health this week and is none too pleased with the team's performance. 'Fucking terrible,' he says. 'The worst I've seen us play all season.'

'You weren't there when this lot beat us 4–2,' I say. Mileson says nothing. He was probably undergoing invasive, life-saving stomach surgery at the time.

Craig Mileson appears as we're dissecting the first half and hands his father a hotdog. 'Where's my onions?' cries Mileson.

'They didn't have any,' says Mileson Jnr. 'They didn't have any vinegar for my chips either!'

'Any chance of catching up with you at the club next week?' I ask Mileson.

'No, sorry, Andrew. I won't be in at all.'

'He's a bit under the weather,' Mileson Jnr says as I leave. As I do, a little girl says to Mileson, 'How are your llamas?'

Mileson beams, the poor performance of the team he's spent a fortune on and his onionless hot dog forgotten. 'They're great. We've even got two babies now. I'll take some photos to show you next week.'

Both teams have clearly had the hairdryer treatment at half-time because they look immediately more motivated in the second half. It is no more than a few minutes old when Airdrie's Neil McGowan and Danny Grainger go in for a 50–50 ball. In the aftermath McGowan punches Grainger. The pair are just yards from the referee who, inexplicably, doesn't even book the Airdrie player. Grainger shakes his head in disbelief.

McMenamin aside, who is so frustrated that he looks like he is about to lash out at any Airdrie player that comes within six feet of him, the Gretna team use the injustice to harden their resolve and midway through the second half they start to play some of the best football of the game. In truth it's the first time in the match that they've got the ball on the ground and played proper football. After a flowing move, Graham cuts the ball back to McMenamin whose shot is deflected just wide.

With fifteen minutes to go Airdrie's Holmes comes closest to clinching the three points, however. A weaving run from McDougall leaves him one on one with Alan Main. Main saves well with his feet, however, silencing a few critics in the crowd who said Main's form might suddenly drop now it seems he's thrown in his lot with Saints for next season. The match ends in stalemate. Astonishingly, it's the first 0–0 draw Gretna have featured in for 110 games.

As the players trudge off the park the other results from to-day's matches are read over the tannoy. Dundee have beaten St Johnstone 2–1. Despite the draw Gretna have been able to extend their lead at the top to ten points. As the result is an-nounced I see Canning walking down the tunnel pumping his fist in celebration. Alexander later tells me, 'We're not really concerned about everyone else.' But it's clear what the defeat of their nearest rivals means to Gretna.

Alexander sums up the game frankly: 'We didn't play particularly well today. Fortunately we managed to gain a point from what was a below-par performance.'

As I dash to catch my train the last words I hear Alexander utter are: 'We have eleven games to go and they might not be pretty.'

I don't think any fan will care as long as they get the results. Eleven nil–nil scorelines for the Black and Whites probably won't be enough. Any more of those and it could be what Alex Ferguson famously calls 'squeaky-bum time' at Raydale Park.

7

A Day of Conflict

14 February 2007

If I've learnt one thing from the last two and a half months doing this book it is that you should always expect the unexpected from Gretna. Today it's the village itself that springs a surprise. I feel something is afoot from the moment I arrive. Two women come running out of a terraced house, jump into a car and start reversing at speed before crashing straight into a road sign. The weirdest thing is that the girls jump out of the car and run off down the street without even so much as inspecting the damage. A moment later three cars fly past in convoy and screech round a corner, knocking over a wheelie bin.

I'm heading for my weekly catch-up with Alexander. Craig Mileson has also assured me that his father will be there. I even confirmed the fact at ten that morning. 'If you get here at 1.30 p. m. he'll have an hour for you,' said Mileson Jnr. I'll believe it when I see it.

It's 1 p. m. when I arrive and, true to form, there's not a trace of Brooks. He's getting harder to pin down than a tent in a force-ten gale but I'm not in any position to complain. It's Mileson's health that's preventing him from being here on a day-to-day basis. For the time being I'll have to make do with our informal match-day chats.

Craig Mileson seems busier than usual. He picks up the phone and starts to read car registration numbers down it. When he finishes the call I say, 'Are you trying to trace which player's got a speeding ticket?'

'No, I'm auditing the club car fleet,' he answers. 'I've got to make a few more calls. Bear with me and I'll go and see if the gaffer is around.'

I lose count of the number of calls Mileson makes. When he takes a break I speak again. 'How many cars do you have in the fleet?'

'We've got sixty between the club and another of my dad's companies.'

And we're not talking about Mini Metros here. The Gretna car park is full of Jaguars, Jeeps, BMWs and Chrysler people carriers. Alexander's top-of-the-range Chrysler has the registration GAO4FER.

Mileson goes in search of Alexander. He's nowhere to be seen, despite having arranged to meet me. It's completely out of character, according to Mileson. 'Maybe he's planning a Valentine's Day surprise for the missus,' he says. With my girlfriend still in the southern hemisphere I'd totally forgotten what day it is.

It's been a wasted trip. Mileson offers me a lift back to Carlisle. It's nearly the last trip either of us ever takes. Driving through the middle of Gretna at speed in Mileson's supercharged Jaguar, a vintage Rolls-Royce that we've been tailing performs a high-speed U-turn, in the process clipping a gatepost. As the Rolls speeds off, Mileson accelerates just as I look up and see the steel barrier connected to the gatepost swing out on to the main road. I shout for Mileson to stop and we do so with a couple of inches to spare. An articulated lorry almost ploughs into us from behind. 'Kerry Fucking Katona!' says Mileson, who looks quite shaken up.

'What?'

'That must be a decoy car for the Kerry Katona wedding.'

A Day of Conflict

15 February 2007

It's Thursday and I'm looking forward to a twice-postponed drink with my publisher in Edinburgh. As I walk to the bar I remind myself not to get drunk and start bombarding him with book ideas. Just behave yourself, I tell myself. Two hours and five pints later and I'm on to my sixth book pitch.

I curse myself as I walk home. Why did I do it? Maybe it's not so odd that, as a writer, I should run every idea I've ever had past the person who could make them all come to life. I feel better about my behaviour when I receive an email from my publisher inviting me to a Derek Johnstone tribute dinner in Glasgow on Sunday night.

17 February 2007
Gretna FC v Ross County
Raydale Park, Gretna

Position	Team	Played	Goal difference	Points
1	Gretna	25	30	50
2	St Johnstone	24	13	40

Saturday football. It's a ritual. I don't think I'll be able to go back to not watching football every Saturday now. I love it. I wake early ... OK, wake early with a hangover of varying degree. Shower and calculate how many layers I must wear to survive the wind coming in off the Solway Firth. Breakfast on whatever I can find in the fridge. Dash to Haymarket. Snooze for an hour (assuming there's no E-number-fuelled infants to disturb me). Wake up as we pass the Michael Douglas Auto Recovery yard outside Carlisle. Get off the train and cross my fingers that there'll be a connecting service to Gretna.

That's a home fixture. If it's an away game I can usually sleep later and not spend seven times longer waiting in train stations or travelling to a match than actually watching it. If it's at Raydale I'm out the door at 10 a. m. and not back till 9 p. m. But the time and travel bother me less than they once did. Learning to deal with my bus phobia aside – I think the official term is Citylinkaphobia – what started as work is now just what I do on Saturdays. Somewhere in the last three months I've become a fan first and an author second. Today, especially, this comes with its own problems.

With Ross County up next I have a crisis of conscience. I try to take my mind off it on the train to Carlisle by flicking through the day's papers. There's a big interview with Brooks Mileson in the *Daily Record* where the club owner plays down concerns over Gretna's impending ground-share in the Central Belt. He says:

> I'm not concerned about attendances and I don't believe we'll be struggling to get people to come and watch us if we're in the SPL. One of the factors that fuels this belief is the amount of support we've built up from outside the Gretna area. We've made a lot of friends and that's why ground-sharing in the central belt is appealing as many fans have taken us to their hearts . . . we're hoping the novelty value we created during our incredible journey will increase the fan base.

Mileson's comments bring to mind another article I saw during the week. On their irreverent Ill Informer BBC site, Tam Cowan and Stuart Cosgrove say of Gretna: 'Great place to get married, shite place to watch football.'

I disagree. I think it has charm though it was great to see the Black and Whites playing at a 'proper' ground like Easter Road.

The Mileson interview is a timely piece both because of my own article in today's programme and because of what I'm told by chief executive Graeme Muir when I bump into him. Muir tells me that he is going to Hampden the following Monday to inform the SFA of the club's ground-share plans. 'It's crazy really,' he says. 'We've not even won the title yet but we've spent so much time on this. It's not even funny. We've got to win promotion otherwise it could all be for nothing.'

A Day of Conflict

I head to the press office and meet Keith Melvin. 'Graeme looks nervous about promotion,' I say.

'It's not that. He's doing Rocky Radio today because the usual guy's been let go – cost-cutting!'

Muir would be forgiven for being nervous about Gretna's promotion prospects because so much is riding on them. While Rowan Alexander and his team keep their feet firmly on the ground – the manager recently confided, 'Football can bring you back to earth with a bump if you look too far ahead, forecasting how many points you have or want to have. It can all get thrown up in the air by a couple of poor results' – it seems that everyone else at the club is compelled to plan for the top flight. For example, the SPL called to request the club crest to be printed on match balls for the following season. It all causes tremendous excitement at the club but no one is getting carried away. The fear of failure is every bit as powerful as the prospect of promotion.

The sun is shining on Raydale Park today and it must be 10°C despite it being mid-winter. It's the match photographers that appreciate the increment in temperature most. 'I've only got six layers on today,' says one as he enters the press office.

'Who are you here for?' I ask. It's the standard chat between media professionals that will be taking place at every ground around the country.

'The *Screws*,' he says, using the media slang for the *News of the World*.

With half an hour till kick-off I kill some time reading the *Screws*' sister paper, the *Sun*. It has noticeably more First Division coverage than usual today. Big hitter Bill Leckie has an exclusive feature about the debt levels at SFL clubs. Gretna's comes in at £2,270,127 (including debts of associated parent companies). It pales in comparison with Dundee's whopping £19-million debt. I show the article to Craig Mileson who, like all senior management, is wearing Gretna tie and club suit today. Everyone, that is, apart from Brooks.

Mileson Jnr dismisses the figures immediately. 'I don't know where they've got that information from but it's garbage,' he says. I'm not sure whether to believe him. Other sources at the club have told me that Mileson Snr may lavish his cash on the club but he is most definitely not burdening it with debt. One thing is clear from Leckie's article, however: Gretna's debts are far from the worst in the division and eminently more serviceable.

To make up for leaving me in limbo during the week, I had received an email from the club with some of Rowan Alexander's thoughts. He explained how he plans for upcoming fixtures: 'We tend to focus on games in threes. If we don't achieve maximum points from one set, it puts pressure on the next lot and that's how we generally work. As we approach the end of the season now, I think if we can muster together seven points out of the nine available from each set of three, we will be on course.'

By Alexander's rationale that leaves Gretna, who have recorded a loss and a draw in their last two league outings, needing six points from today's game. An impossible task but a convincing win against a team that Gretna has beaten twice and narrowly lost to once already this season would go a long way to putting their title challenge firmly back on track.

I'd love to say that it is irrelevant what happens today but it's not. When Gretna last played Ross County a part of me was rooting for the Highlanders. It was a knee-jerk reaction. That was over two months ago, however. Then I was an outsider at the Borders club. Now I'm becoming part of the furniture. I never thought I'd utter these words but I don't want Ross County to win today. There, I've said it. I'm surprised not to be struck down by a thunderbolt from above. Ross County are, after all, as close to the Almighty's team that you could hope to find. Sunday fixtures do not happen in God-fearing Dingwall.

To learn what a conflict today's game causes me it would probably make most sense to reproduce excerpts from my piece in today's programme. I apologise to any County fans and can only say in my defence that it could have been worse. It could have been Inverness Caley.

NATURE V NURTURE
Andrew Ross

County are 'My Team'. But therein lies the problem. There's a rival for my affections. I never meant for it to happen like this. I've never strayed before and I'm wracked with guilt. It started with a few innocent dates. First it was Gretna Green – romantic, yes, but I promised myself I wouldn't get involved. Then we went to Airdrie. I know it doesn't quite match Paris in terms of romance but I was having feelings I hadn't felt for years. From there we met back in Gretna again, where it had all started. By then I was a lost cause and we started seeing each other every Saturday. My promise never to be unfaithful had been broken.

When I arrived to follow Gretna for the season I told myself that whatever else I do I must remain impartial. Having just written a book about a Premiership club and managed to remain impartial throughout I didn't think it would be any different at Raydale Park. But I was wrong. There's a special atmosphere at the club. There's an anticipation of the great days ahead and a feeling that everyone is part of something historic and unique. It's a tremendous reward for the fans who have been with the club since the non-league days but it is no less exciting for people like myself.

Today will be particularly difficult. Ross County are part of my DNA but it's Gretna I've been spending all my time with. Maybe I'll share some of the emotions that Martin Canning will today. Canning was a mainstay of the County defence before his move south and I'm sure he still likes to see them do well. Maybe just not this Saturday . . .

When I wrote my programme piece I only had the Gretna fans in mind. It's an intimate scene at Raydale Park, with everyone seeming to know everyone else, and I just wanted to communicate my growing attachment to the club. I hadn't really thought about any of the thirty-three away fans buying the programme. Therefore I'm shocked, to put it mildly, when I get a text from Stewart, a friend in London, saying: 'a day of conflict i hear?'

The Highland grapevine must be working well today. I've no sooner composed and sent a response to my friend: 'hmmm. it's a gretna scarf, ross county underpants type of day . . .' than I receive a text from another County-supporting friend: 'you traitor. your dad would disown you if he read that.'

Gulp. There's particular relevance as my dad is in the County hall of fame.

'are you here?' I reply, as quick as my fingers will allow. I strain my eyes at the same time as I scan the small band of travelling County fans on the other side of the pitch. The reply comes through: 'in spirit. which is more than can be said for you by the sounds of it. up the county!'

I suddenly regret my forthright views. I wonder if I'll ever be welcome in the Jail End at Victoria Park again? Still, it's done. I have more cause for regret when I realise that the away directors' box is filled with familiar faces. As they take their seats I pull up the collar on my coat and I listen with interest. There are all sorts of outrageous predictions being made. In the midst of it I overhear one director's wife say, 'My husband promised me a belated romantic weekend away for Valentine's Day. This is where he took me!'

The smile is quickly wiped off my face when George Adams, former Rangers head of youth development and Ross County's director of football, takes the seat nearest me. We're only separated by a flimsy barrier. No sooner has he sat down than he's telling me, 'Some of our players aren't even on two hundred pounds a week.' It's clearly a direct dig at Gretna.

County and Gretna are kindred spirits in some ways. Both are from unfashionable, remote football outposts with similarly small fan bases.

After a couple of poor performances in the league Alexander has shuffled the pack.

A Day of Conflict

His 4–3–3 formation comprises:

*Main, Barr, Skelton, Nicholls, Canning, Innes, Jenkins,
Paartalu, McMenamin, Grady, Graham*

Subs: Bingham, Fleming, Grainger, McGuffie, O'Neil

I'm impressed that Alexander has plumped for a bit of much-needed experience up front in the shape of James Grady. His inclusion should take some of the pressure off McMenamin who hasn't scored for a month. I'm yet to be convinced of the new 4–3–3 formation, however. Gretna have scored fewer goals since it was introduced.

With Ross County just above the drop zone they should make for difficult opposition. After faltering last week, Gretna's task is simple. They have to start winning – something they haven't done in three games. I would never have had the fixture down as a grudge match, however. Maybe it's because there's a lot at stake, maybe it's because the refereeing plumbs new depths of incompetence, but whatever the reason, the match is a powder keg waiting to explode.

It's the only thing that will lift the stupor hanging over Raydale Park today. The atmosphere is flat. It is not helped on three minutes when County spring Gretna's offside trap only to be called back by the referee. It's an atrocious decision and the County directors' box springs to life. The rest of Raydale Park remains deathly silent.

The crowd slowly comes to life after ten minutes when Davie Graham cuts in from the left flank and as he shapes to cross is scythed down by Alex Keddie for a penalty. Now I know Keddie has an honours degree in chartered surveying but it really wasn't the smartest challenge in the world. It seems to take an age for referee Chris Boyle to quell County protests, during which the air turns blue in the directors' box beside me. I'm all for appealing against poor decisions but even they must see that it was a stonewall penalty.

135

It doesn't stop shouts of 'You're biased, ref!' or my favourite from a certain Mr Adams: 'You're a balloon, referee!'

When the melee dies down, McMenamin coolly converts the penalty, making it an impressive twenty-four goals for the season. The crowd at last burst into song. From my position behind the home dugout I see that the goal means a lot to Alexander and Irons, who embrace and celebrate as wildly as anyone.

The game as a contest is over just two minutes later when Gretna's no-nonsense midfielder, Davie Nicholls, buries a powerful free kick from twenty yards into the bottom right-hand corner of the net. It causes Adams to turn to me with wild eyes and say, 'The ref's given a free kick! That's not a free kick. Maybe Romanov's right after all.' Adams of course is referring to the comments made by Hearts' colourful owner who claimed that the Old Firm 'buy off' referees.

To be fair to County, they don't lie down at 2–0 and battle for the remainder of the half while Gretna, frustratingly, revert to route-one football despite Irons's shouted directions to 'Hold on to the ball! Play football!'

At half-time I grab a brief chat with Brooks Mileson. As usual he's surrounded by children quizzing him about his animal sanctuary. He was in the paper during the week for a court case he brought against two women who had taken a horse to him claiming it was dying of leukaemia, when, according to Mileson, it had, instead, been severely mistreated. 'It was the worst condition of any animal I have ever seen,' said Mileson. 'Misty was crawling with lice.'

It all adds to the mystique surrounding the Gretna owner and, not feeling like taking him away from his audience of children and locals, I chew the fat with son Craig instead.

In the second half Gretna almost add to their lead ten minutes in through a Canning header. Soon afterwards, for reasons known only to the referee, County coach Davie Kirkwood is sent to the stands. That consists of the rotund Kirkwood hopping over the low wall behind the dugout and standing two yards from where he was.

When the game restarts it does so with some added spice. First Craig Barr fells Sean Higgins with a crunching tackle. As Barr gets to his feet he is pushed over by Keddie who receives his second yellow of the match. The incident sparks off more protestations from the County bench. With the shadows on the pitch lengthening the aggression spills over on to the terraces. A bald, scary-looking Gretna fan shouts over to the home dugout, 'You're going to lose this league the way you're playing.'

At 2–0 up, Alexander and Irons look bemused.

Now Skelton makes a break down the left wing, leaving everyone in his wake. His cross finds McMenamin at the back post, who makes no mistake from fifteen yards. Justifiably, but perhaps foolishly, Irons's reaction is to run along the touchline to find the fan who had berated him and wave his clenched fist in his face. The fan has to be restrained by the police but almost escapes their grasp to 'respond' to Irons.

At 3–0 the game is dead and buried, though there's still time for County to get a consolation goal and for Jenkins to slot home a fourth for Gretna. As the ball hits the back of the net Irons shouts over to the fan he clashed with earlier and holds up four fingers. The fan holds up all ten of his digits defiantly.

With St Johnstone recording an equally impressive victory against Hamilton the title race is still alive. With ten games to go I hear people discussing the mathematics of it as I file out of Raydale Park. 'I reckon we need to win six out of the last ten,' says one fan.

I do the sums. I think it's actually seven from ten but that's only if second-placed Saints win every one of their eleven games. If – and it's a big 'if' at this stage – it goes to the final game it could make for an interesting day: Gretna away to Ross County, who on today's performance will be at the foot of the table. I might need a police escort out of Victoria Park depending how that one ends.

18 February 2007

Sunday night and I'm in Glasgow for a sporting dinner in aid of the Derek Johnstone retirement fund. It's a true-blue night to be sure. I feel sorry for the three women on our table. They are amongst only ten members of the fairer sex at the dinner. By the time the second after-dinner speaker takes the stage the air is truly blue.

As the evening wears on more and more Masonic undertones surface and I decide to leave. It wouldn't be a trip to Glasgow without the customary drunken 'Who do you support, pal?' conversation in the toilets at the end of the night.

'Gretna,' I say to the guy at the urinal next to me.

'Never heard of them,' he slurs.

'You will,' I say as I disappear into the night. 'You will.'

24 February 2007
Clyde v Gretna FC
Broadwood Stadium, Croy

Having only yesterday confirmed the cover design and title for this book I'm feeling a little uneasy about Gretna's return to Broadwood. I hate tempting fate in anything I do so as I pressed send and saw the two lines of text – *'Living the Dream: a season with football's most remarkable club'* – disappear into the ether I felt something like the poor person who named the *Titanic* before it set sail on its fateful maiden voyage.

Before I'm even at the train station today my morning is off to an ominously bad start. I receive a call from my girlfriend who's training to be a surf instructor in Australia. She's dislocated her shoulder. 'That's terrible,' I say. 'At least you'll be back early.'

A Day of Conflict

'Erm . . . I've been offered the chance to extend my trip by seven weeks,' replies Lauren. 'I haven't decided if I'm going to do it or not.'

I've got a sense of which way she'll lean. Another two months of Australian summer or a return to winter in Scotland. Which would *you* choose?

I trudge off to Haymarket ever so slightly crestfallen. It's a lonely shift at the moment but I'll survive, I suppose. It's not as if she's hanging out in her bikini all day with bronzed, hunky surfers . . . *Stop it!* I've got to suppress my envy, be the cool boyfriend. Insecurity is an unattractive trait, I remind myself – I read it on a tabloid problem page so it must be true. It brings to mind something my friend used to say whenever he was apart from his globetrotting girlfriend: 'I'm dealing with it. I'm sure she misses me too but I know it's only a matter of time before a plane carrying a team of well-endowed, sex-starved rugby players is going to crash-land on the beach beside her.' I feel a bit the same. It's how the male psyche works.

My mind is momentarily taken off thoughts of my girlfriend committing multiple adultery with half of Bondi by the sight of fifteen tall Italian men walking down Princes Street wearing Count of Monte Cristo-style outfits, singing their hearts out. I'm disarmed for a second – you're in the wrong place, I think, Sydney is that way – then I realise it's the Six Nations rugby today. Italy are here to face Scotland. I join the procession of Italians with painted faces and blue afro wigs and jolly, kilted Scots. There's no atmosphere quite so good as when two countries that are utterly mediocre at a sport meet each other in top-flight competition.

As I board the train for the short journey to Croy in North Lanarkshire the heavens open. And I mean really open. It's a deluge. Another bad omen for the match? When I disembark into the rain and walk up the hill to Broadwood I see a black cat. Good luck you might say? Far from it: this one is dead on the

139

road, crushed flat. Just then I get a text from my Ross County-mad nephew, Callum: 'gretna r gonna get humped 2day'.

I'm not sure why I have such a bad feeling. On paper it seems that I, or rather Gretna, have no need to worry. With second-placed St Johnstone on Scottish Cup duty today, this is a great chance for Gretna to go thirteen points clear at the top. Then again, if Clyde beat Gretna, they can leapfrog from seventh to fourth place. So the stakes are high and I'm expecting it to be a fiercely fought encounter. Gretna triumphed last time by three goals to nil but were nearly kicked off the park in the process. Who knows what today's match will bring?

I've arranged to meet Brooks Mileson when I arrive and I soon find him and regular travel companion Jack Gass in the stand. Mileson is looking healthier than when I last saw him and Gass is ruddy-faced as ever, bearing more than a passing resemblance to a garden gnome with his woolly Gretna hat and beaming smile. We make an eclectic trio sitting there: the owner-turned-fan, the writer-turned-fan and the fan who's been watching the club for over sixty years.

We discuss possible outcomes of the match. 'It'll be tight but we'll edge it,' says Mileson confidently.

'I'll take a two–one to Gretna,' says Crystal Ball Jack (as Mileson likes to call him).

They're right to be cautious. Clyde are one of the league's form teams and not to be taken lightly. They are much improved from when Gretna last visited, having signed players such as former Rangers starlet Brian Gilmour in the January transfer window. Not that anyone at the club is taking Clyde or any of their remaining ten games lightly. Davie Nicholls said to me during the week: 'Everybody has a chance of winning the title until it's mathematically impossible so we've got to keep working hard.'

With the home and away fans positioned directly opposite each other at Broadwood it's a raucous and confrontational environment. It's not a big crowd either. There are a little over

1,100 here, but with the 150 or so Gretna fans dotted about the stand it's intimidating to face the wall of sound and constant abuse of the wonderfully vocal 'Bully Wee' support.

I try to hold a conversation with Mileson at a civilised volume. Not as easy as it sounds, especially as a lot of the chants are directed at the club owner. I feel a bit sorry for him sometimes because he is a genuinely nice man. He's the salt of the earth and a football man through and through and I doubt anyone could find him objectionable in any way. Still, this is football and the battle lines are drawn. Even today's young mascot says over the tannoy that he fancies an easy 3–0 to Clyde before being urged to wave goodbye to Gretna's SPL hopes.

Last time we were here Mileson was admiring Clyde's impressive community stadium and he does so again. I ask him what the new Raydale Park is going to look like.

'It's going to be a fucking mess,' he exclaims. 'Cramped and overdeveloped because we have no room to extend. I don't know why the council won't let us build a community stadium on a greenfield site. It's a disgrace. And I don't know why we need to have 6,000 seats. It's a complete fucking waste of time. Why can't we build a stadium that is the right size for us?'

As the teams take the field I spot a new face among Gretna's ranks. With Craig Barr suspended, former Motherwell fullback David Cowan is making his first appearance at right back. The twenty-three-year-old has not settled anywhere since a horrific double leg break in 2003 and recently joined the Black and Whites till the end of the season.

The full line-up is:

Main, Cowan, Skelton, Nicholls, Canning, Innes, Jenkins, McGuffie, McMenamin, Grady, Graham
Subs: Davison, Fleming, Grainger, McGill, O'Neil

Alexander has stuck with his 4–3–3 formation.

141

On seeing Cowan I say to Mileson, 'This isn't another mystery trialist, is it?'

He rolls his eyes.

'It's not another Xavier Barrau?' I add.

'Don't mention him to Brooks,' says Gass, breaking into laughter.

I'll take the risk. I know Mileson well enough now to pull his leg. 'Have you offered Barrau a contract yet?'

'What, the "great" player that was on three hundred a week at Airdrie and was let go? You must be joking!'

The whistle brings the conversation to an end with Gass elbowing me in the ribs conspiratorially and winking. I doubt that anyone knows more than him about what goes on behind the scenes at the club.

Despite the morning's bad omens Gretna start brightly on the heavy pitch and almost take an early lead when Grady heads just wide from a McMenamin cross. Even on a muddy surface, the tempo in the early stages of the match is high, though neither team seems able to string together more than a couple of passes. It's scrappy and disjointed and it seems innocuous enough when, on five minutes, the ball breaks to Clyde midfielder Steven Masterson on the edge of the eighteen-yard box. Masterson has other ideas and without a second thought catches the ball on the volley and lashes it past Alan Main into the back of the net. It's a goal from nothing and I doubt this stadium will ever see a better strike.

From there it is downhill for Gretna. They are second to everything. It's only made worse by the delight that the home fans are taking in their slender lead. 'Fuck off, Gretna!' they chant crudely. On twelve minutes Clyde could easily be two up when a good counter-attack sees Ryan McCann unleash a powerful shot on goal. Main makes a great save to keep Gretna in the match, however.

To my eye it looks like Gretna have responded poorly to a change of personnel. It's not helped by the fact that the newest addition to the squad, David Cowan, is having an atrocious debut. He looks timid, off the pace and completely out of place in the combative back line. His performance seems to unsettle both the midfield and defence. After filling the considerable boots of Derek Townsley, Craig Barr has done well in the last couple of games at right back and offers two things Cowan lacks, namely aggression and a willingness to go forward. It's key to Gretna's style of play and with Cowan wilting his teammates stop passing to him. Gretna are restricted to playing everything up the left or pumping long balls down the middle. Rowan Alexander and Davie Irons are tearing their hair out. Even from across the pitch I can make out Irons bellowing, 'To feet, to feet!'

Clyde recognise the uncertainty in Gretna's defence and spend the half bypassing the midfield and back four with some cute one-twos and intelligent movement. The whole thing is backed up by a sold defence, with centre back McKeown winning every high ball that Gretna toss forward. Even the prolific McMenamin and Graham look out of sorts. 'Graham is in one of his lazy moods today,' says Mileson.

Cowan repeatedly fails to stay tight on his man. With Cowan AWOL a three-versus-two attack ends with Masterson through on goal with just Main to beat. Somehow the veteran keeper pulls off the save of the season.

'Cowan! You're going around like a wet raincoat!' shouts Gass in response. It's an astute observation. Cowan seems to hear Gass's comment and other more colourful criticism and becomes even more introspective. The only person in the away stand not to partake in the Cowan-baiting is the elderly fan who sits near me at home matches and shouts indecipherable chants all game. He's at it again today, mumbling, 'Come on, Gretna. Football.' I think.

Just before half-time Gretna do carve out one decent opportunity after winning a free kick on the left. McMenamin heads wide from the ensuing cross, however, causing Mileson to almost jump out of his seat in dismay. Clyde go straight up the other end, their left back getting the better of Cowan again, before unleashing a ferocious shot which is again saved by Gretna's man of the match, Main. 'Terrible!' shouts someone from further up in the stand. I can't disagree.

It's a dismal Gretna performance and as the teams trudge off to get a bollocking in the dressing room Gass trudges off to get us some Bovril. I ask Mileson what he thinks.

'Rubbish,' he says.

'So you'll be on the phone to Rowan after the match?'

'Course I will. I speak as a fan,' says Mileson. 'We speak every Sunday. I tell him exactly what I think.'

In light of goings-on on the pitch, I ask him whether it might have been a mistake to let so many players go and bring in so few in the recent transfer window.

'What's the point? There's no sense in bringing in First Division players now if they're not good enough for the SPL,' says Mileson, echoing Alexander's sentiments. 'We've already got too many players in the squad and some of those aren't even good enough for this division.'

'So why don't you move them on?' I ask.

'We've tried but they're on good money – we've got the fifth largest wage bill in Scotland! They wouldn't get the same money anywhere else so they're happy to sit in the reserves and run down their contracts.'

'So there'll be a few people leaving in the summer, then?' I ask, not expecting any sort of reply.

'There are only a few that are out of contract. Main's one. He's definitely leaving in the summer. Grainger is another out of contract. He's probably not going to be good enough for the SPL. John O'Neil will be leaving too.'

I have to pick my jaw up off the floor. Main's departure has been confirmed for the first time. It's perfect tabloid fodder, if I were that way inclined.

Gretna FC's very own wedding anvil

Just in case you were in any doubt

Gretna's quaint Raydale Park

Alfresco conveniences

Sign in Supporters' Club Bar

My seat at Raydale Park

Rocky the Raydale Rooster

Brooks Mileson

Mileson and Rowan Alexander

Mileson, me and Jack Gass

Davie Irons and Derek Collins

Sir Bobby Robson at Raydale Park

The Scottish First Division Trophy

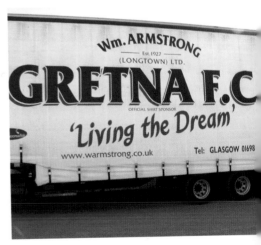

As if we needed reminding

Ross County's O'Carroll makes it 2–2 in final game of season

James Grady keeps his cool to clinch the championship

Grady celebrates his last-minute winner

Irons joins the celebrations

Canning and Baldacchino are mobbed by fans

Danny Grainger at the final whistle

Fans celebrate at Victoria Park, Dingwall

The squad proudly display the trophy

It's the end of an emotional season
for Alexander

Mileson slips quietly away

The team show off the trophy back at Raydale Park

A Day of Conflict

'So there'll be some fresh legs coming in if you're promoted?' I ask.

'Yes,' says Mileson. 'But we have to wait because the players we want need guaranteed SPL football before they'll join us.'

As the second half kicks off Gass returns and promptly proceeds to spill Bovril over everyone. From the outset Clyde pump every ball up the right towards the stuttering Cowan. It's a miracle Cowan is still on the park. A few minutes later it looks like he might not be for much longer. After sliding late into a tackle, Clyde's left back, Imrie, flies up in the air theatrically, arching his back like a leaping salmon before landing in the mud. It's unfortunate that the amateur dramatics occur against a backdrop of the Broadwood Gymnastics Academy, situated behind the goal. I pray that a photographer has captured the image. The referee is not hoodwinked, however. Cowan is granted a stay of execution but only for a few more minutes, when another late tackle leaves him injured and unable to play on.

Grainger comes on for Cowan, much to the relief of the Black and White Army. He slips in at left back with Skelton pushing up to midfield. On the other side Jenkins drops back to right back. McGill comes on too for the ineffectual McGuffie in midfield. It's a better shape for Gretna but as puddles spring up all over the pitch they look no more like scoring.

This is not the Gretna I know. They're uncharacteristically poor. Beside me, Gass watches on with furrowed brow but Mileson is turned sideways in his seat, looking away from the pitch. 'I can't watch,' he says as the clock runs down, not helped by the reluctance of the overweight ballboys to retrieve the ball. 'They're better than the Gretna ones,' says Mileson. 'Last week they were playing football amongst themselves while the players were waiting for the ball.'

Clyde come close again when a poor kick out from Main falls to Masterson, who attacks the goal but shoots just wide. Main's inconsistent kicking will not be missed next season.

As Gretna go on a rare attack and win a corner, Gass says, 'I'm glad I brought a spare battery for my pacemaker!' It's desperate stuff and nervy too. At 1–0 an equaliser is not out of the question. I find myself perched on the edge of my seat. The book – the reason I'm here today – is not even in my thoughts. It's torturous. Though undeserved I pray that Gretna will score. With the clock counting down they win a free kick on the right-hand touchline. It's swung over with venom, missing everyone, and falls to Jenkins at the back post, no more than three yards out. '*Yes!* This is it!' I shout. Jenkins must score. Yet the player proceeds to scoop the ball over when it would have been far easier to score. It's agonising.

Just moments later a long ball is played through to Clyde's Arbuckle. He must be at least eight yards offside but the linesman keeps his flag down. Arbuckle goes on to coolly slot home from seven yards: 2–0. The Clyde fans sing, 'Easy! Easy!' and, 'SPL? You're having a laugh!' It will not be the last time the chant is heard this season. They're almost drowned out by Gass shouting at the six-foot-five linesman, 'You're strutting about there like a bloody ostrich!

Mileson shakes his head and repeats, 'Terrible, terrible.' It goes barely unnoticed when on the pitch Davie Nicholls's twenty-five-yard volley cannons off the post. If it had gone in it would have been every bit as good a goal as Masterson's. The match ends 2–0. It's back to the drawing board for Alexander. The 4–3–3 formation will surely not see another day. Mileson makes straight for the exit with Gass trailing. 'Straight back down the road, is it?' I ask.

'No, we're going to the cabaret. We always do when we're up this way.'

I have no idea where Gass means.

I can tell by people's faces as I file out that the fear of the unthinkable is starting to take hold. Is it possible that Gretna could blow it with just nine games to play? With St Johnstone still ten points behind but, crucially, with two games in hand

and a visit to Raydale Park to look forward to on 7 April, anything is possible. Could what looked like a dream season just days before really be turning into an *annus horribilis*?

8

A Little Local Difficulty

With the trains set to be in disarray on the weekend because of an accident on the West Coast mainline, I spend most of the morning planning my journey to Saturday's match against Queens. If I travel by train my journey will take me at least four hours in each direction. It's inconvenient and, having planned my birthday party back in Edinburgh for 7 p. m. on Saturday night, it will simply not be good enough.

After repeatedly cross-referencing train and bus timetables via Glasgow, Newcastle and God knows where else, and posting a message on the Gretna fans forum asking for a lift, I leave for Gretna to meet Rowan Alexander. The manager is busy but still makes time for a face-to-face meeting. There's still no sign of Mileson at the club. Even his presence on match days goes firmly against doctor's orders.

On the back of last week's defeat I'm intrigued to see how Alexander intends to get his faltering team back on track. And Saturday is not just any old game. It's the local derby. With so much history between the clubs, and with Gretna having knocked no less that twelve goals past Queen of the South in their three meetings this season, it's anyone's guess how it will end. Both teams will be desperate to record a win, not least Queens who have sunk to rock bottom of the league.

Having monitored the Queens and Gretna internet fans forums all week you'd think it was going to be World War Three come Saturday. The animosity between the fans is incredible and I do get the feeling that the Queens fans are bitter about the success of 'The Village People' as they like to call the Black and Whites. Maybe Queens are entitled to be bitter – they are, after all, the only part-time team in the division, and one with a great history – but their criticism of Gretna seems to focus on the money that Mileson invests in the team, the small crowds the club gets and the new fans that the club has attracted. Gretna fans are compelled to respond thus:

> Mileson's investment? No team in the country would turn down the sort of backing he has offered. The small crowds? Gretna has a population of just 3,000. It's not our fault. The new breed of fans? The club is trying to attract new fans to remedy the small crowds so we don't have to listen to people telling us this!

When I arrive at Raydale I can tell immediately that everyone is preoccupied with the match. It's a sell-out and the interest in the local press is unprecedented.

I head straight for Alexander's office. He's sitting at his desk with his hands propping up his head, staring into space. He looks jaded and hollow-eyed. Before we get into our discussion I ask him whether the Queens fans have stopped singing obscene songs outside his bedroom window during the wee small hours.

'How do you know about that?' he asks.

'I overheard your missus telling someone recently,' I reply.

Alexander smiles. 'Ah. Well, that's been . . .' he pauses, choosing his words carefully, '. . . dealt with.'

'How?'

'It would be a good one for the book but I'm no' telling.'

Alexander says he's rushed off his feet and can't spare much time. He's stressed about an assignment he's required to do as part of his UEFA Pro Coaching Licence. He and some of the other young coaches and managers in his class, including Davie Irons, Ally McCoist, Ian Durrant and Andre Villas (Chelsea first team coach), are due to give a presentation. Like schoolkids sharing answers in a test, the managers and coaches have been conferring all week to make sure everyone is ready for the exam.

'It's a good experience,' says Alexander. 'We all help each other and exchange ideas. We'll do club visits here, in England and in Europe to see how other clubs do things. It's good because Gretna are at the stage where we're looking to build links. Hopefully we'll soon have the carrot of SPL football which will help attract players here whether on loan or permanent deals.'

Talk inevitably turns to Saturday's match. I ask Alexander how the players have responded after such a disappointing defeat.

'The lads have been fantastic,' he says. 'They have been really bright in training and are looking forward to getting back on track, and there is no better game to do that than a local derby. They are really up for it. We are into the last quarter of the season and want to start with three points at home. At this stage of the season it's about pulling your sleeves up, winning your individual battles and the collective battle as a team to grind out a result.'

Alexander sounds confident but airs a word of caution: 'Don't forget, Queens are fighting for survival and we have to be equally determined, or even more so. We have something far bigger to aim for.'

I agree with him. Promotion to the SPL is the ultimate prize. Queens have their own motivations. On Saturday it will come down to who wants it most. Alexander fills me with optimism but, based on their performance in recent weeks, his players do not. I'd like to see at first hand how they apply themselves in training and pick themselves up after a defeat.

'When are you training next week?' I ask, angling for an invitation.

'We're in Monday, Tuesday, Thursday and Friday. Monday we do recovery and some small games while anyone playing in the reserves prepares for that night's game. We try and make it fun. On Tuesday we do a warm-down for the reserves and anyone who is fit enough will join the main session. Tuesday and Thursday are double sessions and we do lots of technical stuff – crossing and passing, defending set pieces, etc.'

'How many do you have in the first-team squad?'

'We're down to about twenty-five now,' says Alexander.

'And they're all vying for a spot in the starting line-up?'

'We've got a hard core of first-team regulars which numbers no more than eighteen. We're looking for continuity and if they do well we're reluctant to make changes. After that there are fringe players who are never going to be happy because they are not playing. But you have to manage that.'

'Is their presence not disruptive, though?' I'm thinking of Tosh when I ask. He told me he trained as normal for weeks knowing he was never going to be picked again. I've also been told by sources at the club that right back Mark Birch has been farmed out on loan due to a disagreement with the manager.

'No. All the senior players train together. But by Thursday we have an idea of our squad for Saturday and we take those players away from the rest.'

There's a pause in the conversation. Alexander rustles some papers on his desk. He wants me to leave.

'Do you think I could come and watch the team train next week?' I ask.

'Yeah, not a problem.'

'Great,' I say. My mind is already running away with the possibilities. I need to keep it in check. The same thing happened when I spent pre-season with Wigan Athletic. Once you've been around the players for a week it humanises them, breaks down the barriers. You become deluded that you could do what they do, that it's not too late to give it a go. You're there, for goodness' sake, right there on the training pitch. I swear that I started taking my boots along towards the end of my time at Wigan on the off chance. Maybe it's not so crazy. We're all brought up kicking a ball and dreaming 'what if?' Maybe that's why we love the game, why we never give up hope.

Alexander clears his throat. Our time is up. We shake hands. He seems detached. There's an emptiness in his expression that I can't quite pin down. Little do I know it then but this will be our last meeting with him as manager. I'll never get to attend a training session with him. Indeed, in a matter of days Alexander's whereabouts will be a mystery, doubts will have been cast over his future and the club will have been plunged into a crisis which threatens to ruin their season.

3 March 2007
Gretna FC v Queen of the South
Raydale Park, Gretna

My travel problems are solved by a call out of the blue from a friend, Mike, asking if he can come to the game. A lot of friends have expressed their interest in joining me to watch the Black and Whites but Mike's the first to actually take the plunge. I explain the transport trauma and he offers to drive if I can provide a car. Thus we find ourselves wandering around a shady industrial estate in one of Glasgow's less salubrious suburbs on a Saturday morning looking for an equally shady car hire company. I kill the time, while we wander around lost, explaining the nuances of First Division football and Gretna's faltering form.

We finally find the car hire firm. It is populated with Glaswegian woman with dayglo orange skin. After the briefest of identity checks we hand over £23 and drive off with a Peugeot 206 that looks like it's been driven back and forth repeatedly through a hedge. A little over an hour later we arrive in Gretna.

I'd love to say there's a carnival atmosphere but aside from two policemen standing on a street corner speaking to three Queen of the South fans, the village is as dead as ever. It picks up when we get to Raydale Park, however. As we cross the car park three buses packed full with Queens fans arrive. The buses virtually pogo into the car park, such is the excitement of the fans inside who're leaping around in an alcohol-fuelled frenzy. We make ourselves scarce and head into the ground.

There's a buzz about the stadium that I've not witnessed before. Security is tight too. Mike is relieved of a small plastic bottle of freshly squeezed orange juice by a steward. Outside the press office I bump into Rowan Alexander who is with his family and some friends. He's all smiles, shaking hands and patting children on the head like a presidential candidate. It's totally out of character – I've never seen him with such a relaxed veneer on a match day. Something isn't right. I can't quite put my finger on it. Alexander has said to me in the past, 'I become a different person on match day, totally focused on the game.' Hmmm?

I introduce Mike to Alexander and we chat a bit about the game. While we talk a BBC documentary crew appear and points their camera our way. Alexander promptly disappears to give his pre-match talk. 'I've never seen him look so relaxed,' I say to Mike. 'I don't like it.'

'He's not that relaxed,' replies Mike. 'He almost broke my hand when he shook it. I reckon he's nervous as hell.'

I ponder what Mike says as we head round to take our seats. I don't live in the bubble that is Dumfries and Galloway so maybe I haven't quite grasped what a fierce rivalry there is between the clubs and what pressure there is on former Queens player Alexander to beat his old club. As if to illustrate this, Rocky the Rooster, the Gretna mascot, is being particularly abrasive. He's over on the opposite side of the pitch taunting the away fans. 'He's a braver man than me,' says Keith Melvin when he takes his seat beside us. 'All the Queens fans know who he is and where he lives!'

It's a full house today. That means there's a little over 2,000 inside Raydale Park. But it's creaking at the seams and the Queens fans are making all the atmosphere. What's great about Gretna is that it's a family club but sometimes it lacks that bit of testosterone required to kick-start the singing and chanting.

A Little Local Difficulty

I get the impression that the fans are a bit nervy today. This is a match that needs to be won to put Gretna's promotion quest squarely back on the rails. But Queens are a far stronger outfit than when Gretna beat them 4–0 at Palmerston in early January, not least through the addition of Stephen Dobbie. The former Rangers striker has scored eight times in eight games since joining. Everyone has strengthened their squads in the transfer window, it seems, save for Gretna. I hope it doesn't prove decisive come season end.

After his dismal debut last week David Cowan is nowhere to be seen. Alexander persists with his three-man strike force, however, despite the fact that it drew a blank last week. Talk on the terraces is that there's a lack of creativity in midfield. I can't disagree.

The full line-up is:

Main, Barr, Skelton, Nicholls, Canning, Innes, Paartalu, Jenkins, McMenamin, Grady, Graham

Subs: Berkeley, Fleming, Grainger, McGuffie, O'Neil

The biggest subplot of the day is the resurfacing of the rumour that Alan Main has signed a pre-contract with St Johnstone. I take the rumour as fact following Brooks Mileson's recent revelation. There's more to the story than meets the eye, however. The outcome of the league will decide whether Main – and, indeed, Gretna or Saints – will be playing football at Broadwood and the Excelsior Stadium next season or Ibrox and Parkhead. Main's wage will be better in the top league, too, so, if he does announce his departure and then suddenly starts letting in the odd soft goal, people are going to start pointing fingers.

This is the first of two massive games for basement boys Queens, the second a Tuesday night fixture against Saints. And with Saints facing struggling Ross County today the table could be vastly different by 4.45 p. m. As it stands Gretna have a ten-point lead over the Perth side. That could be seven points with Saints having two games in hand by 5 p. m. The prospect is not even worth entertaining.

The game starts at lightning pace. Both teams create a bucketload of chances in the first ten minutes. First Dobbie delights the Queens fans by rifling in a powerful shot from eighteen yards that draws an excellent stop from Main which the crowd reluctantly applaud. Soon after it's Gretna's turn as both McMenamin and Graham each make penetrating, but ultimately fruitless, runs into the Queens box (sorry, Your Majesty!).

From the outset Queens look a far better-drilled outfit. Steve Tosh, who was a massive crowd-pleaser at Raydale, is on the bench but Jamie McQuilken, who was part of that memorable Scottish Cup Final team, starts. The referee from that historic Cup Final, Dougie McDonald, presides over today's derby. He is card-happy and short-sighted and misses a blatant barge on Craig Barr from a corner that denies the fullback a clear goalscoring opportunity. You can't rely on the referees in this league. It's a lesson Gretna will have learnt by the end of the afternoon.

The Queens fans are creating an intimidating atmosphere all the way up the far touchline. They make this feel like an away fixture for the Borderers. The baying crowd are no more than two yards from the touchline with only the slightest of barriers between them and the players. The noisiest Gretna fan is the one I hear at every game uttering incomprehensible nonsense. He'll shout 'Football!' and 'Gretna!' but everything else he mumbles is indecipherable.

'The world's worst town crier!' says Mike, drawing knowing smirks from the regulars seated nearby. I hear the crier shout, 'Come on, Gretna, pass and go!' but when I look up from my notepad Queens have possession.

It's all Queens as the half wears on. On eighteen minutes midfielder Jim Lauchlan should open their account but he misses with a free header at the back post from a corner. It's a let-off and sparks Gretna into action. The next ten minutes are their best of the game during which Allan Jenkins goes near with a powerful shot from twelve yards. The decent passage of play raises expectations with Gretna fans and when James Grady's clever cross finds Colin McMenamin unmarked eight yards out it looks certain that he'll score with his head. Somehow the league's top scorer conspires to steer the ball wide. It's a similar story on thirty-two minutes when Erik Paartalu heads past from close range.

On thirty-six minutes Queens, buoyed by their vocal support, go close through a Dobbie free kick that whistles by Main's post. Soon afterwards, when a Gretna penalty claim is waved away by the ref after a blatant handball, Dobbie latches on to the long clearance and rifles it across Main into the Gretna goal. I can't help feeling Main could have done better. I'm not alone as Main is roundly castigated by the home support. The Queens fans are still celebrating two minutes later when Davie Graham's spectacular long-range half-volley almost restores parity.

During the interval, chat in the main stand focuses mostly on whether Alexander will persist with the unpopular 4–3–3 formation in the second period. He does, and aside from an early deflected Nicholls shot and a Barr diving header from the ensuing corner which shaves the post, the second half is dominated by Queens. Gretna just don't seem to be able to get hold of the ball. Far from not being able to retain possession, they seem hell-bent on offering it on a platter to their local rivals. If it's not futile long balls up to Gretna's three vertically challenged strikers, it's a sloppy pass across the park in midfield.

Gretna are denied another stonewall penalty on fifty-nine minutes when McQuilken throws his arm at a high cross and punches the ball away. The Gretna fans barely protest – they know it's not going to be their day. It may not even be their season at this rate.

Gretna come nearest to getting off the mark on sixty-nine minutes in the most unlikely fashion. Coming out to gather another wasted long ball trickling towards him, the Queens keeper, MacDonald, loses concentration and watches in horror as the ball slips under his studs and trundles towards goal. The ball rolls just wide, saving his blushes.

On seventy minutes another goalkeeping aberration puts the game beyond doubt when a suspect Main clearance – not his first in the match, I might add – falls to the feet of Sean O'Connor. The number 9 plays a clever through ball to Dobbie who rounds Main with ease and slots the ball home: 2–0. Cue pitch invasion from visiting fans. Game over. Well, almost. There's still time for Tosh to come on to applause from both sets of fans and for Davie Irons to instruct Craig Barr forward to make the formation 3–3–4. It's desperate stuff.

There's also time for another cast-iron Gretna penalty claim to be turned down and for Dobbie to receive a standing ovation when he's subbed off. There's time too for Queens to score a third via a deflected Eric Paton free kick. Main's attempts to repel the shot are comical and start tongues wagging amongst the home support. The look on Rowan Alexander's face tells you words will be had in the dressing room.

When the final whistle goes there's no rendition of 'Living the Dream' played over the tannoy like so often at Raydale. As I wait in the bottleneck at the exit from the ground a fan says to me, 'We should never have let Townsley go.'

Another adds, 'Mark my words: this team will not win the league.' It's a possibility but with Saints only managing a draw at least the gap between first and second is still a healthy nine points. I say as much to the disgruntled fan.

'We should not be relying on other teams' results, though. We could have wrapped this up weeks ago!' he replies.

I wait briefly for Alexander to arrive at the post-match press conference but when he hasn't appeared after twenty minutes we decide to hit the road. I give one of the match reporters a call later to see what was said when Alexander finally did arrive. I'm stunned when he tells me the Gretna manager arrived looking agitated and soaked to the skin. When asked what was on his suit he's said to have replied, 'Well, it's not champagne.'

Somehow, through the disappointment, I've got to get in the mood for my birthday party. I can't get the image of the bedraggled Alexander out of my mind though. I make a few more calls to get to the bottom of it. After some persuasion someone close to the club hints that Alexander and Main might have had some kind of bust-up in the dressing room after the defeat. Director of club development Mick Wadsworth is said to have got dragged into the melee which is believed to have involved a kettleful of water too. Following the alleged fracas, the coaching staff are said to have been summoned to Brooks Mileson's house for crisis talks, though Alexander is rumoured not to have turned up.

It's near impossible for me to get anyone directly involved in the alleged incident to confirm that it happened at all. With Gretna being a small village, it's not long before rumours that seem to corroborate the story appear on the internet:

> Super Ro [Alexander] was obviously feeling quite upset over the defeat by his former employers ... telling the players that they were not trying ... then Super Ro goes into the back to cool down ... By which point Mick Wadsworth has come into the dressing room and tells the players all he has ever done since he came to Gretna was try and help them improve as a team. Alan Main then takes offence to this ... telling Wadsworth that he was a 'lying two-faced c**t'. They then start to square up like two rampant peacocks. Davie Irons gets between the two to calm it down, Alexander then reappears telling Main he is finished etc. Main turns round and tells him to f**k off and that he is ruining the club etc., to which all of the other players respond with a round of abluse [sic]! Rowan has lost the dressing room! After this Rowan goes out on the pitch to talk with Brookes [sic] and after a while Brookes calls Davie over and when he gets over there is Rowan Alexander in tears with Brookes trying to calm him down ... Rowan Alexander is finished at Gretna.

[www.pieandbovril.com]

5 March 2007

It's all go at the moment. While I'm trying to get to the bottom of Saturday's events, Keith Melvin emails me to alert me to the posts being made about me on a First Division fan site. It seems that my article in Saturday's programme, merely highlighting the undeserved negative press that the club attracts, hasn't gone down well with Queens fans. The posting receives well over three pages of responses.

6 March 2007

I'm just tuning my radio to BBC Scotland for the Queen of the South v Saints league match when my phone goes. 'Did you see the news?' asks my dad.

'No, why?'

'It said Rowan Alexander has been given a fortnight off to recover from illness and that Davie Irons is taking over till he's back.'

'Illness? What illness?'

I make a quick call to the club but get no answer. I text Melvin and Craig Mileson but also get no response. Later that evening a statement from chief executive Graeme Muir is released: 'We respect what Rowan has achieved in recent times, but now he needs time and space to recover from this illness. He's seeking advice and that's a good thing. All members of staff have been informed and are supportive.'

Illness? This is news to me. I've spent a lot of time with Alexander in recent weeks and though I found some of his behaviour odd there was nothing to suggest he was in need of medical help. With no explanation of the 'illness' I can only guess what Alexander's ailment is. 'Illness' in football is usually parlance for one of two things: stress or addiction. I have no reason to believe Alexander has a problem with alcohol (any worse than anyone else in Scottish football, anyway). I'd be more inclined to think stress was the cause or, more likely, that he's being eased out of his job through the back door after Saturday's reported fracas. The one thing I can categorically rule out is Alexander throwing in the towel. I just can't see him walking out at this stage after all he's been through in his seven years with the club. He more than anyone has built the club with his bare hands. He'll happily tell you how. Then again, perhaps with his beloved Gretna suffering their worst run of form in three years he's taken it to heart.

It cannot, of course, be ruled out that Brooks Mileson thinks it's time for a change. I know, from sitting next to him on Gretna's travels, that he's been less than impressed with the club's performances in recent weeks. I try to get in touch with the owner but he proves as elusive as ever. Craig Mileson informs me that his father will make an official statement later in the day. When he does it casts no light on goings-on at the club in recent days. On 7 March 2007, Brooks Mileson said:

> I don't want to waste time indulging in tittle-tattle. Rowan hasn't been well for the last few weeks, and it is a credit to the man that he has continued in the job, but he deserves time off to get his health back to scratch. It is nonsense to think there are any other reasons for what has happened over the last 48 hours. I have my own health problems, so I understand what other people are going through. We have built up this club with the benefit of people like Rowan and I find it preposterous that we are even discussing his future.

The silver lining to the day is that Queen of the South continue their march away from the relegation zone with a 1–0 victory over St Johnstone. The result preserves Gretna's nine-point lead over the Perth club, who have a game in hand. It might be just the first time in history that Gretna fans have cheered a Queens victory.

9

Alexander Out – Irons in the Fire

7 March 2007

I'm all set to leave for Gretna – today being the day I usually have a sit down with the manager – when I receive an email from Craig Mileson. He says that the club is being besieged by the press and that the position of trust I enjoy will be best served by staying away. It makes sense. I'm in no rush and I wasn't even sure whether Irons would agree to see me anyway.

I also learn from Mileson that Alan Main has been suspended for two weeks and has indeed signed a pre-contract with St Johnstone. It's impossible to believe that there is no connection to Saturday's rumoured bust-up. Main did not inform the club about his move, however. Mileson's close friend and Saints manager, Owen Coyle, did. I doubt Main will ever pull on the number 1 jersey for the club again. The arrival of twenty-nine-year-old Polish keeper Zbigniew 'Zibi' Malkowski on loan from Hibs until the end of the season seems to confirm it.

9 March 2007

Having had a few days to contemplate, I come to the realisation that, although I've enjoyed a good relationship with Alexander, maybe a shot of fresh blood is what Gretna need. Alexander has shown a reluctance to make tactical changes in recent weeks when the team has been playing poorly. The

163

4–3–3 formation under which the team has been labouring has proved massively unpopular with the fans too. Whether or not Irons changes that on Sunday for the crucial visit to third-placed Dundee will, for me, be the test of whether he's just going to mind the shop while Alexander is away or put his own stamp on the team.

From what I know of him I reckon Irons is his own man. The transition should be smooth. Based on what I'm told by the players, Irons' input on the training ground, touchline and in the dressing room has grown in recent months anyway, with Alexander taking a more hands-off approach. Many in the squad find Irons more approachable. He is universally liked and respected. It remains to be seen whether Irons can cut it as the number one and make the tough decisions the position requires. Or whether he has the tactical nous. Then again, maybe a man called Irons is the right man for the club with an anvil on its badge.

Having not really become acquainted with Irons before, I'm keen to make contact with him before his first game in charge. With a face-to-face or telephone conversation out of the question under the press embargo, I arrange to email the caretaker manager some questions. I ask him if the squad has been able to stay focused on the Dundee match in light of recent goings-on.

'Yes, definitely,' replies Irons. 'It's a massive compliment that they've been able to maintain their focus given the current situation. They have been very professional in everything they have done since the weekend.'

I also ask if confidence is high going into the match with Dundee, particularly as the suspended McMenamin, the only First Division player to appear on both the top scorer and indiscipline charts, will miss the game.

'Colin's been our out-and-out goalscorer so we need other people to stand up and be counted and start finding the back of the net,' says Irons. 'But you don't know what Dundee will turn up. Hopefully it will be the team we played when we won 3–1. Regardless, it's about what we do and I believe we have got the players to go up there and dig out a result that we so badly need.'

As Irons confirms, it's a massive game for the club.

11 March 2007
Dundee v Gretna FC
Dens Park, Dundee

They say a week is a long time in football. Even by those standards it has seemed to take an eternity for these last eight days, between Gretna's ignominious defeat to Queens and today's Sunday fixture with Dundee, to pass. Extra pressure on the team, as if any were needed, is provided by the fact that St Johnstone's victory yesterday has narrowed the gap at the top to six points with what is quickly taking on the appearance of a championship decider between the two looming in a month.

When I arrive in Dundee it looks every bit as grey and uninspiring as when I used to spend time here as part of Dundee United's youth set-up. It will be a trip down memory lane to pass Tannadice on the way to Dens Park. As the train crosses the Tay, the ticket collector says, 'It's a depressing place, isn't it? I cannot think of one redeeming feature whatsoever.' It's harsh, since it's raining and miserable. I think everywhere in Scotland looks like this today.

I'm not sure where I'm going from the station so when I see two people with what look like black and white scarves jumping into a taxi I run after them and open the door. 'Could I share your taxi?' I ask.

'No problem,' says the man in the back seat. I jump in to find that the scarves are dark blue and white. They're Dundee fans. We share small talk about both Dundee's and Gretna's unpredictable form of late. In light of the backlash to my recent programme piece outlining how Gretna seem to be the most despised team in the league, I'm keen to hear the views of some rival fans.

'I don't think people do hate Gretna,' says Graeme, who's a member of the Edinburgh-based Capital Dark Blues. 'Not any more than they do other teams anyway! At Dundee we don't have a problem with the fans or the club. I just think people are worried about what will happen if Mileson pulls his backing. Then Gretna will be unsustainable. That's the real worry.'

It's a fair comment but with Dundee's Dee4life being just one of a massive list of supporters' trusts to receive backing from Mileson, they should know that his involvement in the game is more than a passing fad.

I turn down the kind offer of a pint and head straight into Dens Park. I've decided I'm not going to push anyone at the club to tell me what's really going on behind the scenes at Raydale Park. It's more a case of softly, softly, catchy monkey. I meet Keith Melvin first. I ask him how he's coping with the recent press interest, being new to the job. The look on his face tells me he's been overwhelmed. We chat about today's game before the conversation works its way round to the inevitable.

'What's the atmosphere been like at the club this week?' I ask.

'It's been good,' says Melvin, smirking. 'Davie Irons has taken it all in his stride. In fact I was speaking to Brooks yesterday and he was saying that the team spirit over the last week is the best it's been all season.'

'I don't suppose Rowan is going to be at the game today?' I continue.

'No,' says Melvin nervously, looking around to make sure no one has overheard. 'I don't even think he's in the country. No one knows where he is. Brooks told him to take a holiday.'

When I descend to pitch-side, I see Brendan McGill and Erik Paartalu, who I'm on nodding terms with, watching their teammates warming up. 'You both injured?' I say.

'We've been dropped,' says Paartalu dejectedly.

'Nightmare,' I say.

'Tell me about it. We don't train all week to sit in the stand,' says McGill in his soft Irish lilt.

The pair are chatty but cautious. Like a lot of the playing and backroom staff I'll meet today, they are guarded. 'Relax,' I say to diffuse the tension. 'I promise I'm not going to ask you about last Saturday.'

Paartalu smiles. 'We don't really know what's going on either, mate.'

'Really? You're sure it's not a case of what happens in the dressing room stays in the dressing room?' I say. The more taciturn McGill raises his eyebrow but keeps focused on the pre-match warm-up.

Paartalu seems more willing to discuss the matter. 'These things happen all the time,' says the big Aussie. 'Anything that went on after the Queens game was no worse. You get a lot of big personalities in football and you get a lot of people trying their hardest and lots of differences of opinion so there's always going to be something going on.'

What Paartalu says confirms that 'something', whatever it may be, did happen in the dressing room. Realising his gaffe, he quietly changes the subject and asks me how the book is going.

'Good. It's a bit of an eye-opener coming to all these stadiums,' I say, gesturing to Dundee's dated – but no less charming – ground.

'You and me both,' says the midfielder, eyeing up the two grey tower blocks that cast a shadow across Dens Park.

Out of the corner of my eye I see Brooks Mileson arriving in the stand so head up to take my seat beside him. He seems in a frosty mood so I keep the conversation light. The hundred or so Gretna fans that have made the trip to Dundee are in fine voice around us. There's nothing like a crisis to bring a group together. I don't think I've heard them this lively and up for a game in months. They'll give the 4,000-strong home support a run for their money today. It makes for an excellent atmosphere on a dismal afternoon.

Let's hope the players are as motivated. Apparently they are. No sooner have they taken the pitch than they form a huddle. It's a message to the fans and to the press. Irons, who comes over to the stand and applauds the fans for making the long journey, later tells me, 'We always have a huddle, but we tend to do it in the dressing room. I thought for a change we'll take it out on the pitch and let everyone see how together we are. I think with everything that has gone on in the last week it was important we showed that.'

Irons is already stamping his own mark on the team. Danny Grainger is recalled to left back with Gavin Skelton and Ryan McGuffie returning to a four-man midfield. Davie Graham and James Grady make up the two-man attack. Zibi Malkowski is in goal in place of Main and a new-look bench includes a fit-again Ryan Baldacchino, recent signing Steven Hogg and fringe squad member Neil MacFarlane.

The full line-up is:

Malkowski, Barr, Canning, Innes, Grainger, McGuffie, Jenkins, Nicholls, Skelton, Grady, Graham

Subs: Baldacchino, Berkeley, Fleming, Hogg, MacFarlane

Gretna start with purpose: in the first five minutes Dundee only advance into their half on two occasions. Both of those are high balls up the field. Gretna, meanwhile, seem intent on keeping the ball on the deck despite the greasy surface. They piece together the first of a number of excellent passing moves on ten minutes involving Jenkins and Grady but the striker fails to deliver a decent cross to the waiting Graham.

If the Black and Whites are in crisis they're not showing it. This is the Gretna of old, of when I started following them in late autumn.

They do still find themselves exposed at the back at bit, though. Grainger, who has returned at left back after three games on the sidelines, does still show some of the frailties that led to him being dropped in the first place. It is down the right that Dundee start their best move of the half. It culminates with Bob Davidson's top-corner-bound shot from ten yards being spectacularly saved by debuting Malkowski. On twenty-one minutes Gretna's vulnerability is exposed again when a counter-attack from Dundee sees Gavin Swankie fire over from eighteen yards with just the goalkeeper to beat.

Moments later a speculative long ball from the back sees Gretna's Grady chasing. With him and centre back Gary McKenzie bearing down on goalkeeper Ludovic Roy, who is coming to gather, it seems a fairly innocuous situation. Somehow, under pressure from Grady, the Dundee players collide and the ball is deflected to the lurking Davie Graham, who slots the ball into the empty net from twelve yards. The goal sparks wild celebrations on the pitch, in the dugout and in the stands. Mileson even loosens up and smiles. A group of fans behind me sing, 'Small town in Scotland . . . we're just a small town in Scotland!' in their most ironic tones. A beaming Davie Irons turns to conduct the chorus from the touchline.

Soon afterwards Mick Wadsworth comes up into the stands and sits in front of Mileson. 'Andrew's doing a book on the club,' says Mileson by way of introduction.

'Great,' says Wadsworth brusquely as he almost crushes my hand with his handshake. What is it with this club and crippling handshakes? He eyes me suspiciously, deciding whether to say what he's come to pass on to Mileson.

'Don't worry,' I say. 'I'm not fishing for any gossip. I'm just here to watch the game.' Wadsworth smiles, exposing at least one gold tooth. He's not someone you immediately warm too.

From the restart Gretna almost undo their good work. Dundee go quickly up the field and are only denied a sure-fire equaliser by a characteristic last-ditch tackle from Martin Canning. The Black and Whites soon regain their composure and dominate the remainder of the half. The best move of the game sees Grainger, McGuffie and Graham combine to release Grady into the box. The diminutive striker is upended from behind just as he prepares to shoot but the referee waves away claims for a penalty.

Just before half-time the referee bemuses everyone in the ground when he stops play so a Dundee player can tie his lace. 'I've never seen anything like it,' says Mileson.

When the match restarts a good Dundee move sees a deep cross whipped in from the left to the far post. With the ball going out over the heads of Grainger and Dundee's Davidson, the Gretna player gives the striker a small nudge that sees him go to ground. It takes a moment after the referee blows his whistle to realise he's given a penalty. When you're in the midst of a crisis it is easy to start thinking that everyone is conspiring against you.

I don't think anyone really gives Malkowski a hope. 'Is this a non-smoking ground?' is all Mileson can say as he searches for his cigarettes. Davidson places the ball on the spot. He looks nervous. This is one of those season-defining moments. I can feel it. Malkowski stands tall and puffs out his chest. The goal suddenly doesn't look that big and the Pole is the hero of the hour when he blocks Davidson's weak shot to his left and pounces on the loose ball. All around me Gretna fans celebrate as wildly as they did for the goal. I sense a turning point. Not just in the game but in Gretna's whole campaign. If they do go on to win the title, this will have been a pivotal moment.

At half-time I munch down a gravyless steak pie while fielding a call from my mate Mike – he's a convert to the Black and White cause. Mileson has disappeared for a cigarette and Gass remains, bemoaning the fact that they couldn't find an open fish and chip shop on account of it being Sunday. Gass seems uncharacteristically quiet today and I wonder if Mileson has asked him not to feed me any more morsels of gossip.

Everyone else is in good spirits in the stand. When the tracksuited Paartalu, McGill and McMenamin come up into the stand with pies in hand, the group of fans behind me sing, 'Who ate all the pies?' The three look like they've been caught with their fingers in the cookie jar when Mileson returns to see his elite athletes stuffing their faces.

Mileson doesn't return to his seat next to me, however. Instead he sits in an empty row with Wadsworth. Other than introducing the policy of reducing the average age of the squad, a policy that admittedly has seen the inexperienced side falter, I can't find any reason for Wadsworth's unpopularity. Maybe it's his thorny Yorkshire demeanour or rather his record with his previous clubs. I cannot believe the vitriol dished out to Wadsworth in internet chatrooms. It's not just the Black and Whites' fans he is unpopular with. If you google Mick Wadsworth, you'll see what I mean!

A real worry at the club at the moment, especially in light of Alexander's leave of absence, is that Mileson and Wadsworth might have started meddling in team affairs. Again, these are just rumours – which Mileson has denied when I've asked him – but the two look thick as thieves as the second half restarts. Then again, they *are* the club owner and director of club development, so aren't they entitled to? Adding fuel to the fire, at one stage during the match Wadsworth is seen with his mobile phone to his ear in the stand while Irons is reportedly seen taking a call in the dugout. Not long after, Berkeley replaces Graham on the pitch.

Dundee's manager, Alex Rae, must have given his players a stern talking-to at half-time because, after the interval, they come out fighting. They dominate the first ten minutes during which the former Rangers man enters the fray as a substitute. Rae is as combative as ever and proves a handful for Nicholls and Jenkins in midfield. Though they enjoy more possession Dundee only really create one decent chance. Kevin McDonald's fierce, close-range shot after an excellent run is blocked by the omnipresent Canning on the hour mark, however.

That is the last time Dundee threaten Malkowski's goal. Gretna start to monopolise possession. On sixty-two minutes Grady picks up possession thirty yards out and chips the keeper, only to see the effort bounce back off the crossbar to be turned behind. From the resulting corner Grady comes close again, heading just wide. Later Graham goes on a good run but his cut-back fails to find Grainger or Skelton who're both free in the box. Soon afterwards a weak Jenkins shot is seized upon by Grady who controls and turns in one movement and volleys just wide. Gretna and Grady deserve a goal.

As full time nears, Dundee chase the game, leaving themselves wide open at the back, and twice in two minutes the fleet-footed Matthew Berkeley comes close. By this time the Dundee stands are empty. In time added on they win a contentious corner but Malkowski's confident take sums up the team's resolute, defiant performance.

When the final whistle sounds the relief is palpable. Having not won for three weeks, the celebrations that follow are euphoric. It has been a good win after a very, very difficult week. Irons runs on to the pitch and jumps on Jenkins. Even the normally reserved Mileson must be feeling it because he runs down, leaps the barrier and embraces the pair. It's a great moment. He then comes over to the stands and clenches his fist in the air. The players pause for a few minutes in front of the fans too, milking the applause. Mileson disappears down the tunnel with Irons and the players – something I've never seen him do. Wadsworth remains seated, frowning. Jack Gass beside me raises his eyebrows. Having supported the club for as long as he has, I wonder if there is anything he has not seen.

Irons is still on a high an hour after the game. He's beaming and I can tell how much it means to him and the squad. The dressing room must be a very different place compared with a week ago. I ask him what the result means for the team.

'We had to stop the rot and it's a massive lift to get three points,' he tells me. 'The players gave everything they had for each other. There was such a togetherness and a real desire to dig a result out. It was brilliant to see. If they can show the same attitude and commitment in the remainder of the games then we shouldn't have any problems.'

Goalscorer Davie Graham makes more specific reference to how the result should quell rumours of civil war at Raydale. 'It's been a tough week for everyone involved,' he says. 'There has been a lot of stuff in the papers about fighting in the camp, etc., so we just wanted to show everybody that we're all in it together.'

When Graham says this I pause to consider whether this extends to Rowan Alexander. I wonder what he feels just now, having seen his team return to winning ways in his absence.

14 March 2007

My patience of the last ten days pays off when I get a call from Craig Mileson, inviting me down to Raydale Park the following day to have a coffee with Davie Irons. I almost bite Mileson's hand off because the ground has been a no-go zone for the press for nearly two weeks.

It's the second bit of good news of the day – the other being that Partick Thistle beat St Johnstone in the teams' second meeting in four days to deny the Perth team the chance to narrow Gretna's lead at the top of the table. The result sees the Black and Whites preserve their nine-point lead with seven games to play, though the Saints have a game in hand.

In keeping with Gretna's policy to build for the SPL, the club have signed nineteen-year-old former Newcastle United midfielder Nicky Deverdics. It's another signing with former Magpies number two Mick Wadsworth's name written all over it. Deverdics is high on potential and low on experience.

15 March 2007

When I get down to Raydale Park the squad are midway through a training session. Afterwards Irons emerges wearing jeans, T-shirt and a black lightweight trench coat. He comes to find me in the press office where I'm sitting with Craig Mileson. Irons's mobile phone rings. He's got a country music ringtone. He rejects the call. 'Where shall we go?' he asks.

'Why don't you go into the gaffer's office?' replies Mileson.

Irons looks as if he's been asked to jump into Alexander's grave. He's hesitant as we head over to the manager's office. We take a seat at the meeting table and he soon relaxes. He seems more at ease with my presence than Alexander ever was.

I explain that I'm less interested in asking him what went on last week and more interested in football matters.

'That's OK,' says Irons, 'I think everyone has accepted that Rowan is away for a couple of weeks. As far as I'm concerned he'll be back. I'm just holding the fort.'

No one at the club knows Alexander better than Irons. The former St Johnstone man joined the club in 2002 as a player and has been Alexander's assistant since 2003. I'm interested to know if he detected anything out of the ordinary in the run-up to when Alexander's illness finally got the better of him.

'I did notice a few things actually,' says Irons. 'The Friday before the Queens match I came into this office and he was sitting at his desk. He looked like he was struggling. He said to me that he felt like everything was getting on top of him.'

174

'You mean stress?' I ask – the nature of Alexander's illness has yet to be confirmed.

'Yes,' says Irons. 'Definitely stress-related. After the Queens game Rowan looked terrible. Brooks was concerned. He was worried about Rowan so he advised him to take a bit of time out.'

I ask Irons if he understands how Alexander might have been feeling, having been at the club since day one of its Scottish Football League adventure.

Irons's response is telling: 'Rowan's problem is that he's got this thing about it being his club. It is and it isn't. He can't feel the defeats more than anyone else though he thinks he does. We all suffer when we lose. To be fair, it's been easy the last couple of years and relatively stress-free because we tended to win most games.'

There's logic there, since this must certainly have been Alexander's most stressful spell in his managerial career. It's intriguing to hear Irons's account of events.

'Are you in touch with Rowan? No one seems to know where he is.'

'Yes, we've been speaking a bit,' says Irons. 'We'll be going to the Scotland v Georgia match together as part of our coaching course. I've told him I won't be in touch too much though, because he needs a break from everything. I got a text from him last Sunday after the game. He was definitely happy we'd won,' adds Irons.

'There's such a stigma placed on conditions like stress, especially in football. Do you think there's a way back for him?' I ask.

'How Rowan copes with it is important. He's getting advice and help just now so hopefully he'll bounce back,' he says. 'Stress can hit people in different ways. We're lucky that we haven't had much here in the last couple of years. This year was always going to be more difficult. Hopefully Rowan will learn how to cope with it better.'

We pause for a moment, sombrely. The conversation takes on a more general tone and we discuss the partnership of Alexander and Irons that has become synonymous with the club's success. The pair recently signed rolling five-year contracts.

'I think most people looking in from the outside will think that I'm the loud one, the one that shows his emotions, while Rowan takes a step back,' says Irons. 'It's definitely a double act and it's great to have experienced what we have together. I think if we can reach the holy grail of the SPL it will top everything.'

'But Alan Main won't be there to see it?'

'No. He won't play for the club again,' he says. 'It's a shame the way the whole thing has been portrayed in the media and that his career with Gretna will end like this. Committing himself to our biggest rivals was a problem, though. None of the staff were comfortable with it and the players began to wonder, "Does he really want us to go up?" Only Alan can answer that. What would have happened if Alan made a mistake that handed the title to Saints? If it was any other team it wouldn't have had the same effect. It was best for the team to remove that element of doubt.'

Just then Mick Wadsworth pops his head around the door. 'Do you know Andrew?' says Irons.

'*En passant*,' replies Wadsworth.

Irons looks confused. 'Sorry?' I say.

'*En passant*. It's French for "in passing",' says Wadsworth before he leaves. I quiz Irons about his apparent growing influence at the club.

'I think people look at what's happened at the club and automatically point the finger at Mick,' says Irons. 'They will have noticed that there are more people leaving the club this season than coming in. I don't think the fans saw it coming. Players of that age [thirty-plus] were never going to play for us in the SPL. We had to change the atmosphere at the club, in the dressing room.'

'A lot of people think it would have been better if you'd waited to secure the title first,' I say.

'I'll be first to admit that I didn't know if it was the right time to do it,' reveals Irons. 'Hopefully at the end of the season we'll look back and say that it was the right thing to do. You've got to remember that we still have a backbone of experienced pros in the side. Innes, Skelton, Nicholls, McGuffie – they all played in the Scottish Cup Final and know how to win titles. We may have a young team but we have experience.'

'Are you aware of what the fans think of the transfer policy, and of Mick?' I ask.

'He came in to make decisions that, in my opinion, should have been able to have been made by the people already at the club. For whatever reason they weren't and Brooks identified that and that we needed someone to come in and streamline the club.'

'A hatchet man?' I venture.

'Yes and no. It had to happen. It was totally unrealistic before. We were unsustainable. We had a big squad, a big coaching staff and a big youth academy. I think we'd got carried away with the cup and league success. We had a massive payroll. We got away with it last year because we made money from the cup run but that could be a one-off. You only get about thirty thousand pounds for winning the First Division so we need to be in the SPL to be commercially viable.'

'Do you and Rowan get on with Mick?' I ask.

'Well, obviously we don't always agree with each other,' he says. 'There are differences of opinion but the important thing is that we all come to a decision that we think is right for the club.'

'And what about first-team affairs? Does Mick get involved there?'

'Yes. He's come in as a mentor for Rowan and myself. He has masses of experience and is there to be leaned on. Perhaps he has been leaned on too much this season but it would be foolish of us to ignore him because he's worked at the top level. Personally, he's been a real benefit for me. He's opened my eyes to different ways of coaching.'

We briefly discuss Saturday's match against Livingston. I ask Irons about the team reverting to 4–4–2.

'I wanted to put my mark on the team,' he explains, 'but not change things too much because I'm not the manager.'

'Have the players been affected by Rowan's absence, then?' I ask.

'It's been fine in the dressing room because I've typically been the one who goes around the players before matches to motivate them and interact with them more. All that's different is that I'm picking the side now.'

'So last week's win must have felt good?'

'It was incredible,' says Irons. 'The spirit in the dressing room was as good as I've seen it. I couldn't put it down to one thing. It was a combination of relief, joy from winning, the build-up of what had happened the previous week – all those things. The response from the players was magnificent. They've been sky high ever since, to the extent that they even gave up their day off this week because they want to keep up the intensity. I don't want to tempt fate but the players have a real desire to kick on and go and win this league.'

'Can they keep their nerve, though? Surely the loss to St Johnstone exposed some frailties in the side,' I say.

'Confidence is the thing,' he says. 'It lets your ability shine through. Losing to St Johnstone was disappointing. The dressing room was quiet before that match which meant one of two things. Either the players were quietly confident or they were questioning their ability to win the match. I think some of the players had got it into their heads that if they won there that was the league in the bag, which was wrong. At Dundee the dressing room was quiet too but it was different to McDiarmid Park. There was more of a determination and everyone knew they had a job to do.'

'So, any predictions for Saturday?' I ask.

'It'll be tough,' says Irons, 'but I'll tell you now, we will not lose on Saturday. The players are so determined, so focused and have so much belief in each other.'

17 March 2007
Livingston v Gretna FC
Almondvale, Livingston

I'm feeling bullish today. The title race has entered the comforting world of mathematics. Much more than the 'will they, won't they?' of earlier in the season, it comes down to cold, hard facts. If Gretna win four of their remaining seven fixtures they will be anointed Scottish First Division champions, making it an unprecedented three promotions on the trot.

Twelve points from a possible twenty-one doesn't seem, to use pundit-speak, 'a big ask' for the Borders club. Today's trip to Livingston seems like the perfect place to pick up the first three. Sitting in seventh place, comfortably above the drop zone, Livi have little to play for. With Gretna having beaten John Robertson's side 4–1 in their last encounter, today should be a formality. Saying that, something Davie Irons said to me earlier in the week rings in my ears: 'The teams with nothing to play for can relax and can concentrate on playing good football.'

By the time I reach Livingston South station it is blowing a gale. The nearer Livingston North is closed today so I take my bike to cover the three miles to the ground. My directions are simple: left out of the station, straight on at the first roundabout, straight on at the second roundabout, straight on at the third roundabout, straight on at the fourth roundabout ... you get the picture. You've got to love new towns.

Almondvale is probably the most sensibly sized stadium in the league. Instead of having two large stands on either side of the pitch like so many First Division clubs, Livi have an atmospheric, closed-in arena. It seems far smaller than its 10,000 capacity. Everything about the stadium shrieks sensibility and economy, particularly the punch bags hanging above the desks in the gym-cum-press office.

The first person that I meet at Almondvale is Deacon Blue drummer and BBC Sport presenter Dougie Vipond. It seems the First Division is reaching an exciting enough climax for him to be dispatched to deliver live goal alerts.

I see Keith Melvin next. He reveals that Brooks Mileson is to meet Tourism, Culture and Sport Minister Patricia Ferguson to discuss acquiring an alternative site for Gretna's stadium. Mileson's laissez-faire, man-in-the-street demeanour clearly hides a very sophisticated political operator. The stadium move, which had seemed dead and buried after being opposed at local government level, seems to be very much back on the agenda.

I don't sit with Brooks and Jack today because they arrive late with Mick Wadsworth and reserve-team manager Andy Smith and sit apart from the hundred or so Gretna fans. I take a seat next to Davie Graham's father, midway between two of Gretna's most vocal groups of supporters. They are also about the only two groups of young male adults that you'll find among the Gretna travelling support; the rest is made up of children, families and pensioners.

The shaven-headed Colin McMenamin is recalled to today's starting line-up, with Davie Graham moved back to midfield in place of Gavin Skelton.

The full line-up is:

Malkowski, Barr, Grainger, Jenkins, Canning, Innes, McGuffie, Nicholls, McMenamin, Graham, Grady

Subs: Berkeley, Fleming, Hogg, Paartalu, Skelton

The game is barely five minutes old when Livi's Lee Makel takes advantage of the tail wind to ping a free kick goalwards from fully thirty-five yards. It seems to take Zibi Malkowski by surprise but the Polish keeper dives headlong to turn the effort round the post. Just a minute later, with Gretna struggling to get out of their own half, Livi threaten again through a Neil Teggart header at the back post.

Gretna finally settle and on eight minutes are unlucky to have McMenamin flagged for offside when he latches on to a clever through ball from Allan Jenkins. Moments later Livi's Steven Craig really should have done better when he beats Malkowski to a long ball but somehow fails to see that a simple chip over the stranded keeper into the empty net will give his side the lead.

Jenkins could be accused of similar short-sightedness when he picks the ball up twenty-five yards from the Livi goal and with all the time in the world to fashion a shot decides to play a tight, angled pass which Davie Graham fails to connect with. No one in the away stand seems that impressed and a solo voice singing 'We love you, Gretna!' is forced to struggle on to the end of the verse alone before receiving ironic applause.

With the wind strengthening I can't help eyeing the violently oscillating floodlights and wondering if they'll last the ninety minutes. It's cold, too, but a few poor refereeing decisions in front of the away stand get me up on my feet. Gretna are awarded a free kick for an innocent-looking challenge on Danny Grainger soon afterwards. A voice behind me shouts, 'I can see you in Hollywood, Danny!'

Gretna enjoy their best spell of the half in the run-up to the half-hour mark but McMenamin, Jenkins and Graham all squander decent chances. It's a sucker punch, therefore, when Craig beats Malkowski to a long through ball and atones for his earlier miss by rifling the ball past the sprawling keeper.

The goal sparks off a volley of abuse directed at Mileson and Co. 'Get to fuck, Wadsworth!' shouts one fan. I see Jack

Gass shrink into his seat. Another fan tries to start a chorus of 'Wadsworth out!'

It's clear who the fans blame for the team's recent shortcomings. A few other people around me say, 'Bring back Degsy!' and, 'Come back, Rowan!' A few minutes later and Livi should double their lead in a carbon-copy move of their earlier goal. This time Graham Dorrans shoots wide, however. Lee Makel also goes close with another long-range free kick in the dying minutes of the half. Gretna can think themselves lucky to go in at half-time just a goal down.

It's a relief when it's announced during the interval that Airdrie and St Johnstone are drawing 1–1. 'Looks like we're going to have to rely on Airdrie today!' says a fan nearby. It's a scary thought. Feeling a little like Morgan Spurlock of *Super Size Me* fame, I've pledged to have a break from half-time pies but the biting cold demands one. I have a steak pie and it's rather good. Top marks for pastry.

Gretna emerge unchanged for the second half but look like they've had a good talking-to from Irons. Immediately they win a corner from which Grady heads the ball back across goal only for Canning to head it over the gaping net. Soon afterwards a comic scramble in the Gretna box almost sees Livi double their lead. It incenses the fans, who berate Irons, though one seated nearby jumps out of his seat and points in the direction of Wadsworth. 'That's who you should be shouting at. It's that prat in the corner who's running the team.'

A chant of 'Wadsworth out!' gains more support now and it looks like the director of club development wishes he'd sat in the directors' box, far away from the rowdy Gretna support.

A double substitution on fifty-five minutes seems to change Gretna's fortunes. Though they've looked better this half, they have still struggled in the middle of the park. Paartalu and debutant Steven Hogg come on for McGuffie and Nicholls and immediately look lively. It's the bold type of substitution that I reckon Rowan Alexander would never have attempted. Ex-Manchester United youth Hogg looks a class act.

A solid period of possession culminates in a deserved equaliser for Gretna. When a long throw falls to Grady in the box his snap shot is well saved by Livi keeper Colin Stewart only to fall to Graham ten yards out on the right. Graham shoots instinctively and buries the ball just inside the right-hand post. The game has barely restarted when McMenamin has a fierce shot that is spectacularly saved by Stewart. A goal at that moment would see a Livi collapse, of that I'm sure, but with the scores level they continue to look dangerous on the break. It's Gretna who want, and dare I say need, the three points the most, however. As they fail to capitalise on a decent spell of possession, Irons begins to jump up and down on the sidelines. I can almost see steam coming out of his ears.

It is Livi who nearly snatch victory at the death. As they go on the attack I hear someone behind me in the crowd say, 'Saints have gone two–one up at Airdrie.' No sooner is it said than Livi receive a free kick twenty-five yards out, just left of centre. As dead-ball specialist Makel lines up to take it I have a perfect view from behind him. It goes silent in the away stand. It reminds me of last week's penalty at Dundee. Is this the moment when Gretna's faltering title challenge is going to implode spectacularly? There's a collective intake of breath as Makel takes his run-up. As he strikes the ball everything seems to go in slow motion. The right-footed strike is sweet and flies past the right-hand side of the five-man wall but looks to be heading past. Beyond the crowd of bodies I can see Malkowski scramble across the goalmouth towards the shot which is curling late. The wall dissolves just in time for me to see the ball crash off the post and bounce straight back out. I don't think any one of the 1,748 people there can believe that Makel's strike has stayed out.

The game finishes all square but, with St Johnstone running out 2–1 winners at Airdrie, Gretna's lead at the top is cut to seven points. Irons' prediction that his team would not lose at Livi is proved correct and after the match he says, 'We've taken a draw and four points out of two difficult away games, which is pleasing.'

I doubt many fans would agree. They, like me, want to see Gretna over the finish line and into the SPL as soon as humanly possible. Who is in charge, or pulling the strings behind the scenes, if and when that happens, remains to be seen. There are growing rumours that Alexander's days at the club are behind him.

10

'Come on Gretna, Do Something!'

20 March 2007

It's no surprise when I receive a sneak preview of a press release due out the following day:

> Davie Irons will remain in charge of Gretna until the end of the season as Rowan Alexander continues his recovery from illness. Alexander may return to the club before the end of the season to take on light duties that will assist his recuperation.

24 March 2007

Being back in Scotland is more than just about a book for me. It's been a chance to reconnect with my homeland. Living in London while I pursued a career in journalism, I never felt that I'd lost touch with Scotland. It's just that after a while you stop missing it. It doesn't take long to stop looking for a copy of the *Daily Record* every day, to miss the daily blanket coverage of the Old Firm, to enjoy a TV news bulletin from a studio that doesn't look like it was bought from Latvian State Television in 1974. I even replaced Irn-Bru with ginger beer.

You never miss Tennent's lager, though, so it is therefore ironic that, at eleven o'clock in the morning, I find myself in a bar in Glasgow's Pollokshaws drinking the fizzy, piss-weak beer with a group of mates. Five hours later Scotland have just beaten the mighty Georgia at Hampden with a last-minute scuffed effort to remain top of a European Championship qualifying group including France and Italy.

After the match the majority of the 56,000 fans remain to sing '500 Miles', 'Flower of Scotland' and anything else that comes over the tannoy. It makes the hairs on the back of my neck stand up. It's a sight that you would never see in any other country and I've certainly never seen anything like it. I brim with pride. Having got used to seeing 1,700 every week at Raydale Park I'm completely overcome. My friend Penman nudges me and tells me to get in the party spirit. With a lump in my throat it's all I can do to shout, 'I fucking am!' I'm home.

25 March 2007

The euphoria of yesterday is short-lived when I hear that St Johnstone have beaten Dundee in their Sunday fixture to cut Gretna's lead in the league to a perilous four points. The result makes me feel helpless; Gretna's promotion hopes are dying on their feet.

The friend I'm staying with in Glasgow asks me what the result means for Gretna. They'll still win the league, won't they? I ponder the question for a moment before answering. 'Genuinely? I don't think they will.'

26 March 2007

I'm driven to distraction by Saints' win yesterday. I'm racked with worry that Gretna are poised to throw away all the good work of earlier in the season and there's nothing I can do about it. When Keith Melvin asks me to contribute a piece for the programme for Saturday's game against Partick Thistle I try and convey these emotions. It's time to put our faith in the club and the eleven players on the pitch. I try not to let thoughts of defeat and going into the match with St Johnstone at Raydale Park in twelve days' time with just a one-point lead enter my head.

Yet they do.

29 March 2007

Recent events mean I'm never really sure what to expect from my midweek trips to Raydale Park. New managers ... sorry, caretaker managers, suspended players, mystery trialists, player disposals ... it's like a soap opera, just more dramatic. The last person I've come to expect to be there is Brooks Mileson but it's the affable and elusive owner that I bump into when I arrive.

'Brooks! How are you?'

'I'm rushed off my feet,' replies Mileson.

'Nothing new there then. Don't suppose you've got five minutes for me?'

'Not now, sorry, I'm just stepping into a meeting with the solicitor and then I've got to leave.'

'When would be the best time to catch you?' I ask.

'How about five o'clock in the morning at my house? We're lambing just now,' says Gretna's animal-loving owner.

'OK. I'll bring my marigolds,' I say.

'Your what?'

'My marigolds. You know – rubber gloves.'

'You fucking ponce, we don't use them!' replies Mileson good-humouredly as he heads towards the boardroom.

In the press office I find Craig Mileson and Keith Melvin.

'I just saw your dad,' I say to Mileson. 'He said he's off to meet the solicitor. What's he up to?'

'Trying to figure out how to get rid of the manager!' jokes Melvin. Mileson frowns.

'I thought he'd already done that,' I retort.

'Nah, man,' says Mileson. 'My dad's signing the contract with Motherwell for the ground-share next season.'

'Everyone's keeping optimistic then?' I say. Melvin and Mileson don't respond. They are as nervous as I am about Gretna's title hopes.

Fresh from an interview with ITV, Davie Irons appears at the press office door and asks me to join him in the manager's office. When we get there I notice that Alexander's desk is like the *Mary Celeste*. It looks like the absent manager has just popped out to lunch.

Irons asks if it's OK if his newly anointed number two, Derek Collins, joins us. We all sit down around the large meeting table that's far too big for the narrow Portakabin.

'I thought you'd already be up at Firhill, Davie,' I say, referring to the rumours in the newspapers linking him to the newly vacant Partick Thistle manager's position.

'When it comes to this club, don't believe everything you read,' replies Irons.

'So Rowan's really not coming back this season then?' I say.

'Not on a day-to-day basis, no,' he says. 'He'll undertake some scouting duties but he won't be back in the dressing room.'

'How have the players reacted?'

'They're fine,' say Irons. 'No disrespect to Rowan but as this season has gone on he's stepped back more and allowed Derek and me to get more involved. So it's not been such a shock for the players that he's suddenly not around.'

'But you expect him back?'

'Brooks has stated that he'll be back next season so we'll see what happens. He's part of the club,' says Irons.

'Surely there must be a temptation that if you both do well between now and the end of the season that you might not need Alexander?' I say.

'That's for Brooks to decide. We'll do the job to the best of our abilities.'

'Come on Gretna, Do Something!'

There's an uncomfortable pause as we all ponder what's been said. 'Big game on Saturday?' I say, breaking the silence.

'Yes. It'll be tough because Partick have lost their manager and you never know what response they'll get from their players. It's one we have to win, though.'

What the pair say next surprises and encourages me. It reminds me that while I urge fans not to surrender to pessimism in my piece for this week's programme, I've been guilty of exactly that.

'If we beat Partick and Airdrie in our next two games,' says Irons, 'we can win the league by beating St Johnstone. It's as simple as that. It's a big if, though.'

I'm suddenly looking at next week's showdown with Saints in a different light. I'd been so blinkered in my pessimism that I hadn't even bothered to consider the best-case scenario. I ask the pair if this belief runs right through the squad or if they're learning that some of their squad do not posses the mental toughness to finish the job.

'You're right. The mental side is important,' says Irons.

'Some of the players have been over the course before,' adds Collins, 'but we can't see which ones are going to flourish and which ones buckle until they step over that white line on to the park.'

'Once they take the field there's only so much we can do. If they play badly we feel the frustration as much as the fans,' says Irons. 'There is pressure on every team, though. Pressure to avoid relegation, pressure to catch us. We're the only team where it is in our hands. We're comfortable with that and want to maintain it till that trophy is in our hands. Whether that's next Saturday or the last game of the season we'll have to wait and see.'

'The sooner the better,' says Collins. 'We're assuming that St Johnstone will win all their games now. We've had a streak of luck there so far but we don't expect them to slip up again. The margin for error is slim.'

'We're in a very good position, though,' says Irons. 'That's the way we look at it. We knew it was going to be tough this season. Brooks was saying to me this morning that he never expected us to be in the position we're in. He thought we'd be top four so all credit to the players. They've worked very hard and I hope they get the success they deserve.'

'Is Brooks getting any more involved in the football side of things since he's got back?'

'We speak every day,' says Irons. 'He's very hands-on. If he doesn't like something he'll tell you exactly what he thinks. He's very frank and it's difficult sometimes but ultimately it's his club.'

'So, if something happens on the pitch that he doesn't like, he'll call you on Sunday and tell you?' I ask.

'He doesn't even wait till Sunday!' says Irons before he excuses himself to go and do a radio interview.

I remain chatting with Collins for a while. He's thoughtful and eloquent. Something he says strikes a chord. 'We all work extremely hard here but we'll never be a big club support-wise,' says Collins. 'We get bored reading about it in the papers every week. But does that mean we should not be allowed to dream about reaching the SPL?'

31 March 2007
Gretna FC v Partick Thistle
Raydale Park, Gretna

Position	Team	Played	Goal difference	Points
1	Gretna	30	29	57
2	St Johnstone	31	17	53

I've been fretting about today's game all week, allowing myself to drown in the negativity emanating from the press and Gretna fans alike. Am I being overdramatic about today's game? I hardly think so. The match is the first of a trio that could see Gretna embark on the most exciting chapter in the club's sixty-one-year history. The outcome of today's game and that between St Johnstone and Livingston at McDiarmid Park will decide whether Gretna continue to live the dream or are about to endure a nightmare.

With the changing of the clocks, spring seems to have been ushered in. I alight from a remarkably incident-free journey in Gretna Green to a flawless blue sky and warm, bright sun. It's the first day that I've ever felt overdressed for a match at Raydale Park. My four layers seem excessive as I mingle with short-sleeved children in their black and white replica tops outside Raydale Park.

If it's spring in Gretna it's a winter of discontent at Firhill. It's a makeshift Partick side at best today, due to injury. The only source of optimism is the appearance of former England captain Terry Butcher in the dugout alongside caretaker manager Jimmy Bone. Though the aggregate score in meet-ings between the two teams this season is 12–2 in favour of the Black and Whites there's a lot of nervous tension in the air. It only intensifies when it is announced that the mercurial winger Ryan Baldacchino, who was scheduled for a first start since August, has pulled a muscle in the warm-up and will not make the starting eleven. When you mention Baldi at Raydale, supporters' eyes glaze over and the superlatives flow.

Irons' starting line-up has a familiar feel, save for the inclu-sion of recent signing Nicky Deverdics on the bench.

The full line-up comprises:

Malkowski, Barr, Skelton, Jenkins, Canning, Innes, Paartalu, Nicholls, McMenamin, Graham, Grady

Subs: Berkeley, Deverdics, Fleming, Grainger, McGuffie

Steven Hogg, who impressed in his first-team debut, is injured. He's fallen victim to the curse of the match-day programme.

Hogg is the featured player. He may not be playing but at least we know his favourite drink is 'pint of Carling' and favourite food 'Sunday roast'.

Raydale Park seems to be bursting at the seams today – not that it takes much to do so. The ageing ground could just about house the entire population of the village. How many clubs could say that? The hush of expectation, broken only by the familiar cries of 'Come on, Gretna! Football!' from the man my mate Mike calls the town crier, is broken as the match kicks off by some welcome singing from the five busloads of Thistle fans. The last thing I want to do is go on about the home fans, who have again turned out in impressive numbers, but I don't hear a song from the Black and White Army all day. I put it down to nerves. I'm not exactly singing arias myself.

With a strong wind blowing uncharacteristically from left to right (towards the Solway Firth) in the face of Thistle, they barely enjoy a single foray into the Gretna half in the first seven minutes. All the while I bring reporter Jon Coates, who's returned from the Cricket World Cup in the Caribbean, up to date on what's been going on in the First Division while he's been away. On five minutes a sweeping move from left to right sees Allan Jenkins bearing down on the Partick goal only to be halted by a physical and illegal-looking challenge. 'Penalty!' I shout.

'You've become a proper fan since I've last seen you!' exclaims Coates. I can't deny it.

With appeals for a penalty waved away by referee Mike McCurry, it's not long before Gretna are on the attack again. They look inspired today. They've got the bit between their teeth. They look like they're back to their good old (winning) selves. And not a moment too soon. Before the match Davie Irons said to me he had something up his sleeve that he was sure would motivate the team. Whatever it was it's working. Skelton wins a throw on the far side of the pitch that is promptly launched into the box by Erik Paartalu. It reaches as far as Colin McMenamin at the back post and the striker swivels and hits a looping overhead kick goalwards. The striker looks destined to add to his twenty-five-goal tally for the season but has his effort, which leaves Thistle keeper Jonathan Tuffey beaten, hooked clear by a last-gasp lunge from Barry Smith.

Thistle continue to look out of sorts, despite the scare. A volley from Adam Strachan from a corner on ten minutes that is blocked by a forest of Gretna legs is their only real chance of the half. It looks increasingly like it's a case of 'when' and not 'if' the Black and Whites will break the deadlock. On the bench I notice that the normally animated Irons is more composed today, while Derek Collins marshals the touchline, kicking every ball.

Davie Graham, on his way to another man of the match performance, goes on a direct run into the box before laying off to Paartalu midway through the half. With the Thistle defence split, the ball bounces off the big Aussie to shouts of 'You've got a touch like an elephant!' from the town crier. Next McMenamin volleys over from seven yards after controlling with his hand. Then it's Grady's turn to squander a good chance when his volley on the turn sails wide of the post. Five minutes later Graham and McMenamin combine cleverly in the box and Graham's cute lob glances the top of the bar. Soon after, a Jenkins in-swinging free kick from the left misses everybody and almost sneaks in at the back post.

From the ensuing corner the Thistle keeper gathers and as everyone moves downfield for his kick out McMenamin, sensing it's not Tuffey's day, cheekily stays on the line behind him in the hope he'll dribble it out. Shouts of 'He's behind you' alert Tuffey to the danger. Moments later McMenamin gets a chance that's bread and butter to a player with his scoring record. A Skelton cross is flicked on by the omnipresent Graham to the number 9 who controls, shrugs off the challenge of Robertson and pokes the ball under the spreadeagled keeper from six yards out. There's a collective release of breath from the home support. Maybe there's life in their team after all.

Gretna FC – Living the Dream

The goal sees Gretna strengthen their grip on the game and Grady wastes an easy chance for a well-deserved second by heading over from six yards. It may be Graham and McMenamin who regularly garner the plaudits at Raydale Park but no one can beat Grady for effort and sheer persistence. It's why Brooks Mileson personally ratified the extension of his contract when it seemed more likely that he would leave the club. As Davie Irons said to me earlier in the week, 'James will admit he's not the most technically gifted player but one thing you know when you pick him is that you'll get one hundred and ten per cent effort.'

Despite the lead there's a few tense expressions in the stand when news filters through that St Johnstone have kept up the pressure on Gretna by taking the lead in their game. As long as the Black and Whites keep their heads in front here it's irrelevant.

I walk over to the Corries Stand to grab Brooks Mileson for a chat at half time but, as I'm doing so, I see the club owner coming the other way. He's wearing a suit and tie, though his trademark knee-length leather jacket and cigarette hanging out of the corner of his mouth make him look more like a petty criminal on his way to court than a multimillionaire football club owner.

'Very smart. What's the suit in aid of?' I say.

'Don't ask,' says Mileson, shrugging his shoulders unenthusiastically. 'I've got to go and entertain one of today's sponsors.'

Going back to my seat I thumb through the programme, looking for my own column. I read it and feel guilty for being so pessimistic. Mileson signs off his own column saying, 'Three games in a week – win them all and we've done it. Who would have thought little Gretna would be in this position?'

Gretna start the second half even brighter than the first – a real belief has returned to this side, that has been sadly lacking in recent weeks. It seems a new hand at the Gretna tiller has reinvigorated the team that had won just one out of Alexander's last five matches in charge.

'Come on Gretna, Do Something!'

Following a flurry of wasted Gretna chances, the visitors' best spell in the match is early in the second half. In quick succession Strachan goes on a good run before squaring the ball to Mark McChrystal, who shoots across the face of goal. Soon after, a Thistle break sees Robertson receive the ball in acres of space before shooting over the bar (and the Corries Stand) from eighteen yards.

Thistle's resurgence causes the crowd to get noticeably more vocal as the halfway point of the second half nears. As if in response, Davie Nicholls steals the ball in midfield and plays through Graham, who shoots high and wide of goal. On sixty-nine minutes Nicholls again breaks down a Partick attack and launches a counter. He passes it short to Jenkins before receiving it back and spreading it wide to Graham. It's the best move of the match even before the forward crosses with pinpoint accuracy on to the forehead of Grady, who makes no mistake from eight yards: 2–0. We can all breathe easy.

On seventy-two minutes, just as Jenkins prepares to take a Gretna corner, my mobile phone rings: private number calling. I'm going to ignore it but as I haven't heard from Lauren since she left for a camping and surfing expedition to 'a really isolated area with amazing, if shark-infested, beaches', I answer. The line is terrible so I do the unforgivable: leave my seat, and the match, to take the call.

'It's noisy there. Where are you?' says Lauren.

'I'm at Gretna's most important game in their history! You're not shark bait, then?' I say.

'No! Hey, do you know what the Arsenal score was?' she asks.

'They got beaten four–one by Liverpool. Look, I've got to go back, the crowd are going crazy about something. Are you going to make it back for the last game of the season at Ross County?'

'I hope so. I haven't booked a return flight yet,' says Lauren non-committally.

I get the feeling she's not going to leave sunny Oz until she's kicked out. I still adore her, though.

'Keep me posted. Look, I've got to go now. I miss you.'

I dash back to my seat, ashamed to have missed eight minutes of action. At the moment I see the slightest thing as a bad omen. 'What have I missed?' I ask Coates.

'Nothing really. Oh, someone said that St Johnstone have conceded an equaliser and had their keeper sent off.'

'Nothing! That's excellent news!' Coates raises an eyebrow at my complete lack of impartiality. Then word comes through that Saints have gone behind. A cheer rings around Raydale Park. On the pitch, Gretna break from defence and are soon three on two with Jenkins on the ball and Graham and McMenamin in space on either side. It's one of those moments when you can't help but rise from your seat. When the whole season seems somehow captured in that one fraction of time. As if what happens next will determine the destination of the title. It's like the penalty save at Dundee and the free kick off the post at Livi. Even as they occurred you knew they were significant.

Jenkins, who has worked tirelessly in midfield, shows a complete lack of respect for the occasion, however. He chooses to go it alone and shoots agonisingly wide. I'm not sure what it means in the grand scale of things.

At the final whistle Davie Irons runs on to congratulate his players. With the Saints game playing injury time, celebrations in the stand are more muted. As the stadium empties Brooks Mileson materialises out of the crowd, making a beeline for the supporters' club bar. I follow and join him and around sixty fans with eyes glued to the full-time scores filtering through on Sky Sports. There's an agonising delay before the immortal words '4.52 ft st johnstone 1–2 livingston' come up on the screen. A huge roar spreads around the bar and Mileson is mobbed. He looks a little uncomfortable with the attention. I drag him aside.

'It's within touching distance,' I say.

'Come on Gretna, Do Something!'

Mileson the numbers man, the sharp-minded businessman, rolls his eyes to the top of his head as he does some sums. 'If we win on Wednesday then we can win it back here if we draw against Saints – is that right? – wait . . .' he says.

Mileson frantically tries to figure out the permutations as the celebrations continue all around us. He's not just contemplating what could happen in the next two matches, however. He must have thoughts of headier times ahead, of many more hundreds of thousands, if not millions, required to be invested if the SPL becomes a reality. He looks as if his head is spinning. He's brought back to the present when a chorus of 'Ro, Ro, Super Ro!' breaks out in homage to the absent Rowan Alexander. I turn back to Mileson to ask if there's a good time to catch up with him during the week and, as I do, I just catch a glimpse of him disappearing out of the bar.

Spirits are as high in the dressing room as they are in the club bar. As I walk past it Irons is holding court. I grab him for a chat. 'Whatever you did to get the boys going seemed to work,' I say. 'What's your secret?'

'Al Pacino,' says Irons.

'Sorry?'

'Pacino. I played the boys a speech he makes in the film *Any Given Sunday*. The boys were glued to the television screen. It's all about going that extra couple of inches for your team and those inches together making a big difference. You could see it in their eyes and on their faces when they went out on the pitch – they were really up for it.'

Irons really is putting his own stamp on the team. I can't help feeling that the longer Alexander is away from the dressing room, the harder it will be for him to come back. But Irons is proving to be an able, if not spectacular, stand-in. Like every fan making their way home from Raydale Park tonight I have a renewed belief in Gretna's promotion credentials. Despite ourselves, we're probably all thinking the same thing: the champagne is on ice, but for how long?

197

1 April 2007

What a difference a day makes. I wake to Sunday newspapers full of talk of Gretna's inevitable promotion to the SPL. It's astonishing, really. Many of the reports talk about a return to form after a slump – is seven points from three games (including two away from home) really a slump?

Another story that grabs my attention before I remember it's 1 April concerns Kenny 'Dr Goals' Deuchar. It's reported that Gretna's on-loan striker has landed a role in BBC hospital drama *Holby City*. A local paper picks up the story and runs a full-page feature on it, then files a complaint when they realise they've been hoodwinked.

Later that day I attend the Edinburgh derby where I meet *Scotsport* presenter Andy Walker. Between mouthfuls of excellent steak pies and stewed tea we fall into conversation about the First Division. Walker knows the SPL inside out but he freely admits he knows little about Gretna. I suggest that, as the most likely addition to the SPL in August, the occasional mention on *Scotsport* wouldn't be out of the question. Walker agrees.

'Why not invite someone from Gretna on the show?' I propose.

'Who would we ask?' says Walker. 'Alexander? Is he back? What's the story?'

'He's still off – stress-related,' I say.

'Every job in football is stressful,' says Walker. 'I just don't buy it.'

'There is talk of a dressing-room bust-up too.'

'The same thing goes. I've see hundreds of fights in dressing rooms over the years. It's nothing out of the ordinary.'

'I think it's a combination of both,' I say.

'Maybe. Looking from the outside I can't say what's gone on but people I know in the game seem to say that this guy Wordsworth is behind it all.'

'Wadsworth?' I say, correcting the ex-Celtic striker.

'Yeah, him.'

'It's a popular view but stress is the official line. What about getting Brooks Mileson on the show instead?' I say. 'He'd be good value.'

'It's a non-smoking studio!' says Walker, laughing.

Maybe he knows more than he's letting on.

3 April 2007

I don't get a jot of work done today. There are two reasons for this. One, I stayed up to some ungodly hour last night watching *Scotsport* in its graveyard slot in the hope Walker would mention Gretna. When I gave up, there'd still been no mention of the Black and Whites. Second, tree surgeons are swarming over my back garden like ants and their death-defying feats – namely climbing trees and felling them from the top down – is compelling viewing. It's like a mortal version of the children's game Ker-Plunk. I keep my camcorder on standby in case of any mishaps and check that *You've Been Framed*'s £250 offer for clips still stands.

4 April 2007
Airdrie United v Gretna FC
Excelsior Stadium, Airdrie

Position	Team	Played	Goal difference	Points
1	Gretna	31	31	60
2	St Johnstone	32	16	53

It's the best day of the year so far – a sweltering 20°C when I meet my brother in Glasgow before heading out to Airdrie for the evening match. A couple of swift pints later and we're on the train. I explain to Stuart that Drumgelloch, where we disembark, can be edgy and to keep his wits about him. He looks more than a little scared. 'What's the deal?' he says. 'Am I here to watch the match or be your bodyguard?'

Bathed in sunlight, Drumgelloch looks slightly less grim than when I was last here but it's no less threatening. We look like fish out of water here and a gang of teenagers wearing Rangers scarves soon take an unwelcome interest in us. I think we're only saved from a confrontation when a rival gang, adorned with green and white scarves, appear on the scene in the nick of time to preoccupy the group.

We make a sharp exit and head directly to the supporters' club bar in the Jack Dalziel stand. It's like a gentrified working men's club and only has two types of beer on tap: Tartan Special and Miller. 'I didn't even know Special was still being brewed,' I say to my brother.

'Only for Airdrie,' says the testy barmaid. 'What you for, brown or yellow?'

'Brown or yellow what?' I ask.

'Beer!'

Some bottled Stella saves the day and puts us in the mood for the match. I dearly hope Davie Irons' boys are in the mood tonight too because three points will leave them needing just a point in Saturday's showdown with St Johnstone to win a fairy-tale promotion. All the Gretna fans look at ease and in good spirits when we join them in the main stand. There's no sign of Brooks Mileson so we take a seat behind the town crier who, along with at least 120 others, has made the long journey here for tonight's game.

The weather and Gretna's lofty league position lend the evening a carnival-like atmosphere but I'm starting to feel a bit uneasy about all this talk of the 'champions elect'. Gretna need four points from five games. Not impossible but it's not inconceivable either that they could fall short of the mark. I won't rest easy until it is mathematically impossible for the club to be caught.

'Come on Gretna, Do Something!'

Despite the jovial atmosphere, Airdrie's mascot is nowhere to be seen. I learn later that the mascot bears a striking resemblance to Gretna's and is even called Rocky the Rooster. The previous mascot, Diamond Jack, was retired when, according to the club website, 'the original costume had become cheap and nasty looking'.

Having missed dinner we buy a couple of £1 pies while we wait for kick-off. They are the worst pies in the league by a long way, filled with the most suspect of grey mystery meat. It reminds me of a half-time chant recently heard at Clyde: 'You don't know what you're eating!' Genius.

As we force the pies down, grimacing, Celtic and Scotland midfielder Paul Hartley arrives with two burly minders and sits nearby. I really can't make the connection to him being here, in the Gretna end. It's tempting to start a 'Hartley for Gretna' rumour. Stranger things have happened!

On the back of Saturday's victory Irons has picked an un-changed side of:

Malkowski, Barr, Skelton, Jenkins, Canning, Innes, Paartalu,
Nicholls, McMenamin, Graham, Grady

Subs: Berkeley, Deverdics, Fleming, Grainger, Hogg

Having only taken a point off Airdrie in three league encounters this season I'm not taking anything for granted tonight. With Airdrie rooted to the bottom of the league they are playing for their survival. Thirty-six-year-old James Grady summed it up earlier in the week when he said, 'They have something to fight for and so have we. But they will have a little bit more pressure on them because they might lose their jobs if they go down.'

He's right. It's life or death for Airdrie and they'll be no pushovers, especially with over a thousand vocal fans behind them. My brother doesn't take much persuasion to cheer for the Black and Whites – he's a Ross County fan and knows that a defeat for Airdrie increases the faltering Highland club's hopes of survival.

It comes as no surprise that the opening exchanges are cagey. Both teams seem nervous and no one really enjoys any significant possession. A series of long balls in either direction makes the match resemble a game of tennis rather than the beautiful game. About five minutes in I see Brooks Mileson and Jack Gass arrive. Moments later I'm surprised to see Rowan Alexander appear in the stands to a ripple of applause. Alexander and Mileson sit apart and don't seem to acknowledge each other, however.

It's ten minutes in before Airdrie have the first meaningful chance with a free kick outside the Gretna box. The opportunity is wasted and Gretna go on the counter-attack with the lively-looking Davie Graham chasing down the field after a long ball, only to be beaten to it by Robertson in the Airdrie goal. His clearance only goes as far as Grady who is immediately fouled some forty yards from goal. The resulting Jenkins free kick reaches Chris Innes in the box but his header back across goal is gathered by the keeper.

It's scrappy stuff and it's being played at 100 miles per hour. Another wasted Airdrie free kick sees Gavin Skelton break down the left wing before crossing the ball just behind McMenamin who's on the six-yard line. Keeping apace, Airdrie go straight on the counter and a Gary Twigg solo run is only ended by a lunging Martin Canning tackle on the edge of the box. There are appeals for a penalty but they're waved aside by the ref. It's a surprise because he seems whistle happy – before the game is out he'll have booked eight players and sent one off in a match that's as good-tempered and sporting as I've seen all season. It causes Davie Irons to remonstrate with the linesman, 'You've got to have a word. He's blowing for every tackle.'

The scrappy, stop–start nature of the half is getting to both sets of fans. In the row in front the town crier repeats his trademarks shouts, 'Come on, Gretna! Football!' or my own personal favourite, 'Come on, Gretna! Do something!'

The Black and Whites' best chances of the half come on forty-five minutes when a cross-field ball from Paartalu reaches Graham, who squares it to McMenamin. The league's top scorer makes a marauding run into the box and a powerful shot aimed at the top corner is only kept out by a spectacular save from Robertson.

During the interval I bump into Alexander. He looks refreshed but his handshake is as crushing as ever. We don't get much chance to speak because he's soon surrounded by well-wishers. I later bump into Mileson. I tell him I've just seen Alexander. 'Really?' replies Mileson, looking mystified.

When I take my seat again I see Craig Mileson making his way from the directors' box to join his dad in the stand. He stops for a quick chat.

'It's fucking morbid over there,' says Mileson.

The disappointing first half is causing a few fans in both ends of the one open stand to look anxious. A point apiece wouldn't be terrible for either team but three points would make a world of difference to both. There hasn't been a more important three points up for grabs all season for either team. Sensing this, both managers make a change at half-time. Gretna bring on Hogg for Jenkins. Airdrie replace McDougall with the pacy McGuire.

The game picks up from where it left off, however. Neither team even comes close to breaking the deadlock. On forty-nine minutes Airdrie's best move of the match sees a lengthy build-up prise open Gretna's defence, leaving Kevin MacDonald with a free shot from sixteen yards. The midfielder shoots just wide, however. Moments later a decent Gretna move sees Grady upended on the left edge of the eighteen-yard box. A Hogg free kick finds Grady but his header is pushed round the post. A throw-in soon afterwards finds Skelton on a rare foray forward. The left back's shot whistles just wide of the target. I glance over my shoulder to Alexander. He looks composed on the exterior but inside I think there's a raft of emotions battling to get out.

'This has got nil–nil written all over it,' I say to my brother.

'No shit?' says Stuart. It's not the most insightful prediction I've ever made.

On the hour mark Gretna go close again when Innes meets an inch-perfect Hogg corner and heads goalwards. The vertically challenged Robertson jumps to clearly tip the ball over. With the linesman signalling for a corner the referee awards a goal kick. A fan sitting next to me says, 'I've seen a referee spoil a good game before but here he's spoiling a bad one!'

Despite Gretna having more chances, it is Airdrie who look like they want the three points more as we enter the final third. McGuire is causing no end of problems, his penetrating cross-field runs pulling the Gretna defence out of shape. With Davie Nicholls tiring, Irons brings on another young midfielder in the shape of Nicky Deverdics. His entrance prompts Airdrie manager Kenny Black to switch McGuire to the left where Paartalu is also tiring.

With ten minutes remaining Airdrie twice threaten, only to see decent through balls cut out by Barr and Canning. The physical Barr, who is Gretna's man of the match, finally succumbs to the pressure and is cautioned by the referee for a clash with Brian McPhee in the corner. Moments later, after Barr becomes involved in an exchange with an irate Airdrie fan, Barr and Paul Lovering come together for a crunching 50–50 challenge. Common sense would dictate a booking apiece at worst but Lovering's ensuing histrionics see the referee issue Barr with a straight red. With the crowd incensed, the extendable tunnel has to be pulled out to shield Barr from the torrent of abuse and various objects raining down from the stands.

I begin to worry about my own safety. Some Airdrie fans sitting just three yards away, separated only by a plastic cordon, have started issuing threats that I'm sure are far from empty. I feel it's only a matter of time before we're invaded by the menacing group. A few harsh words are exchanged with another fan near us. He's clearly from Carlisle. It prompts one Airdrie fan to say, 'What type of accent is that? At least we won't make fools of ourselves in the SPL next year.'

When the furore dies down, Airdrie realise they still have the best part of ten minutes to make the most of the one-man advantage. Gretna have everyone behind the ball and resist all that Airdrie can throw at them in the dying minutes. The final whistle comes as a relief to the Black and White Army. A point apiece seems like a fair outcome under the circumstances.

After the match Irons tries to explain why his team, who are twenty-nine points above Airdrie in the league, could not secure the win: 'I could sense a wee bit of apprehension amongst the players as we approached the game. They are the first to admit that they didn't perform. Hopefully we will have a reaction from them on Saturday. We said before the game that we couldn't win the title tonight anyway. We knew we needed four points in the next two games and we've still got the chance to achieve that. We want to go and win the league against St Johnstone on Saturday.'

Saturday's showdown with Saints should be an incredible occasion. Win and Gretna are promoted. Lose and the squeakiest of squeaky-bum times will follow.

With the last train from Drumgelloch beckoning we make the nervy one-mile walk back to the station. When we get there a handful of people are waiting for the train. Sensibly, none are wearing black and white scarves. There's a Swiss couple who have flown over specifically for the game and look a little on edge. We bump into a Gretna fan we saw in the bar before the game too.

'Terrible match,' I say.

'Awful. Still, there's plenty of time to get back to Glasgow and get a hooker,' he replies, deadpan. 'Where are you off to?'

'Home,' says my brother, laughing nervously. 'Look, there's a bench along at the end of the platform.'

11

It Ain't Barcelona

5 April 2007

I confess that we didn't go straight home last night. A drink for the road in Glasgow's Merchant City before the last train back to Edinburgh became three. Two hours later and we're buying a carry-out from a bar and heading back to my brother's flat. Not the smartest thing to do as I'm due down at Raydale Park in the morning to interview a couple of the players ahead of Saturday's self-styled championship decider.

Predictably, I sleep in and am in no condition to be doing interviews. I salvage the situation by carrying out a telephone interview with Chris Innes. The Gretna captain, who took the biggest gamble of his career when he joined Third Division Gretna from SPL Dundee United two years ago, can't help but emphasise what a massive encounter it will be on Saturday.

'I don't think they come any bigger than this,' he says. 'It's going to be a fantastic game to be involved in. If we win on Saturday – *if* we do, as I don't want to tempt fate – I can't tell you how much it means. I'll probably just break down on the park.

'I really believed Gretna could get to the SPL when I came down. I believed in Brooks's ambition and Rowan and Davie's foresight to get the club this far. I don't think a lot of folk thought we could progress as quickly.'

6 April 2007

Nothing to do with Gretna but I'm listening to *Talksport* as I'm prone to do of a morning when Mike Parry and Micky Quinn start discussing Fulham manager Chris Coleman's wife using spy technology to track his movements. 'I don't know what all the fuss is about,' says Quinn. 'My wife has been bugging me for years.'

7 April 2007
Gretna FC v St Johnstone
Raydale Park, Gretna

Position	Team	Played	Goal difference	Points
1	Gretna	32	31	61
2	St Johnstone	32	16	53

It's a beautiful, sunny day in Edinburgh. Having wallowed in pessimism all week, the sunlight brightens my mood. I'm groggy, having struggled to sleep because of nerves, but despite having a massive sense of foreboding last night I feel more positive in the broad light of day, especially when I realise that my journey has come full circle. It has been eighteen weeks – 126 days – since my first match at Raydale Park. Then, on a bitterly cold December afternoon, Gretna eased past St Johnstone by two goals to nil on their march to the top of the league. I cling to the memory, praying for a repeat scoreline that will see the biggest party in memory hit the small village.

In a rush to get ready, my bedroom looks like a whirlwind has hit it. It's all open drawers, wet towels on the floor and coat hangers on the bed. Lauren could almost be back, instead of continually extending her Antipodean adventure. Rushing around, tidying up the mess before I leave, my eyes are drawn

208

to my sock drawer. There amongst a sea of black and blue I spot a flash of red – my lucky socks. The socks began as a bit of a joke. Last season Lauren claimed that Arsenal were going to win the Champions' League and it was all down to her lucky Arsenal socks. My red socks became lucky by proxy on the night of the Champions' League semi-final. Having got a pair of tickets, making me the best boyfriend in the world for ninety minutes, Lauren arrived late, out of breath and lucky-sockless. 'It's OK,' I said, improvising, 'I've got *my* lucky socks on.' Arsenal went on to beat Villareal that night and the lucky socks were born. I grab them and stuff them in my bag. I think Gretna will need all the help they can get today.

I pass an again strangely incident-free train journey reading the day's papers. There is unprecedented coverage of the First Division, with at least three of the nationals running full-page previews. I lose count of the number of times the term 'champions elect' appears. Sports editors across the land have finally woken up to the fact that Gretna are on the threshold of a historic achievement.

I begin to get a feeling for what a big occasion it is going to be at Raydale Park when I see some football fans on the train from Carlisle to Gretna for the first time. There is a mix of home and away fans, both looking as excited as they are nervous. Trailing the Black and Whites by eight points, it is make or break for St Johnstone today. A win for Gretna sees them in dreamland. A loss makes things very interesting for the final three games of the campaign.

When I arrive at Raydale I'm appalled by what I see. It's like a village fete. There are balloons and flags everywhere, kids with painted faces (with slogans such as 'SPL here we come') and an all-round party atmosphere. You've heard of 'after the Lord Mayor's Show'; well, today is a case of *before* the Lord Mayor's Show. All this joviality and expectation feels premature. OK, the fans deserve their day in the sun but this is far from over. The task that Gretna have ahead of them

209

today is no walk in the park. I can't help feeling that the club are setting themselves up for an almighty fall.

I bump into a tired-looking Craig Mileson and he seems as disgusted and anxious as I feel. 'I didn't sleep well last night,' he says. 'I woke up at 6 a. m. and couldn't get back to sleep. Then I had to go and buy some champagne this morning. I didn't want to do it, man. I didn't want to tempt fate.'

Just then Rocky Radio announces, 'Welcome to Raydale Park where Gretna can make it a historic three promotions in a row!'

Mileson shakes his head. 'I don't like all this one little bit.'

Hanging around the players' tunnel I bump into Gretna captain Chris Innes. He looks worried, admitting, 'There may be a little bit more pressure today. Saints will give it everything.'

Davie Irons looks vexed. He says, 'It's great to be in a position where we can actually win the title at home. But we couldn't have picked a harder game. They will come here and give it everything. It is their last shot at catching us.'

The Gretna players look focused but nervous as they warm up. Sitting on the advertising hoardings watching them I'm joined by the suspended Craig Barr.

'You must be gutted to be missing the match,' I say.

'It's torture. I wish I could be out there.'

'Imagine how Rowan feels,' I say. 'Did he come in the dressing room at Airdrie?'

'No. We saw him on the bus, though,' says Barr. 'Someone said he's watching Hamilton today ahead of next week's game.'

'Do you think he'll be back next season?' I ask.

'We haven't been told what's going to happen. It's been OK, though, because Davie's very popular in the dressing room. Some people find Rowan quite hard to speak to.'

While Barr joins his teammates in the dressing room I spot BBC Scotland's Chick Young marching around with microphone in hand. It's pandemonium at Raydale and there must be at least thirty photographers here, compared with the usual five, and about forty reporters and radio commentators, including all the big hitters. Most are congregated at the mouth of the retractable canvas tunnel waiting to interview anyone they can. I don't think any of us expect to see Sir Bobby Robson appear, accompanied by Mick Wadsworth. I can see it now: 'Robson for Gretna' splashed across the back pages of tomorrow's newspapers. Rocky the Raydale Rooster comes over and shakes Robson's hand. I hear the former England manager say, 'What are the birds like around here?'

Barr rejoins me while his teammates make final preparations before taking the pitch. 'Did you see Robson?' I say.

'Yeah. He just came into the dressing room. We all started clapping. He took one look around and said, "It ain't Barcelona, is it, boys!" He said to the guys who were playing, "If you go out there today and each of you win your personal battles then you'll win the game." Then he went over to Colin [McMenamin] and Ryan [McGuffie], who he knew from their time at Newcastle. I think they were surprised he remembered them.'

We're joined by a nervous-looking Brooks Mileson. He is carrying two packs of Marlboro Lights and sparks up a cigarette before taking a seat next to Robson on one of two office chairs that have been hastily placed like thrones on the grass behind one of the goals. I head to the main stand to take my own seat but when I reach it someone is sitting there. Raydale is so packed that there is not an empty seat in sight so I settle down on the stairwell to watch the match.

The teams emerge out of the tunnel to the Proclaimers' '500 Miles'. They are greeted by a cacophony of clicking camera shutters. This is it. First versus second. A potential title-decider – one of the biggest games that many of Davie Irons's squad will have ever played in. Even the most imaginative of Hollywood screenwriters couldn't have scripted a better finale to the season. (Or so I thought at the time.)

The tension is palpable. You could cut it with a knife and as the teams take their positions a huge cheer spreads around the ground. Saints have brought at least 300 fans – the away terrace is packed. The rest of Raydale Park is bursting at the seams – not for the first time this season – with fans desperate to see that First Division champions' flag hoisted above the ramshackle ground. I thought I'd seen it full before but this is a whole new ball game. For all the foreboding the scene is perfectly set for Gretna. In ninety minutes they could be in the SPL.

In the absence of Barr, Irons has drafted in McGuffie at right back. It doesn't fill me with confidence, especially as he'll be up against the best player in the league in Jason Scotland. He's not everyone's cup of tea but he is effective. In midfield Hogg comes in for Jenkins.

The full line-up is:

Malkowski, McGuffie, Skelton, Paartalu, Canning, Innes, Hogg, Nicholls, McMenamin, Graham, Grady
Subs: Berkeley, Deverdics, Fleming, Grainger, Jenkins

On paper the Saints' line-up looks a little stronger and significantly more experienced.

The match starts brightly and, in the first five minutes, there is no evidence of the nerves that will creep into Irons' side as the half progresses. Indeed, Gretna look the better team. On six minutes a Gretna breakaway is halted when the flying Davie Graham is cynically fouled on the halfway line by Martin Hardie. It's Hardie who squanders Saints' best chance in the opening spell when he receives the ball in the box after a penetrating Jason Scotland run but shoots into the side netting. The incident causes Irons to shout to Chris Innes, 'Tell Canso [Canning] he can't drop off Scotland.'

Almost immediately Gretna are on the counter through Graham. After cutting in from the byline at pace, the young

212

winger shoots from twenty yards. Raydale Park erupts, thinking the shot is dipping in, but the powerful drive rattles the crossbar. I've lost count of the number of times he's hit the woodwork at the Corries Stand end this season. Irons shouts from the bench, 'Keep it up, Davie. They're [Saints] shitting themselves.'

From that moment on Gretna begin to look more and more impotent, however. They can't build on their strong start and seeds of doubt begin to be sown. Saints seem certain to get on the scoresheet first. On twelve minutes Zibi Malkowski collides with Peter MacDonald when coming to gather a dangerous cross. Both players fall to the ground. While the crowd falls silent, it seems to take an eternity for Innes to clear the loose ball.

With McGuffie toiling against Scotland and MacDonald at right back, and Skelton having a torrid time of it on the left with Filipe Morais, Robson's words about winning personal battles must be ringing in their ears. Having one makeshift fullback, in the form of Skelton, is one thing. Playing with two in a match of this significance is virtual suicide, and so it proves when Scotland scores an inevitable opener for Saints. The goal is a travesty. An innocuous cross-field ball going away from goal should be easily dealt with by McGuffie and Canning. Scotland is third favourite to get there but McGuffie somehow attempts a back header when he could easily have kicked the ball out of play. The weak header evades Canning and drops right at Scotland's feet. He takes just one touch before shooting powerfully at goal from eighteen yards. His opportunistic effort seems destined for Malkowski's arms until a wicked deflection off Canning's outstretched leg takes it past the keeper.

Gretna look rattled by the goal and it sends the Saints fans wild. Saints manager Owen Coyle shouts, 'Let's get another, Jason.'

I don't doubt it's possible and with Gretna looking ever more toothless, despite a rare sniff at goal when McGuffie slices past the post from ten yards, I get the feeling that Saints have only just got going. A speculative through ball that sees Canning and Scotland in hot pursuit hammers home the point. There's only going to be one winner in that race and, having outsprinted Canning, Scotland coolly slips the ball under the spreadeagled Malkowski for his second of the match: 0–2. The half-time whistle is a relief, with Saints threatening a rout.

It's almost impossible to move in the stand during the interval. I work my way down to pitch-side in the hope of a quick word with Robson but he's nowhere to be seen. I do get the chance to enjoy the Annan Angels' unique brand of dance-based chaos close up, however. When they leave the pitch they ask their attractive troupe-leader, 'How was that, Miss?'

'Don't call me Miss!' she hisses in reply, glancing round to see if any of the Gretna and Saints squad players sitting behind her have overheard.

Bobby Robson's team talks may have been good enough for Barcelona, England, Porto, PSV and Newcastle but with it having little effect at Gretna, Irons needs to put a rocket up his team if they're to turn this match around. The atmosphere inside Raydale Park is deflated. It's exactly what I'd feared. In desperation Irons brings on three subs just after the interval à la Sir Bobby, however. Jenkins comes on for McGuffie, Grainger for Skelton and Deverdics for Paartalu. It's rash – Gretna's last throw of the dice with half the match still to play.

From the kick-off Grady grabs the game by the scruff of the neck. You get the feeling that if the title race goes down to the wire it will be the no-frills players like him who'll stand up and be counted. Grady goes on a mazy run that sees him reach the six-yard box before being dispossessed. Moments later a Hogg corner finds McMenamin unmarked in the box only to head over from six yards.

It Ain't Barcelona

Had it gone in, the header could have changed the course of the match. As it is Gretna barely have another shot on goal in the entire half. Irons' three substitutions never really have the desired impact. On fifty-five minutes it should be 3–0 to the visitors when Morais receives a clever pass from Scotland but shoots wide with an open goal at his mercy. Four minutes later and Morais is sent off after a second yellow card for kicking the ball away. With half an hour to play Gretna should really take advantage but having made all his substitutions Irons's hands are tied. His eleven men are left to toil against St Johnstone's more determined ten.

It's a miracle that the Perth side don't extend their lead in the final twenty minutes. Scotland looks like he will score every time he takes possession in the Gretna half. It's a relief when he's subbed off on eighty-one minutes and he receives a deserved ovation from away and home fans alike. It's very much a case of Scotland 2 – Gretna 0 ... It's an insult to Scotland when it's announced that the sponsor's man of the match is ... Davie Graham, of course!

By eighty-nine minutes the visiting fans are chanting 'Easy! Easy!' and 'Cheerio, cheerio!' to the departing Gretna fans. A chorus of 'One Bobby Robson!' is even audible. At the final whistle boos ring around Raydale Park and a few fans start a chorus of 'Ro, Ro, Super Ro!' in homage to their absent manager. 'Keep the Faith' blasts out over Rocky Radio.

It takes Irons forty minutes to emerge from the dressing room after the match. When he does he says, 'The way we performed today, we had to get it out in the open and try and put it right for Saturday. We just didn't perform on the day. After the sending-off they dug in and had experienced, quality players to see the game out. Whether it was nerves or a combination of nerves and poor performances from individuals, it has cost us the game.'

It's the second time I've heard Irons hint that ridding the club of experienced campaigners so early in the season might have been premature. It's a worry that's long been voiced on the terraces.

There are no excuses to hide behind for today's lacklustre performance. Brooks Mileson even admits his team were second best. 'We played very, very poorly,' he says when I bump into him. 'St Johnstone were the better team by miles.'

I trudge away from the ground, head bowed, disconsolate. Gretna blew it today; there's no way to sugar-coat it. Although tomorrow's sports pages will see reporters replace 'champions elect' with 'The champagne is still on ice', I still have some nagging doubts as to whether or not this roller-coaster ride is going to end with Gretna in the SPL. A five-point lead with three to play would look safe if Gretna were playing well but they are not. Worse, they are utterly erratic and unpredictable. Suddenly that gap doesn't look so comfortable. I hope the champagne is on plenty of ice because I think this is going to the wire.

Walking back to the station with a cloud over me I reach into my bag, pull out my 'lucky' socks and throw them with all my might into a nearby field. I receive a rare text from Lauren asking if Gretna won. I reply: gretna beaten 2–0. i am convinced this is going to end badly.

Having started to hear from Lauren less and less, I hope the same cannot be said of our relationship. Like Gretna's promotion push, sometimes you just get a feeling about something. It's going to take a lot to persuade me otherwise on both fronts.

8 April 2007

In a search for some enlightenment and guidance as to what the next three weeks holds for Gretna and St Johnstone I turn to the unlikely oracle that is William Hill. The bookie has

Gretna at 25–1 *on* for the title even after yesterday's defeat. Saints are, in my view, a very reasonable 9–1.

9 April 2007

I end up partying quite hard over the Easter weekend to blot out the disappointment of Gretna's loss. In the more contemplative moments, I wonder whether my involvement is starting to be a jinx for the club. I seem to have a history of being a nearly man, whether it be education (yes, I went to a good university but I got the worst possible pass in my degree), sport (yes, I played football but never at the highest level) or my career (yes, I wrote a book about Wigan Athletic but its release was postponed while the team toiled at the bottom of the Premiership).

I'm always coming second best in things. I am the second son of three. I was even born on March ... yes ... the 2nd. I live in flat 2, at number 2 on an Edinburgh street. This is even the second book about Gretna, for goodness' sake. I hope this does not rub off on the club. Second best in the First Division doesn't amount to a hill of beans.

13 April 2007

Friday the 13th. I've been fixating on the league table and the remaining fixtures for days now and the final game of the season versus rock-bottom Ross County is starting to look ominous. Is it possible that I'll travel to Victoria Park on 28 April for a match that could determine whether Gretna are crowned champions and whether Ross County are to be relegated for the first time in their history? They way things are going, I wouldn't bet against it.

14 April 2007
Hamilton Academicals v Gretna FC
New Douglas Park, Hamilton

Position	Team	Played	Goal difference	Points
1	Gretna	33	29	61
2	St Johnstone	33	18	56

Forgetting football for a moment . . . after a series of fraught calls late last night I think Lauren and I are indeed on the buffers. It hurts like hell. Thus I'm extremely hungover, tired and strung-out as I take the train to Hamilton for the first of Gretna's final trio of fixtures in the 2006/7 campaign. The state I'm in I shouldn't be let loose in any public place, let alone amongst professional footballers, managers and club owners.

I'm super-nervous about today's encounter. The Black and Whites' recent form gives me no indication of which Gretna team are going to turn up: the team that capitulated to St Johnstone, the team that played out a dire 0–0 draw at Airdrie, or the team that annihilated Hamilton 6–0 on the first day of the season?

Hamilton at New Douglas Park is a completely different proposition, however. Due, according to many, to its artificial pitch, they've only lost here once all season. Sitting third in the table, they are desperate to catch Saints and make second place theirs. Gretna lost 3–1 here in late October too so it'll be no easy task for the visitors today. I daren't say it but I think a point would be a good outcome, leaving Gretna needing just one win (or for Saints to lose just once) from their final fixtures to guarantee promotion.

If the weather was balmy at Raydale last week it's positively tropical in Hamilton. As I walk from station to stadium I bake in the sun and alcohol-tainted sweat oozes from every pore. Nice. Outside I bump in the perma-frowned Mick Wadsworth. I've noticed that he seems never to stop to talk. Maybe it's just

218

me? If you meet him and want to have a conversation you must trot along beside him obediently.

'Nice day for it,' I say, trying to keep apace.

'We should be playing cricket,' replies Wadsworth as he walks straight past me.

New Douglas Park is empty when I enter, save for the few groundsmen pottering about and the odd tracksuited player. Wanting to get a closer look at Hamilton's controversial playing surface, I walk down from the stands and out on to the pitch. As I kneel, running my fingers through the artificial blades of grass, a cloud of rubber pellets – which underpin the whole thing – flies up. I'm joined by a Hamilton squad member.

'What do you think of the pitch?' he says.

'It looks all right. Is it really such a big advantage for you?' I ask.

'Yeah, I'd say so. We train five days a week here so we're used to it. The ball does bobble when it's hot like this though, but we know how to use it to grind out a result.'

'What do you reckon today?' I ask.

'We'll win. The bookies don't think so. They've got us at four to one so I've put quite a lot of money on us.'

Far out to the right I see assistant manager Derek Collins laying out some cones for the pre-match warm-up. He looks preoccupied.

'How are you doing?' I ask.

'Ask me that after the match!' replies Collins.

'Are the boys up for it today?'

'I think they know they've lost their way in the last few weeks,' he says, 'but they're really determined to come out and prove to certain parties in the press that they're up to the task and not going to bottle it. There is a lot of anger in the dressing room. They're really psyched up and just want to finish off the job.'

A rather anxious-looking Davie Irons joins us. With Alexander still in limbo, the pressure is now firmly on the square shoulders of the man who used to be Alexander's number two. He seems to be lacking a little bit of the vim and vigour he had earlier in the season. I dare say that his empathy with Alexander grows by the day.

'You'll be hoping for maximum points today, then?' I say.

'Hopefully. The players have a positive attitude and we're very confident that we can do the job. If we do, Clyde might even do us a favour on Tuesday night by beating Saints and we'll have won the championship. It would be nice to win this game, knowing we are going to miss one or two key players through suspension next week.'

With the players filing out for their warm-up I move to the touchline where senior squad member Davie Nicholls is standing. 'You not playing today?' I ask.

'No. I've got conjunctivitis,' says the midfielder dejectedly.

'Gutting,' I say. 'Are the boys going to finish this off today?'

'There's a lot of aggression and determination. Someone wrote in the press last week that the stench of dung at Raydale Park on Saturday didn't come from the fields but from the players' performances. If that doesn't motivate us to come out and prove what we can do, nothing will.'

'That's a bit uncalled for.'

'I couldn't believe it,' says Nicholls. 'I've played a lot of places and I can tell you that Gretna is a good football club, full of good people. There's no big-time Charlies here like the press make out. If there were, they'd get a fucking slap and be out on their arse.'

'What went wrong against Saints, then?' I ask.

'It was like a fucking carnival. People just expected us to turn up and win but there were eleven other professionals who wanted to stop us from doing that just as much. All the fanfare spurred them on,' says Nicholls.

'Do you think their added experience helped?'

220

It Ain't Barcelona

'Maybe. But if you look at how young our team is in comparison you appreciate how well we've done this season. If someone had said we'd be five points clear with three to play at the end of the season we would have bitten their hand off.'

'I believe a lot was said in the dressing room after the Saints match?' I say.

'I think everyone just needed to take a look at themselves and ask why we've faltered lately,' says Nicholls. 'There were no fingers pointed but we knew we hadn't given the best account of ourselves. There'd been a few nerves since the Airdrie game so it was just a good time while the defeat was so fresh to take stock, put it behind us and look forward to getting our season back on track. The boys know they've only got three games to do it.'

With kick-off beckoning I head up into the stand. There must be about 200 Gretna fans here. I spot Mileson and Jack Gass and, as soon as I sit down, Mileson starts on about the pitch. 'This pitch shouldn't be allowed. It's a bloody disgrace. It's not even the best artificial surface available!'

Before kick-off the stadium announcer says, 'Would the away fans please be aware of the strong sunlight today and regularly apply sunscreen.' A first in Scottish football!

New Douglas Park is comprised of two stands – a main stand and one behind the left-hand goal. Beyond the far touchline is a retail park. There, two Morrison's supermarket workers appear holding brooms. They spend the following ninety minutes laboriously sweeping the car park, taking in the game.

Gretna line up in their blue away kit with a number of changes from last week. Barr comes in at right back before a two-match suspension takes effect, while Deverdics and Hogg come into midfield.

The full line-up is:

Malkowski, Barr, Skelton, Paartalu, Canning, Innes, Deverdics, Hogg, McMenamin, Graham, Grady
Subs: Berkeley, Fleming, Grainger, McGill, O'Neil

McMenamin, who's been nominated for the Scottish PFA First Division Player of the Year award, will be desperate to break Gretna's three-match goal drought. From the very beginning it's obvious that the playing surface is going to dictate the outcome of the match, however. The ball continually bounces and spins erratically. They may be involved in a life-size game of pinball but at least Gretna look focused and cohesive. The nerves of recent weeks have been shrugged off.

Hamilton look good too but it's Gretna who enjoy the lion's share of early possession. It's good humoured up in the stands. There's a summer feel. Mileson is in shirtsleeves, Jack Gass is sunburnt and, in the crowd, the nerves that were evident last Saturday have eased too. Players and fans alike share one pragmatic thought: a win today and we're probably home and dry.

As early as three minutes Steven Hogg tests Sean Murdoch in the Accies goal with a curling free kick. A moment later a searching long ball from Nicky Deverdics finds James Grady who hits the ball on the half-volley. A cloud of black rubber pellets rises from the playing surface as the ball dribbles impotently towards goal. On grass it would have stung Murdoch's palms.

It's a fast-paced, exciting first half. Some good pressure from Gretna sees Grady pulled down out near the corner flag. A perfectly flighted free kick from Hogg sees Paartalu head over from close range. In midfield Deverdics's industry is causing problems for his opposing number and after a series of rash challenges Hamilton's Alex Neil is booked.

The Accies' first real chance of the half comes when, under no pressure whatsoever, Malkowski slices a clearance out of play. A voice behind me in the crowd shouts, 'Straight out of the Alan Main coaching manual!'

From the quick throw-in Richard Offiong's snap shot whistles past the post. The chance marks a turning of the tide. On twenty-four minutes Brian Easton charges through the Gretna midfield unchallenged before shooting powerfully at goal.

Only a decent tip over from Malkowski keeps the score level. From the ensuing corner Malkowski saves well again from a close-range header.

Around the half-hour mark Hogg has to come off injured. Skelton moves up to midfield with Grainger coming on at left back. On twenty-nine minutes Gretna have their best chance of the half. A decent one-two between Graham and Grady on the right culminates with Grady firing across goal just four yards out. McMenamin meets the low cross at the back post and heads down at the gaping goal, only for the textbook header to rebound high off the artificial surface and over. No one can believe it's stayed out.

On thirty-eight minutes Gretna have another gilt-edged chance to take the lead when a fierce McMenamin drive is well saved with the loose ball falling to Grady. His shot is saved too and loops high in the air, spinning towards an open goal. Skelton reacts quickest and as the ball drops he heads it down towards goal even though it is going in anyway. Again, astonishingly, the ball bounces up and over the bar to collective groans from the visiting fans. Just what do they have to do to get the ball in the net?

At half-time the sprinklers come out on the pitch. The water is said to lessen the erratic bounces and behaviour of the ball. Only, the whole pitch isn't watered. Just the half Hamilton will attack in the second half. A prize draw is carried out on the other side of the pitch. Third prize is a fitted carpet. I wonder whether it might per chance be 100 yards long, green and lumpy?

Hamilton's trademark passing game begins to pay dividends after the restart. In the opening exchanges of the half Neil stings the palms of Malkowski, who is tending the goal in front of the Gretna fans. Soon afterwards a David Winters free kick from twenty-five yards just slides past Malkowski's right-hand post.

On sixty-four minutes, after some concentrated pressure from the Black and Whites, Grady whips in a low cross that just eludes the outstretched leg of Deverdics at the back post. Beside me Mileson flinches, kicking out his leg in empathy like a passenger looking for the brake pedal in an impending accident. I notice that Mileson is tense, tenser than I've ever seen him. He's appeared quite disinterested at some stages during the season but, now promotion is within touching distance, the façade has dropped. Mileson is kicking every ball. I'll end the match with black-and-blue shins as a result.

Davie Graham is not having one of his better games. When he fails to challenge for a high ball, Mileson exclaims, 'He didn't even jump, the lazy little shit!' Graham is replaced moments later by Matthew Berkeley, whose pace proves a handful for the tiring Hamilton defence. The game begins to look stretched and when McMenamin is fouled twenty yards out a trademark Grainger left-footed free kick is netbound but for the intervention of the keeper. Groans and shouts of frustration rain down on me from all around. The fans sense the three points are there for the taking and that there may never be a better chance to clinch the title.

On seventy-five minutes the referee awards Hamilton a soft free kick just twenty yards out from goal. Mileson is out of his seat in a flash, berating the referee. He looks at me, wild-eyed, and says, 'Imagine if we lose a goal here. Doesn't the referee know what's at stake?'

With the true extent of Mileson's investment in the club a guarded secret I think only he truly knows the true consequences of missing out on promotion.

The opportunity is wasted by Hamilton but the incident has wound Mileson up like a coil. He's on the edge of his seat and I reckon he'll go off like an incendiary device if there's a goal at either end. With just moments to go I try to engage him in conversation: 'What do you reckon? Is it a good point or two points dropped?'

'It's a bloody good point!' he replies. 'If we can't hold on!' Around us some of the Gretna fans have started a chorus of 'Championes, championes'. It doesn't feel right. The job is far from done. It's a fact echoed when in the dying seconds Hamilton's James McArthur makes a run from deep. He shrugs off a couple of weak challenges and somehow digs the ball out from his feet to lift it over the advancing Malkowski. We all rise out of our seats. I glance at Mileson, whose red, sunbathed face drains of colour in an instant. He's deathly white. The ball seems to fly through the air for days. Gretna and Mileson's SPL dreams hang in the balance with it. As McArthur's shot sails over Malkowski's head towards us it looks like a certain goal – a goal that will leave Gretna's promotion aspirations in tatters. All the 1,889 minutes of football I've watched this season flash before my eyes.

While everyone freezes, McArthur's shot seems netbound. But it is spinning and somehow – God only knows how – the ball catches the very inside of the left-hand post and rebounds out across the goal line. Malkowski is rooted to the spot. So too are the Gretna defence and the Hamilton attack. The fans are all slacked-jawed with awe. The ball is cleared. It's a sensational let-off for Gretna.

With only seconds remaining Gretna somehow manage to bounce back from the scare and charge upfield. Berkeley charges down the field like a whippet before crossing towards McMenamin, who misses making a connection by inches. From Hamilton's next attack, Deverdics manages to wrestle back possession and lofts a long ball forward to McMenamin. With the referee consulting his watch, the Gretna striker flicks on for Grady who shoots just wide when he should have netted. It's the last kick of the match and it is agonisingly close. These are the margins between success and failure in this league where only the champions are promoted.

In the aftermath, Irons seems sanguine. I think he knows it's a good point but all his earlier optimism has disappeared.

With furrowed brow he says hurriedly, 'There is no guarantee [of promotion] the way this league is going.'

Mileson is a wreck. I think the match has taken more out of him than anyone else here. He looks ill and weak. 'We can still do it,' I say. Mileson exhales loudly but says nothing. We shake hands. After he leaves I have a bit of a realisation. While our plans to meet to talk on record have become a running joke, I've overlooked the fact that, as the season has progressed, I've actually been given the best access that Mileson has ever granted. I'm seeing him at his most relaxed, and often at his most passionate, elated or disappointed. I get to see the sheer joy when Gretna win and the sheer terror when they sail too close to the wind like today. I get instantaneous comment on club rumours, results, tactics and individual performances. I'm told stuff I can't reproduce here and much that I have.

I started this project wanting to get to know Brooks Mileson the eccentric multimillionaire football club owner. In that quest I've failed. But it's a glorious failure because instead I've got to know Brooks Mileson the football fan, and it is then, not when he has a microphone shoved in his face, that you see the real Mileson. He's just like you and me, plus a few zeros on the bank account that have enabled him to buy a club he first started following from the terraces, and still does.

I guess he and I are not so different. Gretna was not our first love but, for different reasons, we're both here week in, week out. From an initial suspicion has grown a mutual re-spect. I know this sounds schmaltzy but Mileson has become a friend – he's just one of the guys I watch football with every Saturday. The fact he pays the players' wages is neither here nor there. It sums up my time with the club, where an initial nervous nod to players and staff has become a warm hand-shake. In the future that warmth will still linger with me. I don't think it will ever leave.

12

'They Will Win Promotion, Won't They?'

18 April 2007

Another opportunity presents itself for Gretna to clinch promotion when Saints travel for a rearranged Tuesday-night
fixture at Clyde. The long and short of it is that on Saturday
Gretna need only match Saints' result tonight to clinch the
title. A loss for Saints would gift the trophy to the Black and
Whites – Gretna are *that* close.

I regularly check Ceefax for updates but there's no score
as the match enters the final twenty minutes. Then 'Goal – St
Johnstone – Martin Hardie, 74 mins' comes up on the screen. I
know Clyde won't bounce back from this.

21 April 2007
Gretna FC v Clyde
Raydale Park, Gretna

Position	Team	Played	Goal difference	Points
1	Gretna	34	29	62
2	St Johnstone	34	19	59

This whole thing is getting to me. Everyone I meet wherever
I go is asking if Gretna have done it yet. 'No, they've bloody
well not,' I answer. 'And they may never at this rate.' It's
all I can do to get a wink of sleep the night before Gretna's
penultimate game of the season against Clyde. The maths

of the situation are simple. With Saints having won again in midweek, Gretna just need to win today and the league title is theirs. Similarly, if Saints lose today they cannot overhaul Gretna, who enjoy a far superior goal difference.

It sounds simple but it's not. Gretna could have clinched the title in any of the last three games but they have not. Worse, they have failed to score in four – a first not just for this season but, dare I say it, in their entire league history. Excitement has built to such a level that even my parents have made the long trip down from the Highlands to accompany me to the match.

'We want to be there when they win the league,' they said.

'Don't hold your breath,' I replied, deadpan.

On the journey down in the car I'm unimaginably tense and nervous. I've hardly been able to eat or sleep and everything else in my life is suspended until this situation is resolved – including my failing relationship with Lauren. Even my publisher is getting jittery. 'They *will* win promotion, won't they, Andrew?' he asked earlier in the week.

'Of course they will. And even if they don't against Clyde, think how exciting it will be for it to go to the last game of the season!'

He didn't sound convinced. It heaps more pressure on my shoulders.

I'm so nervous that I've forgotten to arrange a couple of tickets for my folks. It's only when we get to the ticket barrier that I remember. Having left my wallet in the car I think on my feet. I tell my parents to keep quiet and when I pick up my ticket I tell the steward that the journalists from Germany have finally arrived. '*Willkommen* to Gretna,' he says to my bemused-looking parents.

Despite the fact that Sunday's papers will portray Raydale Park as a 'party waiting to happen' it is nothing of the sort. It was true for the recent visit of Saints but today there's a more muted realism amongst the fans. It's not about rubbing your rivals' noses in it. It's about getting across the finishing line by any means necessary. No sooner am I inside the ground than I bump into Gretna's chief executive, Graeme Muir. He looks nervous. 'Surely today, Graeme?' I say.

'Hopefully, hopefully, hopefully,' he replies with hands clasped to the heavens. It's like a mantra. On my way to the press office to pick up a team sheet I see Rowan Alexander. He's speaking to someone so I just shout over, 'Hello.' Alexander waves back. What Alexander said after the defeat away to St Johnstone in February has been on my mind of late: 'If [the players] are still making the same mistakes with us that they were making before they came here then we've got a big problem. We are not going to go too far. It's as simple as that.'

In the press office Keith Melvin looks impossibly nervous. He has hollow eyes and looks like he hasn't slept for days. He can barely hold a conversation so, with twenty minutes till kick-off, I head round to see if I can grab a word with any of the players. I sees Innes, Barr, Hogg and Berkeley. They're all looking wantonly at the pitch, gutted that they'll play no part in what could be the most important game in the club's history. I ask Barr what the mood is like in the squad.

'The boys are right up for it,' he replies. 'We all believe that we can finally finish off the job today. There's no doubt in anyone's mind.'

It's exactly what I, and the 1,800 fans here today, want to hear. I grab a quick chat with Davie Irons as he heads up the tunnel to prepare his pre-match motivational talk. I sense that we're beyond the realms of Al Pacino and Bobby Robson now. If the prospect of promotion is not enough in itself to motivate the team, the sheer fear of being known as the team who threw away a twelve-point lead with a handful of games to play certainly should be.

'Are you expecting a tough afternoon?' I ask.

'We know it will be a difficult game. But we're confident as we have talented players and there is such a great spirit in the camp. The boys have worked so hard all season I think they

229

deserve success,' says Irons, adding, 'but I know it doesn't work like that,' as he disappears into the dressing room.

Irons has a vaguely resigned tone in his voice. I know that he shares my fearful premonition that the title race will go down to the wire. I hope it doesn't filter down to the players who, as they trot back up the tunnel, have expressions ranging from sheer determination to abject terror. I'm not sure if I'd rather swap places with them. We fans are equally as nervous but ultimately helpless. The players, at least, can have a say in all our destinies.

Those players selected for the penultimate game of a roller-coaster season are:

Malkowski, Cowan, Skelton, MacFarlane, Canning, Grainger, McGill, O'Neil, McMenamin, Graham, Deverdics

Subs: Baldacchino, Fleming, Grady, Jenkins, Paartalu

Craig Barr, skipper Chris Innes and Davie Nicholls all miss today's game through suspension while Ryan McGuffie and Steven Hogg are injured. John O'Neil and Neil MacFarlane, neither of whom has started a match since September 2006, are drafted into midfield with Brendan McGill back on the right. Up front James Grady is dropped to the bench. A shuffle of the pack might be just what this team needs.

Ominously the first five minutes of the crunch match are dominated by Clyde. Indeed, it takes an early shot from the visitors' Ryan McCann that flashes wide to kick-start the home side. Their response is immediate and from a long, high ball to Supporters' Club Player of the Year Davie Graham, Colin McMenamin picks up possession and shoots directly at David Hutton in the Clyde goal. He has an uncanny propensity to do so. It's a habit he'll have to change if he wants his football career to progress.

Graham looks completely out of sorts today. One of the youngest men on the park, he looks as if the pressure is getting to him. One of his only other meaningful contributions is a composed square ball to Gavin Skelton early on which the left back drags wide of the target.

After a few early chances, the game settles into the type of mediocre encounter that has seen Gretna pick up just nine points in their last nine games. The same spell has seen Saints pick up double that number. It's terrible to watch. Not even the so-called town crier can be heard shouting his muffled instructions from the stand. His replacement, perhaps, shouts, 'This is terrible. Come on, Gretna. You get to play Celtic and Rangers if you beat this crowd.' All those around him laugh but as the implication of what he says sinks in they become nervous sniggers.

On twenty-three minutes it is Clyde who almost break the deadlock when the impressive Ruari MacLennan draws a good save from Malkowski with his eighteen-yard effort. The scare seems to finally settle Gretna's nerves and five minutes later a pinpoint McGill cross is met by McMenamin, who somehow heads over from six yards. He's scored twenty-six goals this season but it could easily have been thirty-six. McMenamin turns provider moments later when his flick-on is met on the half-volley by McGill some twenty yards out. The first-time strike has David Hutton scrambling across goal to push the opportunistic effort past.

The atmosphere inside Raydale Park is tenser than ever. The fans can sense that one goal today might just be enough. A tractor driving along the road beyond the low-slung away ter-racing stops. The driver peers into the stadium to see what all the fuss is about before looking nonplussed and driving off.

As the break nears Gretna have a stranglehold on the game yet can't quite get off the mark. At the back, stand-in captain Martin Canning is winning everything in the air and Grainger alongside is more than acquitting himself, though a rare slip-up gives Clyde midfielder Brian Gilmour one of the best chances of the match. His poorly executed lob sails over the bar, however.

As half-time looms, veteran midfielder John O'Neil floats in a free kick that is met by the unmarked Canning who heads just over the bar. On forty minutes, just as a whisper is spreading around the ground that Saints have scored in their match, McGill swings in a dangerous cross towards the far post where McMenamin arrives at pace to volley inches wide. Somehow the sides leave the pitch on forty-five minutes with nothing to show for their endeavours.

The interval can't be over quick enough for me and with no stomach for a pie I go and speak to Rowan Alexander, who is seated next to Brooks Mileson in the Corries Stand. Alexander looks refreshed and relaxed. 'How are you doing?' I ask.

'Good,' replies Alexander.

'What do you reckon to the match?' I ask.

Alexander shrugs his shoulders. 'Clyde have had the best chances,' he says. 'There's too much chopping and changing with Gretna for my liking though.'

Just then Mileson returns to his seat. He looks nervous. 'You OK, Brooks?' I say.

'Yeah, good, Andrew.'

'Don't suppose I'll be seeing you for a chat until all this is resolved?'

'Probably not,' replies Mileson, smiling. 'I'll see you at County next week though.'

As I walk back to my seat Rocky Radio's DJ says, 'It's nil–nil. I'm still a believer. Are you?' He then plays 'I'm a Believer' by the Monkees. Worse will follow at the final whistle.

Both sides emerge unchanged for the second half. With Gretna still unable to unlock the shaky Clyde defence there's talk all around of when fit-again wing wizard Ryan Baldacchino will make his bow. The stage is set for the Raydale favourite.

Both teams start with purpose in the second period. Irons' men know what they must do but Joe Miller's team are show-ing that they're not prepared to lie down and hand the title on a plate to the Black and Whites. Early on Gilmour again wastes a decent chance, shooting wide from close range. The feeble effort will prove to be a rare one for Clyde as Gretna, to a man, give everything in pursuit of the three points. It is to be the most scintillating, nervy, exciting forty-five minutes of football I've seen in a very long time and absolutely fitting for the occasion.

As soon as the out-of-sorts Graham makes way for the hungry James Grady on fifty-three minutes, an onslaught on the Clyde goal commences that could easily see Gretna gain not one but five goals. The first decent chance comes after a clever interchange between McGill and O'Neil on the right sees Grady receive the ball in the box before squaring it to Nicky Deverdics. The young midfielder is flattened by Clyde's keeper but the ref somehow waves away the penalty claim. Gretna don't dwell on it. A matter of minutes later the Clyde keeper has another rush of blood to the head. When he's beaten to a through ball by Grady he simply jumps on the diminutive striker and as the two fall to the ground the loose ball trickles agonisingly out of reach of the advancing McGill. The crowd are all out of their seats. It's unbearably stressful. Everyone wants Gretna to finish it here. I don't think anyone can handle three years of hard work coming down to ninety minutes of football far away in the Highlands on the last day of the season.

The very prospect spurs on Irons' team. Another missed header by Canning sees heads drop on the pitch momentarily. A Steven Masterton free kick for Clyde that misses everyone and almost slips in at the back post sends the fear of God through the crowd. A very red-faced fan pleads with the Gretna bench, 'Come on, Davie! Get them going!'

It's clear that it's going to take a Herculean effort to do something they did at will earlier in the season – hit the back of the net – and the players, at long last, seem up for the challenge. On sixty-seven minutes I truly believe that Gretna are going to do it. The best move of the match sees McGill cross low from the right. Grady steps over the cross, leaving it for McMenamin who repeats the action, leaving the ball to run to Deverdics at the back post. Just ten yards out and with an open goal at his mercy Deverdics somehow rattles the top of the crossbar. There hasn't been, and probably never will be, a more straightforward chance for Gretna to clinch promotion to the SPL. It was on a plate for the young midfielder.

I can't see a single face amongst the Gretna support. They've all got their heads buried deep in their hands. They can barely watch events unfolding on the pitch. The Clyde support, never backward in coming forward, sing 'SPL? You're having a laugh!' gleefully as news comes through that St Johnstone are now three up in their match with Queen of the South.

With Gretna realising that if they are to win this title they must step up and do it the hard way, they heap the pressure on the Bully Wee. Just two minutes after Deverdics' miss a Grady header is cleared off the line as far as McMenamin who, from nine yards, fires it straight at the Clyde keeper. You'd put your mortgage on him to score from there. Just not today. Whereas a goal seemed inevitable moments earlier it suddenly seems that no matter what Gretna do today the ball will not end up in the Clyde net.

The introduction of Baldacchino and Jenkins gives Gretna a much-needed boost and gives the fans a final glimmer of hope. Baldi mesmerises each time he gets the ball and on a couple of occasions his dangerous crosses evade McMenamin and Grady by inches when only a touch would turn them into the net. I don't think I've been this tense or nervous for years. I feel physically sick, jittery, have sweaty palms, a dry mouth. My voice is hoarse from shouting. I turn to match reporter Jon Coates with wild eyes: 'Surely they deserve a break, an own goal, anything?'

Coates shakes his head. 'They don't deserve anything. You're a lost cause. Your impartiality went out of the window a long time ago!'

I realise then that although I enjoy the company of the press at home games, I have been sitting in the wrong place for weeks. My conversion is complete. I look around me and see twenty composed media professionals. At the end of the row Keith Melvin and I are white as sheets, on the edge of our seats and have bitten our nails down to the cuticles.

With time running out McMenamin finally has the ball in the back of the net. I can barely believe my eyes. Raydale Park goes berserk. But the striker's excellent finish is chalked off for handball as the striker rips off his top and charges towards the delirious Gretna fans. It's devastating but it's the correct decision; McMenamin had handled the ball in the build-up.

With Gretna pushing for a much-deserved, and desperately coveted, goal, Clyde's MacLennan almost catches the home side off guard in the dying seconds when he receives the ball thirty yards out. A goal now would render all Gretna's efforts meaningless and deny them a vital point. The flame-haired midfielder swivels and unleashes a venomous long-range effort that is only deflected from its rightful resting place in the top corner by the outstretched fingertip of Malkowski. How different things could be next Saturday if that had gone in.

As the final whistle looms Raydale falls eerily quiet. It seems that another chance has passed for Gretna to decide their own destiny. Then, miraculously, on ninety minutes a Grainger free kick from the halfway line falls to McMenamin. All 1,800 fans rise out of their seats simultaneously. It's a carbon copy of an earlier chance with the striker just nine yards out with the goal at his mercy. Yet, incomprehensibly, unbelievably, agonisingly, disastrously, McMenamin succeeds in firing a low shot straight at the stranded keeper. No one can believe Gretna's goal machine has failed to find the back of the net, least of all the keeper who has kept one of the most unlikely clean sheets of his career.

With hopes fading, Gretna's final chance of the match sees a goalmouth scramble result in the ball getting trapped under Grady's feet just three yards out. As Grady does his best *Riverdance* impression to free the ball, a heavy tackle sees it cleared and rolling tantalisingly close to the outstretched limbs of three Gretna players. No one can get a touch on it, however. It sums up the afternoon.

As we enter the final minute of injury time I resign myself to the fact that the title race is going right down to the wire. We could be here for another three hours and the Clyde goal would not be breached. Before the final whistle is even sounded some of the match reporters lean over and ask how long it takes to drive to Dingwall. This whole promotion circus is going on the road.

I'm drained after the match but I don't think anyone is surprised that this is going to go to the last game. This is uncharted territory for the club. Perhaps unhelpfully, Rocky Radio plays 'Under Pressure' by Davie Bowie and Queen as the players drag themselves off the pitch, spent by the sheer effort of the last forty-five minutes. I pop my head into the supporters' club bar. It's full of glum faces. Even the club clown looks down. She's rubbing her eye and wiping away tears. 'Come on, look on the bright side,' I say.

'It's not that. A fly flew in my eye – it's a clown injury!'

I overhear people making plans to travel up to next Saturday's game. I think every last one of them will be required to help Gretna over the finish line. I pop into the press office for the post-match interviews. It's hard to see at the moment but I'm sure there are positives to be gleaned from today's encounter. Irons walks in, looking wired. If the Ross County game could be played right now I think he'd prefer it. The wait will be agonising, especially after the frustrations of the last forty-five minutes.

'We go away and prepare for the biggest game of our lives,' says Irons resolutely. 'It's frustrating as we did not get the result today that the players deserved. I thought the boys played brilliantly and I cannot fault them for their attitude or commitment. But that could be a vital point for us as St Johnstone also have to go to a difficult place next weekend.'

Someone asks just what Gretna need to do to score a goal at the moment. 'Hopefully one of them will stick one in off their backside next week,' says Irons. I don't think anyone would begrudge them it if they did.

A tired-looking Neil MacFarlane sums up the mood in the dressing room: 'We wanted to finish it here and we haven't so we know what we need to do next week. There are no more chances after that. I would be kidding people if I said we weren't nervous because everyone is. It will be a hard game.'

The mood with the rest of the Gretna camp seems better than I thought it would be. They're keeping things in perspective. The twelve-point lead they enjoyed earlier in the season must be forgotten. So must St Johnstone who, after a tremendous run of results, trail the Black and Whites by a single point. Now this is about Gretna's players winning just one match or spending the rest of their days thinking about it.

Clyde manager Joe Miller won't be the only person thinking that Gretna have blown it, however. 'Saints have been in the SPL before and I believe they're heading towards the title,' he says. 'They've got a few experienced boys who have been there before.'

It is a cruel reminder of how Gretna's gamble on youth may yet be their downfall. It's a depressing thought. As I head for the exit I see Keith Melvin. 'We've blown it, we've blown it,' the press man says with a pained expression on his face. 'I just can't see us winning at Ross County. They've got to win to avoid relegation.'

It's an unwelcome reminder that my boyhood club are clinging on to their First Division status by their fingertips. 'We'll do it,' I say. 'Trust me on this one.' I knew I was lying. This is the type of finale I'd dreaded. It's ironic, exciting, heartbreaking stuff but I'm beyond caring about the conclusion of my book. This is real life and the hopes and dreams of thousands of people hang in the balance.

22 April 2007

I wake in a cold sweat having had a second dream in as many weeks about Gretna winning promotion. This time it seems to be clinched with a 2–1 win by the Black and Whites. James Grady, who didn't even start Saturday's match, scores the winner . . .

24 April 2007

With massive momentum behind them St Johnstone announce that they have sold all their ticket allocation for their final match of the season at Hamilton. It's a shred of comfort that the Saints must overcome both a youthful, talented Accies side and their atrocious artificial pitch to have any chance of catching Gretna. With Gretna's superior goal difference a draw will not be enough for the Perth side.

26 April 2007

An early start in Edinburgh sees me arriving at Raydale Park a little after 10 a. m. for Gretna's final training session before the biggest game in the club's history. When I get there the session has just got under way. There's no fitness stuff today, just a practice match followed by some shooting drills. After drawing a blank against Clyde I wholeheartedly approve of the latter.

I expect the atmosphere to be flat. I expect everyone to be on edge. Nothing could be further from the truth. The sun is out, it's warm and the place is buzzing. My own nerves and anxiety about Gretna's fate are assuaged considerably. While Irons and Collins put the team through their paces on the pitch, Wadsworth wanders around the perimeter seemingly more interested in his mobile phone than the training session.

When he passes my way I ask him if he's got a couple of minutes.

'No,' he says.

'Seriously?'

'I'll give you some time after Saturday but not until then.'

By Saturday I won't need to speak to Wadsworth. By then we'll know if Gretna are in the SPL and whether his divisive policy of trading experience for potential has worked. He'll never be a hero to the Gretna fans but if they fail in their task on Saturday he will certainly be a big fat zero – he'll be hung out to dry by the Black and White faithful.

Wadsworth takes a seat beside me. 'When are you travelling up to Dingwall?' I say.

'You're persistent, aren't you?' he replies.

'It's my neck of the woods up there.'

'So you're a teuchter, are you?'

'In a manner of speaking. County are my team,' I say.

Wadsworth eyes me suspiciously. 'Really?'

'Yeah, well, they were,' I say. 'It's a big game for them too.'

'Shut up!' he says, only half-jokingly. 'I'm not interested in them. It's a far bigger game for us. We've got massive expectation and a massive prize at stake.'

With that Wadsworth wanders off to make another call. Out on the pitch the training session is winding down so I grab Colin McMenamin for a chat. He's just been telling his team-mates about a relegation scare he had with Livi when they needed a draw in their last game to stay up and conceded a late equaliser. 'That's pressure,' says McMenamin. 'After the game I was so drained I couldn't even stand up in the shower.'

While we talk the young striker stays out on the pitch doing some extra shooting practice, betting £5 a go that he can strike the crossbar from thirty yards out. After a few misses he starts to find his target with alarming regularity. It's this skill that saw McMenamin voted First Division Players' Player of the Year. I ask him what the accolade means to him.

'It means a lot,' he says. 'It's not very often that players get to recognise their peers so it was a great honour. I was very surprised because Gretna are viewed as outsiders and are the subject of a lot of jealousy in the First Division. Not really with the players but more so with the fans and at board level.'

I ask if, in light of the award, he feels under pressure to end his four-game goal drought and score the goals that win the title.

'I'm dying to score but everybody will want to be the hero,' says McMenamin. 'It's the biggest game of my career. Not just for me but in terms of what we can achieve for the fans, the club and the community in Gretna. It's a massive game.'

I ask the young striker about his last spell in the SPL with Livi and what it would mean to return with Gretna.

'I want to play at the top level and in Scotland that's the SPL,' he says. 'I feel I deserve to be there. I had offers from SPL clubs in the transfer window but I knew that if I signed here for another couple of years we would get there. Hopefully that's what happens on Saturday and I'm justified in my decision.'

'And if it doesn't?'

'If it doesn't then I'm sure we'll get there next year. But we'd have bitten anyone's hand off at the start of the season if they'd said we'd be in the position we're in now. It's in our own hands. It's as simple as that.'

McMenamin rejoins the squad in the centre circle. As he does so I hear him butt into a conversation, saying, 'Saints will be five–nil up at half-time anyway. Forget about their game!'

I grab Gavin Skelton for a quick chat. He's the club's longest-serving player and has seen the Black and Whites go from the

UniBond Premier League to the cusp of the SPL in five years. Promotion to the top flight would be particularly sweet for the man who used to combine his playing duties with a job fitting electric fans in chicken sheds.

'Promotion to the SPL would finish off a great journey,' says Skelton. 'It might take years for the magnitude of it to sink in because I'm so involved in it. I haven't even watched the Scottish Cup Final video since we were in it. The only thing I've thought about is how good it would have been to see our name on the trophy for 2006. I don't want to have to think that about the First Division title too.'

I ask whether he'll spare a thought for Rowan Alexander on Saturday. The pair have seen the club rise up the ranks together.

'I will, yeah. It's difficult for me to comment, though. I can't really say more. He started the journey and I'm sure he'll be there to see us finish it off.'

'Are you feeling confident?' I ask.

'If we were going into it off the back of some poor performances I'd be worried but we're not. We've played well the last two games and all that was missing was the goal. That'll come on Saturday.'

Skelton is summoned to join the rest of the squad who're seated like schoolchildren at the feet of Davie Irons. Irons looks contemplative and a little nervous. He's about to deliver an inspirational team talk that Churchill would be proud of. As he begins I look around, wondering if I should make myself scarce. No one tells me to so I sit just fifteen yards away with open ears.

'I want to thank you all for the effort you've put in since I took over,' Irons starts. 'Your application, your honesty, your endeavour: I couldn't have asked for more. I know there have been some difficult times and I know we haven't got the results we wanted but I appreciate your effort. It's been a pleasure and an honour to try and help you over that finish

241

line. If there is any justice, and there is justice in the world, you'll get what you deserve on Saturday.

'After Saturday's game someone I respect massively[1] came up to me and said, "You'll win at Ross County. Go in there and tell your team. Tell every single player that they'll win." And he told me why. It's not rocket science I suppose: positive thinking. Every one of us here, whether you're playing on Saturday, whether you're coaching, the kit man, a fan or a player travelling up to sit on the sidelines, we've got to start thinking positive. I'm a great believer in it. It circulates, especially amongst a tight-knit group like this who want the same thing. It could be that one per cent, that togetherness that might make the difference between success and failure.

'Because we *are* going to win on Saturday. We *will* win the championship. There is nothing else I am more confident of. Does anyone not believe me? I want you to believe me. So start believing. Start thinking, start transferring, start using that thought. Are you ready?'

All the players nod solemnly.

'Good,' says Irons. 'I'll see you in the morning. Let's get in that positive mindset and let's go out and finish the job.'

As the squad applauds Irons he moves in my direction. 'The boys seem really up for it,' I say. 'Has it been difficult to get them motivated for Saturday?'

'I don't really need to motivate them at this stage,' says Irons. 'They know what's at stake. They've got a great chance to win the championship. What other motivation do they need?'

'So Brooks hasn't put any promotion bonuses in place?'

'No. The players aren't even thinking about that,' he says. 'All credit to them. They haven't even mentioned it. It's the last thing on their minds. It's about the glory for them, the prestige of winning the championship. That's all that matters.'

---

[1] I learn later that the person Irons was talking about was a sports psychologist and not the senior football figure that he led his team to believe.

'They Will Win Promotion, Won't They?'

I ask Irons if, with pressure mounting, he's getting a better understanding of Alexander's condition.

'I've been there with him for the last three seasons so I know what he's gone through. Yes, ultimately the buck stops with me now but it's something I'm relishing, even enjoying. I think I show a bit more emotion than Rowan did but that's the type of person I am. Maybe that helps.'

Talk of Alexander always draws a sombre response. Changing the subject, I ask if Irons will be getting updates from St Johnstone's match at Hamilton on Saturday.

'Yes, we'll keep an eye on it but there's nothing we can do. What the score is there might effect how we approach a period of the game. But if we win it doesn't matter what happens anywhere else. That's all that's in our minds.'

I shake hands with Irons and wish him luck. I'm joined on the pitch by Craig Mileson. 'Did you get everything you wanted?' says Mileson, helpful as ever.

'Yeah. Don't suppose your dad's around, is he?' I ask, already knowing the answer.

Mileson shakes his head while he digs a ringing mobile out of his pocket. He looks at the screen but doesn't answer. 'That's Karl Hawley from Carlisle United calling on my dad's phone. What the fuck does he want? His contract must be up at Carlisle.'

If Gretna win promotion on Saturday I sense Mileson will be receiving many more such calls.

'So I'll see you at the game?' I say.

'Yeah. You'll be sitting with me and my dad, won't you?' asks Mileson.

'Wouldn't miss it for the world.'

13

Living the Dream

28 April 2007
Ross County v Gretna FC
Victoria Park, Dingwall

Position	Team	Played	Goal difference	Points
1	Gretna	35	29	63
2	St Johnstone	35	22	62

I wake from a fitful sleep. I'm not nervous, just excited. Outside the sun is already high up in the sky and there's not a cloud in sight. I'm stripped of expectation. I have no predictions for this final game of the 2006/7 season. I genuinely don't have a clue what's going to unfold. I can't deny that St Johnstone have the momentum and don't doubt they'll win at Hamilton. If Gretna are going to finally clinch promotion they've got to do it themselves. Win and they're in the SPL. It's that simple. Well, simple if you call beating a team that's rock bottom of the table and fighting for their First Division lives. If Gretna are to guarantee an incredible, unprecedented third promotion in a row they will have to relegate Ross County for the first time in their long history.

Ah. Ross County. There go the heartstrings. I've been in denial about today. I've been in denial all season. It's only now I'm back in County heartland with so much at stake that I realise what conflict today is going to cause. What is my ideal scenario? Gretna to be promoted and County to avoid the drop. What needs to happen for that to become

245

a reality? Saints must lose and County must at least draw with Gretna and hope second bottom Airdrie lose their game against Queens (who've nothing to play for). There are other permutations but they are extremely unlikely. This is going to be a fight to the death with three points sought by Gretna and County at all costs.

Over breakfast I look at the morning papers. It's all Saints this and Saints that. The hacks have decided: Gretna are chokers. Promotion is the Perth club's for the taking. In the search for guidance, for a sign, for something, I seek out my horoscope. It reads: 'The best prediction for the weekend is to expect the unexpected. *Also* expect it to be exciting, breathtaking and maybe life-changing.'

Ten miles away Davie Irons and his players are settling down to breakfast at the Inverness Marriott. They've been calm and focused all week but the big day has arrived and some are looking edgy. The anxiety doesn't last for long. At the top of the table Davie Nicholls, who's been up since 5 a. m., almost chokes on his cornflakes after reading an interview with Saints chairman Geoff Brown. He mounts a scathing attack on the club and an unprovoked personal attack on Brooks Mileson.

It is an extremely ill-advised interview – an attack on Mileson is an attack on every single person connected with the club. Nicholls reads out the offending passages to the squad. All vestige of nerves disappear there and then. They're fired up to a man, none more so that the combustible James Grady who has promised Mileson that he'll fire the club into the SPL. It's time to shut up the outspoken Saints chairman, to silence all Gretna's critics. It's time to finish off the job once and for all. Irons doesn't even have to read his pre-prepared speech. His boys are already in the zone.

In the early days I never doubted that Gretna would win the league but I'd never paused to think what it might feel like if they did. That's because at the outset I was detached. I was an outsider. I wasn't involved. Now it's different. I'm a fan whether I like it or not. I know what winning this title would mean, what it has taken to do so. I know the unfettered joy that the title would bring to so many people today. I also know the incredible despair that failure would cause.

I've been a football fan all my life but never before followed a team's fortunes so religiously and at such close quarters. I've never wanted something as much as I want this small club from the Borders to get what they deserve. But for the fact that today's opponents are Ross County I'd have my replica Gretna top above and not beneath my sweater.

It's hard being with my family today. They are County to the core. My dad's picture hangs on the wall in the club's hall of fame. He and my mother will stand with the County fans today. My brother Iain, who I'll meet after the match, and my nephew Callum will both be in Victoria Park's Jail End too. I'm the proverbial black sheep and you might well ask how I can abandon my beloved County in their hour of need. But how can I desert the Black and Whites after all we've been through together in the last six months?

The drive to Dingwall is taken in silence. No one knows what to say. The only talking point is that the Kessock Bridge we need to cross is closed because someone is trying to jump off it. Not today of all days. This can't be happening. Unbeknown to me, the Gretna team coach is one of the long line of vehicles held up on the wrong side of the bridge. Reserve-team coach Andy Smith soon tires of waiting and walks up to a member of the Northern Constabulary who's marshalling the situation.

'Can you let me through?' says Smith.

'Why, do you have experience of these sort of situations?' replies the officer.

'No, I'm going to go and give the fucker a push.'

The situation is soon resolved and the traffic gets moving again. As we speed silently through the Ross-shire country-side I stare out of the window, barely able to believe that after

247

nine months of football it has come to this. My attention is grabbed by the village, near Dingwall, where my brother lives. The sight of it brings home a staggering truth. It is no bigger than Gretna but the prospect of it producing a team capable of playing in the SPL is impossible to comprehend. It's mind-blowing and reminds me that if Gretna can somehow drag themselves over the finish line it will be the most astonishing achievement in the history of the game. That is what today is about. Not about whether Gretna can cut it in the top flight. Not about how many fans they'll bring to Inverness Caley on a rainy Wednesday night. Not about one man's millions. This *is* a modern-day fairy tale in the making. I pray Irons' men can provide the perfect ending.

We arrive in Dingwall a good hour before kick-off and I head into the National Hotel for a quick pint with Brooks Mileson and his entourage. I feel guilty even doing this knowing my brother will be in the favoured County pre-match pub nearby. Having left Gretna at 7 a. m., Mileson, son Craig, Jack Gass, former Gretna captain Mick Galloway and assistant grounds-man Phil Smith stopped for a fry-up in Ballinluig and a pub lunch in Inverness. There are no fish and chips for Brooks and Jack today. I pray that it is not a bad omen.

Mileson looks nervous. In fact he looks unwell.

'How are you feeling?' I say.

'OK, Andrew. OK,' replies the ashen-faced club owner. 'My doctor told me not to make the trip. He said it was too long a journey. But how could I miss a day like today?'

'You couldn't,' I say. 'That's out of the question. Are you feeling confident?'

'I've got to, don't I? We've got to do it. It's the biggest game in the club's history.'

Everyone nods in unison. Outside, legions of fans in black and white tops swarm around Dingwall town centre. I hear a car horn beeping and a Highland accent shout, 'We're going to murder you lot today!'

Living the Dream

'What do you reckon, Jack? You're always good for a pre-diction,' I ask Gass.

'It'll be tight, very tight,' replies the lifelong Gretna fan. 'But I think we'll do it.'

I leave the group to their thoughts and head to Victoria Park. Walking over the railway bridge I realise it's a journey I've made hundreds of times before. This area is woven into the fabric of my life. My brother got married in the registry office ahead with me as best man. I won an amateur league cup final on the playing fields to the left. My other brother Stuart was born in the hospital beyond the stadium. And the stadium itself? What a field of dreams it has been for the Ross family. In 1964 my dad scored three goals in ninety seconds for County to enter the record books. It stands as the fastest hat-trick in football. That is why this club is in my blood, why I have a lump in my throat as the enormity of the occasion floods over me.

I'm praying I don't bump into anyone I know while I'm in this state. I busy myself with making sure my Gretna top is not visible above the collar of my jumper. I keep my head down. I just want get into the away stand – somewhere I've never sat in thirty years of watching County. I'm focused on getting past the home turnstiles without being spotted. It is never going to happen. Above the din I hear someone shouting my name. I turn. It's one of my oldest friends though we haven't spoken in two years. We've stood in the Jail End cheering on the dark blues more times than I care to remember. He was there the first time I went when we were small enough to walk straight under the railings on the terrace, when the pies seemed as big as flying saucers.

'How's it going?' he says as we embrace. 'It's been ages. What's new?'

'You know, not much,' I reply sheepishly.

'Where are you going?' he says. 'Aren't you coming in this way?' He hasn't heard about my book.

'I'm just going over there to speak to someone,' I lie.

'OK. I'll wait.'

'Seriously, it's OK. I'll see you in there,' I say, fiddling with my collar nervously.

I see my friend eyeing it. He must see a flash of black and white because he looks confused, hurt almost. He's as diehard as County fans come. He's a big enough man not to mention it though.

'You *are* coming in the Jail End, aren't you?' he says.

'Erm . . . look. I've been doing a book on Gretna. I'm going to sit with them,' I say, shrugging my shoulders.

'That's great,' says my friend. 'But that's work . . . isn't it? Come with us. Come on – it's where you belong.'

I ponder what he says for a minute, feeling our friendship slip through my fingers like grains of sand.

'I can't. Not today. I'm sorry. Listen, maybe we can meet up after the match?'

'Maybe,' says my friend as he turns and dissolves into the crowd. I know this is 'just' football but I also know we won't meet after the match and that our friendship will never be the same again. In this most familiar of surroundings I suddenly feel very alone and even a well-meaning good-luck text from my ex does little to help.

I compose myself and head through the away turnstiles, head bowed. The first person I meet inside is Rowan Alexander. He looks as out of sorts as I feel. He must be finding today ten times more difficult than I am. We shake hands. 'Good luck today,' I say. 'You deserve promotion.'

'Thanks,' says Alexander with sad eyes. 'Let's hope we both get the ending we deserve.'

I head to the press box to see my media cronies for the last time. I meet Jon Coates. We discuss the helicopter the SFL has chartered to deliver the trophy to here or to Saints at Hamilton come final whistle. At this moment the chopper is sitting in a field in Braemar, approximately halfway between the two stadiums. 'What do you reckon?' I say.

Living the Dream

'I still can't see it,' says Coates. 'Saints will win today; it's just a question of whether Gretna can.'

As much as I can't sit with the County fans today, I can't sit with the press. I don't belong there any more. I belong with the Black and White Army who are 600 strong today – that's a little under a quarter of the village population. As the teams warm up under the hot sun I take a seat in the midst of a sea of black and white. My phone rings. It's my brother, calling from behind the goal that Gretna will shoot towards in the first half. I'm seated to the right of the opposite goal. I ignore his call. I can't speak now. I'm tapping my feet uncontrollably. On the pitch Irons' team looked fired up. In between drills, Gavin Skelton pumps his fist and gives a war cry at the top of his voice.

My excitement and anxiety as kick-off nears are indescribable. I can only imagine what is going through the minds of the players. Mileson and Co. join me. At least three times before kick-off, Brooks disappears behind the stand for a cigarette. I'm seated behind Mileson, Mileson Jnr and Gass, next to Phil Smith and Mick Galloway. Behind us is a fan who has flown from Manchester to Aberdeen, then taken a train, bus and taxi to get here. Beside him is a man with sharp features who hasn't missed a Gretna game in five years. Gass has barely missed one in sixty years. I'm in good company.

As three o'clock nears 'The Final Countdown' blasts over the tannoy system. It's a full house with 6,216 somehow squeezing into Victoria Park for the most dramatic denouement to a title race in any league for years. To my right the Jail End is packed and noisy. To my left and all around me the Gretna fans are in fine voice. It's the ultimate cup-tie carnival atmosphere.

I look at the team sheets for the first time. The only changes from last week see Nicholls in for MacFarlane and the out-of-sorts Graham making way for Grady. The diminutive striker has only found the net twice so far this season but he'll run through brick walls for the cause. It may take more than that today.

Club captain Chris Innes misses today's game through suspension, as does right back Craig Barr.

The full line-up is:

*Malkowski, Cowan, Skelton, Nicholls, Canning, Grainger,
McGill, O'Neil, McMenamin, Grady, Deverdics*

Subs: Baldacchino, Fleming, Graham, MacFarlane, Paartalu

Come 3 p. m. the teams have still not taken the pitch. As if the atmosphere couldn't get tenser it is announced that kick-off will be delayed by five minutes. Come 3.05 p. m. there's hysteria inside the ground. Both sets of players have so much to play for and so much to fear. It's unbearable on the terraces. Mileson is a bag of nerves. His son has a look of sheer terror on his face. I lean over and shake both their hands. 'They're going to do it,' I say, unconvincingly.

'I bloody hope so,' replies Mileson.

From the outset both teams start at a million miles an hour. Neither has any reason not to. Gretna are playing for unthinkable glory. County are playing for their professional lives. In the opening exchanges it is Gretna who look the most lively and the first real chance falls to veteran midfielder Davie Nicholls after a clever pass from fellow old-stager, John O'Neil. Nicholls doesn't trouble Samson in the County goal with his volley, however.

Having failed to score in the last four games, Colin McMenamin is goal-hungry. A slick one-two between Skelton and Grady sees the ball slid through to the striker whose powerful shot is blocked. On ten minutes McMenamin is in the thick of it again but a through ball from Nicholls is just out of reach.

On twelve minutes County mount their first decent attack. The lively Michael Gardyne makes a powerful run from the halfway line, cuts inside Danny Grainger and shoots just inches wide of Malkowski's right post. It's a let-off for Gretna.

252

It seems to provoke the correct reaction. Grady picks up the ball forty yards out, passes wide to Brendan McGill who advances before unleashing a powerful shot on target. The ball rebounds off Samson to the waiting McMenamin whose snapshot flashes into the side netting. From where I'm sitting it looks like it's gone in. All around me people are out of their seats before they realise their mistake.

While the action continues on the pitch, off it I hear the crackle of portable radios all around. I've been resisting checking the St Johnstone score for all my might but I know immediately what's happened when I hear a collective sigh. 'Saints are one–nil up,' says someone behind me.

I'm not sure if the news reaches the players but Gretna suddenly seem to wobble. Their fluid football of the first twenty minutes is forgotten and they revert to the long-ball game that has proved so unpopular and ineffective in the latter part of the season. 'Come on, Gretna! On the ground!' shouts a voice. I recognise it. It's the town crier. For once he's spot-on. I'm somehow reassured by his presence.

I get a sense of the type of afternoon it is going to be in the following minutes. No sooner have Gretna squandered two chances from a Canning header and a Nicholls daisy-cutter from thirty yards than McMenamin has the mother of all misses. After good work down the left wing, Skelton's pinpoint cross is whipped in on to the head of the diving McMenamin, who somehow heads on to the post from six yards. Six hundred voices groan in unison. Two minutes later, when a Grainger free kick is floated in towards the back post, it looks like Gretna will finally break the deadlock but the unmarked Canning's stabbed volley somehow flies over the bar.

By the half-hour mark the County defence is at sixes and sevens but the longer Gretna go without scoring, the shorter fans' fingernails are going to get. Phil Smith turns to me and says, 'What have they got to do to put the ball in the back of the net?' I don't have an answer for him.

Just as Smith is speaking County's Gardyne shows exactly what's required. He receives the ball twenty yards out, shimmies and fires the ball high into the Gretna net: 1–0. The Jail End erupts. By the time the game restarts Gretna's promotion dreams seem to be in tatters. To add insult to injury, the irrepressible Martin Hardie has doubled Saints' lead at Hamilton. It's a sucker punch.

If we're ever going to see if Gretna have got the nerve to turn this situation around it will be in the next fifteen minutes. 'We've got to get one back before half-time,' says former club captain Galloway. He's right. He knows it will make Irons' half-time team talk a far easier task.

Gretna respond like true champions. I don't think anyone expects them to bounce back so quickly. From looking defeated and on the ropes they somehow conjure up an equaliser against the run of play. With County invigorated by their goal they sense they can finish this off before the interval but they're shell-shocked when, on thirty-four minutes, Nicky Deverdics heads home from close range after Grady's initial header is parried by Samson.

The celebrations are brief but wild. There's a lot still to do and the players know it. The atmosphere inside the ground is electric. Gretna are back in it but it's anyone's game. No sooner have the Black and White Army allowed themselves to dream a little than the atmosphere sinks noticeably. Jason Scotland has extended Saints' lead over Hamilton to three.

With news filtering through that County's relegation rivals Airdrie are 2–0 up in their game, the atmosphere in the ground sinks further. It's a massive blow for County who know they've got to better Airdrie's result by at least two goals to survive. It saddens me but I'm so caught up with Gretna's hopes and dreams that I barely give it a second thought. It's eerily quiet in the ground for a moment. Some of the players look around, wondering what could possibly have happened.

Living the Dream

Two minutes later, County's fate looks inescapable, and Gretna's looks secured. After finding the back of the net just eight minutes before, the Borderers score for a second time when an angled Deverdics through ball allows Grady to spring the County offside trap and race through on goal. I think every one of the 600 Black and Whites fans watch Grady fire the ball under the advancing keeper through palms fixed to their faces. The relief is palpable: 2–1 to Gretna. They can relax. Just a little. This is only the halfway point of the most incredible finale that this league has ever seen.

At half-time I can't face a pie. Neither can anyone else. All around me half-eaten pies litter the terrace. Mileson disappears for a cigarette and returns with a tray of drinks. He's shaking so much that it's a wonder there's anything left in the cups. I can't get any of the fizzy cola down, though. I'm paralysed with fear. Gretna are in the driving seat but for how long? For once in my life I want something I'm involved in to end well, to surpass my institutionalised, low, Scottish expectations. Can't Gretna just have their moment in the sun, I plead to the football gods? Can't I? Just this once?

News that Hamilton have pulled back a goal on Saints doesn't really lighten the mood. As it stands Gretna are in the promised land but all around me I can tell people share my fear. This is going to go down to the wire. There will be more goals at both grounds to come – I've never felt surer about anything in my life.

Half-time seems to take an eternity to pass. I can only imagine what Scott Leitch is saying to his players. They are effectively relegated. Irons' job is simpler. I can imagine him telling the team to keep it tight, sit on the lead and hurt County on the break when they chase the game late on. If Gretna can hold their lead I think they could go on to finish the job in style. If County nick an early goal I fear Irons' team might never bounce back.

No sooner has the second half kicked off than my worst fears are realised. A goalmouth scramble sees Diarmuid O'Carroll bundle the ball over the line for a County equaliser. It's the worst possible start for Gretna and sends the advantage back to St Johnstone. One hundred miles away the pilot of the SFL-chartered helicopter begins to check the coordinates for Hamilton while the SFL representative looks out the blue and white ribbons. In truth he probably already has them on the trophy.

At least the early goal leaves forty minutes for the Borderers to fashion a winner. That's forty minutes of sheer unadulterated agony for everyone connected with the club. From Mileson – who's fidgeting in his seat and learning why his doctor forbade him to make the trip north – to each and every fan wondering how much more drama and agony they can take. I look over my shoulder far to the right and see Rowan Alexander. He looks tense. His eyeballs are bulging and a vein in his forehead looks set to burst.

Gretna don't look as rattled as I thought they'd be. Their precarious position is hammered home on fifty-four minutes, however, when a slick County move ends with Martin Scott shooting just wide. County's defence may be shaky but their young, pacy front line is causing no end of problems for Gretna's makeshift back four.

A flurry of County chances makes the atmosphere impossibly tense. Some Gretna fans start to sing the names of Baldacchino and Graham – the two players they feel could inject a bit of pace into the tiring Gretna midfield. Irons makes the change on fifty-eight minutes. It's Paartalu and Graham for Deverdics and Nicholls. Baldacchino remains on the bench. He, I suspect, will be Irons' final throw of the dice.

The changes have an immediate effect. County's flat-footed defence is no match for Graham's pace and trickery and the imposing Paartalu makes the middle of the pitch his own with a long-overdue good performance as the game descends into attack and counter-attack. On sixty-five minutes a McMenamin flick sees Graham cut in from the left wing and shoot just wide. On seventy-one minutes, just as news filters through that Hamilton have reduced Saints' lead to one, offering a glimmer of hope – a draw for Saints will not be enough – the tireless McGill pelts down the right and rifles in a deep cross to McMenamin at the back post. Just thirty yards from where I'm sitting he rises above Alex Keddie and heads goalwards from four yards. The header grazes the top of the bar and flies over. McMenamin seems fated not to add to his season tally of twenty-six goals. It is time for one of his teammates to stand up and be counted.

It looks increasingly like Gretna are not going to do this. The worst thing is that, with them chasing the game demonically, they're leaving massive gaps at the back. At any given time County could score and shatter Gretna's ever-receding title hopes. Yet the Borderers must chase the game, keep taking chances, even if it does mean that in the stands our hearts are in our mouths. It's so unbearable. 'It's not going to happen, is it?' says Smith next to me. In front Mileson has left his seat for a cigarette. He comes back looking upset and unwell. He is a deathly shade of white and soon disappears again for the remainder of the match. Unable to watch, Craig Mileson and Gass soon follow, leaving myself, Galloway and Smith on the edge of our seats.

McGill's last contribution in the match brings the crowd to their feet. A direct run though the middle sees the midfielder unleash a powerful shot that is blocked by a County defender. The ensuing corner almost sees Gretna's dreams die on their feet. A break from Don Cowie releases Gardyne, whose drilled effort at goal requires Malkowski to dive at full stretch to preserve parity.

With fifteen minutes remaining, Baldi comes on for McGill. I learn later that Irons considered replacing Grady but was told in no uncertain terms by the thirty-six-year-old that he wanted to play on. Despite suffering from cramp no one was going to drag him off that pitch today. It would prove to be the most astute decision of his career.

The substitution gives Gretna fans renewed hope. If anyone can turn this game around it is the fleet-footed, golden-booted Baldacchino. With the game stretched, his impact is immediate. It lifts the crowd though the pressure is reaching unprecedented levels. It is crushing – I feel like my head has been plunged deep under water. Why after thirty-five games, after 3,150 minutes of football, must it come down to the last fifteen?

With the Saints game having kicked off five minutes before the one in Dingwall it is entering its final ten minutes. On the eighty-one-minute mark Hardie scores again for Saints to make it 4–2. Game over, surely. Simultaneously a good move involving Graham, McMenamin and Grady sees the visitors get two shots on target in quick succession only to be blocked by the face of one County defender and the back of another. The delay while they are treated is unbearable.

Gretna can't buy a goal today while at Hamilton they can't stop scoring. However, despite a late consolation by former Gretna player Brian Wake, Saints run out 4–3 winners. It's a great win and as it stands Owen Coyle's team are champions. Their fans and players start to celebrate wildly. It takes a few moments for the news to filter through that the day's other big match is running five minutes late. With the match on a knife-edge at 2–2 they must endure the same intolerable suspense as the Gretna faithful.

By this stage I have my head firmly planted in my hands. I'm drained. I don't know how much more of this I can take. On eighty-five minutes another good County attack draws another spectacular save from Malkowski. This is torture. Never, never, never, never, never is this going to happen. Gretna have blown it. They're still pressing, not giving up, but they look more likely to concede than score. There's no midfield to speak of now. It's end-to-end stuff with little in between. This is echoed when Skelton takes matters into his own hands and charges the length of the field in *Roy of the Rovers* fashion only to shoot millimetres wide. He stays up the field afterwards. He's spent. Everyone is. Everyone is out of position. I don't know how much longer Gretna can run, how much they have left in the tank.

From a dangerous County break, a long Malkowski throw starts off a counter-attack. Graham charges down the right wing to pick up the clearance and his early drilled cross arrives on the six-yard box between Grady and the County keeper. It must be a goal! It's just too close to Samson, however, and his brave block starts off another County attack. It's frantic. Everyone in the stadium is on their feet, looking at their watches. The full ninety minutes is up. We're into injury time.

With no more than ninety seconds remaining, Gretna continue pressing County but it looks like it's all going to be in vain. Around me I see 600 familiar faces resembling Edvard Munch's *Scream*. I imagine my own is the same. Next to me Smith is red-eyed. Galloway can't watch. A fan behind me rocks forward and places a hand on my shoulder to steady himself. His grip almost draws blood. In Braemar coordinates are set for Hamilton. The helicopter rotors start spinning slowly on their wide arc. At New Douglas Park the foil is removed from numerous champagne bottles. The wire casings are slowly loosened. The pressure inside the bottles slowly eases the corks out.

Then impossibly, unbelievably, Malkowski pulls off another crucial save from County's Mark McCulloch. The referee is already consulting his watch as the Polish keeper launches the ball skyward for what must be the final attack. His sliced kick looks like it's going out of play until Baldacchino rises to flick the ball on to McMenamin, who charges down the right flank. Showing incredible composure under almost unbearable pressure, the striker picks out Graham on the opposite wing with an inch-perfect pass. With time seeming to morph and slow, Graham moves towards goal and considers shooting before spotting Grady unmarked, six yards out. His slide-rule pass to the right is perfect this time. No one in the crowd can believe what they're seeing. It's the final minute of the final match of an incredible season. The ball seems to take an eternity to reach Grady but when it does he makes no mistakes. He slides the ball under the spreadeagled Samson. The look of joy and relief on his face is an image I will take to the grave. Grady says of the moment, 'The ref said we were in injury time so when Davie passed I was shitting myself but I just slipped it under the keeper. It was an incredible feeling.'

Once Grady's shot hits the back of the net, time snaps to fast forward and he charges towards the Gretna fans behind the goal for the wildest celebrations I've ever witnessed. He's mobbed by the ecstatic, disbelieving fans and soon engulfed by every one of his teammates. My brother will later tell me that in the Jail End someone was on the phone to a St Johnstone-supporting friend. He said, 'You've got to send me a bottle of champagne. We're holding Gretna ... wait ... oh shit, they've scored!'

I'm in shock. I turn to Smith and Galloway and grab them. We leap in the air, barely able to believe what we've seen. Down on the touchline Irons runs the length of the pitch with his hands fixed to his face and his eyes on stalks like a cartoon character. From behind, a group of fans spill over, knocking me to the ground and my notepad, camera and pen with me. I don't care. I pick myself up and turn to the stunned Smith and embrace again. We pause, unsure what to do next. Then leap up and down again, elated. Far behind me Alexander is out of his seat. He has tears in his eyes and a look of astonishment on his face. Below, I see Gass running up the stairs to see what's happened. He has tears streaming down his face too. 'Unbelievable,' says Gass repeatedly. He's euphoric. The chopper in Braemar is stopped in its tracks.

Living the Dream

It takes five minutes to restart the game. When it does, the referee looks as if he's about to blow but then County go up the park and nearly score. However the shot is deflected for a corner. From it a frantic scramble ensues before the ball goes out for a Gretna goal kick. A moment later the referee finally blows. A pitch invasion ensues. It's pandemonium. I break down in tears. I never thought I'd see this day. I run on to the pitch with arms aloft. I see Mileson out of the corner of my eye in a tearful embrace with his son. Craig Mileson is having to hold his father up. His knees have buckled. I leap over the barrier and join them, helping the elated club owner to his feet.

'This is great! This is amazing!' I exclaim.

Mileson is speechless. He's soon mobbed by well-wishers. He says of the moment: 'My legs had gone, everything had gone. My son was holding me up and when the goal went in that was it – I was going to collapse. I was totally drained.'

I barely notice the County fans filing out dejectedly. I go back on to the pitch where everyone is running around wildly. No one knows what to do with themselves. Nobody has prepared for this moment or thought that it would ever happen. Only in Hamilton is the disbelief greater. Tears are being shed on the terraces and in the dressing room.

In amongst the fans I bump into some of the players. 'I told you we'd do it. I fucking told you we would do it, didn't I?' says Davie Nicholls.

Craig Barr sees me and hoists me up in the air. 'Ya fucking beauty!' he says. 'I can't believe it!'

Gav Skelton goes running past and I grab him. 'You!' he says. 'It's brilliant, isn't it? I told you we'd score today!'

Then I see Irons in the players' tunnel. I run up to him and he leaps and offers me a high five. He's jubilant and emotional. 'I've never seen anything like it,' shouts Irons. 'We were down, we were out then we were in ecstasy! What these boys showed, to go to that level, to push themselves so far, is unbelievable. They're magnificent!'

'You made us all wait for it, though!'

'I didn't imagine it would take the last kick of the ball! It was the most unbelievable finish you could imagine. With two minutes to go I thought it was curtains but we always hoped we'd get one more chance and by God we got it. A quarter of Gretna's population came here today, Andrew. That's why we kept going right to the end. For them and for Brooks. It means the world to all of us.'

All around people have expressions of sheer joy. It's chaos but I see familiar faces everywhere I look. People criticise Gretna's modest support but they're a group more involved in their club than any other I know. This means everything to them. I meet Smith again and we dance a jig, looking stupid. We don't care. Then I see Gass. 'Unbelievable,' he's still saying. 'I can't take this in. There's been days at the club when we couldn't even pay the wages. In sixty years I've never witnessed scenes like this.'

The celebrations go on and on and on. Through the forest of bodies I see Alexander up in the stand, looking uncertain, excluded almost. He is soon surrounded by fans. They don't want to leave him out. I push my way over and reach up into the stand. 'Amazing!' I exclaim, shaking his hand.

Alexander smiles and nods before being mobbed from all sides. He's pulled over the barrier on to the pitch – to his rightful place. He's earned this. This is his day too. Whether he'll be around next season to reap the rewards is a question for another time.

With the players being relieved of their strips, boots and shorts they retreat to the dressing room to don their First Division Champions T-shirts. On the back is emblazoned the lyrics to the favoured song of visitors to Raydale Park: 'SPL? You're having a laugh'. This is a moment to be savoured by players and fans alike. They've proven the doubters wrong and made history. 'Little' Gretna *are* going to the SPL.

Someone hands the players a banner. It reads, 'We're just a small town in Scotland – SPL here we come!' Another dig at

the club's many detractors. The final riposte is when the players break into an ironic chorus of 'One Geoff Brown, there's
only one Geoff Brown!' Mileson, who's recovered enough to
join the celebrations, says when prompted by a reporter, 'Geoff
Brown, who's he? Ah yes, he's that chap in charge of the team
that finished second.'

Then it's all about Gretna. With the helicopter carrying the
First Division trophy expected in twenty minutes, stewards
clear the pitch. I see Ron MacGregor, Gretna's chairman and
one of football's gentlemen. Like Mileson he is shunning the
limelight, happy to let his players take centre stage.

'Well, Andrew,' says MacGregor. 'You've got the ending you
wanted.'

'Who cares about the book? What a day for Gretna!'

'Yes, from the UniBond League to this in five years. It's unthinkable,' says MacGregor. 'It's a great end to the fairy tale.'

'It's not the end. You're in the SPL next year!' I say. MacGregor
shakes his head in wonderment at the possibilities.

Back in the main stand the players have climbed up into
the directors' box. Irons is conducting a chorus of 'One Brooks
Mileson, there's only one Brooks Mileson!' Then he jumps
down to embrace the owner, screaming, 'I love you!' It's a moment of raw emotion. Irons then sees Alexander. The two hug
and tears flow freely before Irons sees Derek Collins standing
alone, away from the celebrations. He runs over, puts his arm
around his assistant and the two walk out into the centre of
the pitch, enjoying a quiet moment to let their achievement
sink in.

There's joy all around. Even the small group of County
fans who've stayed to spoil the party are soon moved on. My
nephew is among them. He looks devastated. A full hour after
the final whistle the party is still going. Just when it looks like
faltering the helicopter carrying the trophy looms into view.
It's a majestic sight. Having been dragged, reluctantly, into the
melee, Mileson joins me. We stand shoulder to shoulder, as

we have for so much of the season. 'I can't believe my eyes. I never thought I'd see this day,' says Mileson emotionally. We're joined by a fan who has the match ball. Mileson signs it. The three of us stand transfixed by the sight of the chopper carrying the much-coveted silverware.

By the time the trophy is carried into the ground I've moved up to the stand. I want to savour the atmosphere. I find myself next to the press box. Inside, forty busy hands rewrite match reports that were no doubt ready to be sent before Grady struck the late winner. I've spent afternoons this season being jealous of the journalists who turn up, get paid and then leave it all behind at the final whistle. But not now. Jon Coates looks up at me. I can only imagine what a bedraggled figure I cut. I'm soaked in champagne and damp-eyed. 'You finally got your ending,' he shouts. I did, I think, and so much more.

Out on the pitch Chris Innes steps forward to receive the trophy his team wanted so badly. When he raises it above his head the party starts over. Each player takes a turn to raise the trophy to rapturous applause. Zibi Malkowski even steals a policeman's hat for his hurrah. It's all good-natured stuff.

After much persuasion Mileson takes the trophy in his hands. He studies it briefly before holding it aloft to the de-light of the fans. In that instant I can tell the self-deprecating club owner enjoyed it, that he'd dreamed about it and that the most can-do of individuals I've ever met even knew that this would happen one day.

Up in the stand I sense someone behind me. I turn. It's County chairman Roy McGregor. 'Your dad told me about the book,' he says. 'You'll sell heaps of copies now.'

'Thanks,' I say. 'I wish it didn't have to end like this.'

'Don't worry. We deserved what we got this season. We'll bounce back. You enjoy the moment,' says McGregor. It's an incredibly magnanimous gesture under the circumstances.

On and off the pitch the party rages on. People eventually start to drift off. Some have to start the long journey south to continue the party in Gretna. Some of the players are even off in quiet corners of the ground relaying news to absent loved ones. Players like Grady, Nicholls and McMenamin are surrounded by reporters. Grady tells one, 'When I left the house on Friday the last thing my son said was, "Daddy, bring me back a medal please."'

The players won't get their championship medals today but later that night Grady will go in to see his sleeping son, give him a hug and leave the cheap, plastic medal he won in Friday night's team quiz by his bed. Josh Grady will not remove the medal from his neck for the better part of a month.

All the players are heroes today, not just Grady. In tomorrow's *Sun* the Team of the Day section will feature the entire Gretna squad. It's a first.

Mileson is being press-ganged too but is making plans to leave. I lean over the tunnel wall as a few of the players drift up to get changed. 'Well done, Zibi,' I shout to the on-loan keeper who'll be back at Hibs on Monday.

'Are you coming back on the bus with us?' he asks.

It's tempting but I decline politely. I've promised to meet my brother. I turn and see Keith Melvin for the first time since the start of the match. He looks shell-shocked. 'I still can't believe it,' he says. 'What just happened?'

'I don't really know,' I reply. 'What now?'

'Back down the road,' says Melvin as Craig Mileson joins us. 'No parties?'

'Maybe later. There's one for the staff and players on Thursday. You're invited,' says Melvin.

'Great. I'll see you there.'

I meet my parents. It's some three hours after the final whistle but it barely seems like ten minutes since Victoria Park erupted to the loudest cheer of the season. We walk to meet my brother. I'm choked, emotional and play the events of the day over and over in my head. I can barely hold a conversation. I can't even get a pint down. I need to process what's gone on, what Gretna have achieved ... and how. I'm sure I'm not alone.

Though in good spirits, I feel out of place amongst County fans. I feel guilty. Guilty that they've been relegated and guilty that I've deserted them. I'm not sure if I'll ever be welcome back in the Jail End again. I decide to leave.

As I walk to the car, exhausted, emotionally spent and barely able to utter a word, I see a group of Gretna fans piling into a car. With every superlative, every cliché, every platitude used up in the four hours since Grady scored the most important goal in the club's history, they look similarly tongue-tied. As we pass I recognise one of them. He was sitting behind me during the game. We shake hands and embrace, teary-eyed. 'I'm speechless,' I say. 'How are we ever going to top that?'

The fan pauses for a moment, deep in contemplation. He seems to be playing some of Gretna's amazing achievements over the last five years through his head. The consecutive Third and Second Division titles – and now the First, won at the death; the Scottish Cup Final; the UEFA Cup. He seems lost in reverie but there's a flicker in his eyes. A smile breaks across his face. He beams and shouts at the top of his voice, 'SPL – four in a row! Come on, Gretna!'

The dream lives on.